WORD ASSOCIATION

WORD ASSOCIATION

PHEBE CRAMER
Institute of Human Learning
University of California
Berkeley, California

1968

ACADEMIC PRESS   New York and London

COPYRIGHT © 1968, BY ACADEMIC PRESS INC.
ALL RIGHTS RESERVED.
NO PART OF THIS BOOK MAY BE REPRODUCED IN ANY FORM,
BY PHOTOSTAT, MICROFILM, OR ANY OTHER MEANS, WITHOUT
WRITTEN PERMISSION FROM THE PUBLISHERS.

ACADEMIC PRESS INC.
111 Fifth Avenue, New York, New York 10003

United Kingdom Edition published by
ACADEMIC PRESS INC. (LONDON) LTD.
Berkeley Square House, London W.1

LIBRARY OF CONGRESS CATALOG CARD NUMBER: 68–14652

PRINTED IN THE UNITED STATES OF AMERICA

PREFACE

Over the last fifteen years, psychological investigations of verbal behavior have been increasing rapidly. Directly or indirectly, a large number of these studies have made use of the word association test—either as a technique to assess the effect of some experimental variable on the production of verbal responses, or as a source of calibrated material from which experimental stimuli have been selected to study the relationship between associative strength and other cognitive functions. Although the focus of these two types of experiments is slightly different, both rely on the word association test to provide critical information. For this reason, it would seem important to know the conditions under which associations may be expected to remain stable, as well as the ways in which associations may be modified.

This book was begun out of the need to bring together and coordinate the available experimental information on word association. A comprehensive survey of this material should be valuable to any investigator who is planning to use the word association test in either of the ways indicated above—i.e., as a dependent variable measure or as a source of experimental material. The present book reviews the large majority of word association studies published between 1950 and 1965, and organizes these into chapters based on those variables which have been shown to modify associative processes. Knowledge of the effects of these variables should help investigators to design more closely controlled experiments and to rule out sources of variation which are irrelevant to the main point of the study.

In addition to this reference function, it is expected that some readers will find the studies reviewed here to provide a provocative springboard for speculations about the structure and functioning of thought. This use of the word association test has been the primary source of the author's interest in the topic. Throughout the book, I have attempted to point out the implications of the studies presented for some broader conceptions regarding cognitive processes.

In addition to these two functions—of providing reference material and as a potential source for theoretical speculations—there was a third factor which was influential in prompting the writing of this book. It has been my opinion that the psychodiagnostic use of the word association test should provide a wealth of useful information both about the personality and cognitive functioning of clinical patients. Yet, in practice, the clinical insights gleaned from this test seem to be less than might be expected. Probably for this reason, many clinical settings no longer include word association among the standard battery of tests. In fact, in some senses it seems that word association has been increasingly taken over by experimental psychologists as a useful technique for investigating verbal behavior, while being abandoned by clinicians as a psychodiagnostic technique. The potential usefulness of this method for study in both areas and for bridging the gap between the two—and it does seem that the study of cognitive processes must span that hiatus—certainly has added to my interest in word association.

In writing this book I have benefited from several sources of interest and support. I began the preliminary outline and survey of the literature during a summer spent at the Austen Riggs Center, Stockbridge, Massachusetts, which was generously supported by NIMH grant MH-10504-01. The conception of turning the review into a book was the outgrowth of discussions with colleagues at the Institute of Human Learning, University of California, Berkeley. It was there, during a year's visit as a Research Fellow, while on leave from Barnard College, that I wrote the major part of the manuscript. I am deeply appreciative of the Institute's support for this year, and for the interest and encouragement given me by the Director of the Institute, Dr. Leo J. Postman. Other colleagues at the Institute who have been especially helpful include Dr. Edmund S. Howe, Dr. Neal F. Johnson, and Dr. Geoffrey Keppel. To my many other colleagues and friends who have expressed interest in this project I am also thankful.

Berkeley, California PHEBE CRAMER
June, 1967

CONTENTS

Preface	v
Introduction	1
Prologue	10

Part I. TASK AND ENVIRONMENTAL VARIABLES

Chapter 1. **The Stimulus Word**

Stimulus Affectivity	41
Summary and Discussion	53
Stimulus Familiarity	56
Summary and Discussion	63
Part of Speech of Stimulus	67
Summary and Discussion	70
Semantic Level of Stimulus	73
Summary and Discussion	76
The Stimulus Defined in Terms of the Responses Evoked	77
Summary and Discussion	80

Chapter 2. **Verbal Context**

Manipulation of the Associative Environment	82
Manipulation of Other Aspects of the Verbal Environment	86
Examples and Instructions	91
Summary and Discussion	93

Chapter 3. **Repeated Stimulus Presentation: Originality or Satiation?**

Studies of Originality Training	99
Studies of Satiation	103
Summary and Discussion	106
Further Thoughts on Originality Training	111

Chapter 4. Reinforcement

Positive Reinforcement	115
Negative Reinforcement	116
Positive and Negative Reinforcement	119
Summary and Discussion	120

Chapter 5. Stress

Stress as a Subject Variable	124
Experimentally Induced Stress	127
Summary and Discussion	131

Part II. SUBJECT VARIABLES

Chapter 6. Demographic Variables

Age	141
Summary	149
Sex	151
Summary	153
Educational Level and Socioeconomic Status	154
Summary	155
Discussion	156

Chapter 7. Organismic Variables

Intelligence and Verbal Ability	159
Summary	163
Values and Interests	164
Summary	167
Personality	168
Summary	172
Response Sets and Cognitive Styles	174
Summary	177
Selected Subject Groups	178
Summary	180
Discussion	181

Chapter 8. Pathological Conditions

Functional Pathology	191
Altered States of Consciousness	203
Organic Pathology	205
Summary and Discussion	208

Chapter 9. **Cultural Differences**

Chronological Changes 217
Cross-Cultural Studies 221
Summary and Discussion 223

Chapter 10. **Concluding Remarks** 226

Epilogue 242
Bibliography 243
Author Index 261
Subject Index 267

INTRODUCTION

This is a book about word association. In it are reviewed more than 300 studies which appeared in the literature between 1950 and 1965. An attempt has been made to include all English-language publications during this period which used some form of a word-association test as a measure of the dependent variable. With but few exceptions, unpublished dissertations, convention papers, and foreign-language publications have not been included. Inevitably, some investigations will have been overlooked; yet it is the author's belief that the main and reliable findings are represented adequately.

This is not the first book which has been devoted entirely to the consideration of word association. Nearly 50 years ago, C. G. Jung (1918) reported the results of his own experiments and those of colleagues, stressing the relationship between these findings and his theory of psychological complexes. Other shorter reviews of word-association studies have appeared (e.g., Levy, 1956; Rabin & Haworth, 1960; Rapaport *et al.*, 1946; Woodworth & Schlosberg, 1954),* but on the whole, interest in this approach to the study of personality and of thought processes decreased after Jung's early work. Nevertheless, during the period 1950–1965 a reversal in this trend occurred. This renewal of interest in word association in large part reflects the general increase in investigations of verbal learning and verbal behavior and, perhaps, an increasing interest in the study of cognitive processes.

Considering the large number of investigations which recently have been conducted in this area, one might reasonably ask why so many people have been interested in the study of word association. Although the determining cause for each individual experimenter is in some senses undoubtedly unique, several general sources of interest can be pointed out. These general reasons can be grouped into two broad areas. For some investigators, the identification of natural language associative habits is but a first step in the study of other cognitive processes. Implicit in these studies is the assumption that associative connections among words are important and meaningful factors in determining these processes. In fact, such associations

---

*Since the writing of the first draft of the present book, another review has appeared; see J. Jung (1966).

have been shown empirically to be powerful predictors of such behavior as organization in free recall, facilitation of transfer, and ease of concept attainment. In this type of study, then, the interest in word association is in providing calibrated experimental materials so that associative strength may be used as an independent variable. Thus, knowledge about word association is only a preliminary phase in developing some further study. In addition to these learning experiments, there have been attempts to explain other aspects of cognition on the basis of word-association studies. Noble (1952), for example, has dealt with the problem of meaning and meaningfulness in this way, and S. A. Mednick (1962) has formulated a theory of creativity based on associative factors. In this book, we shall not be concerned further with this role of association as an independent variable.* However, it is clear that factors which affect associations themselves must in turn play an important role in determining any other cognitive functions which are based on these associations, and this would be reason enough to study them in more detail.

But beyond this interest, there is another reason why investigators have studied word association, and here the interest has been more in the associations themselves. This interest is based on the belief that associations *per se* reflect something basic about the nature of the mind and its thought processes. It is these investigations of word association—where the association is considered as a dependent variable, to be explained as a function of other factors—with which this book is concerned. The interest of this group of investigators in word association can be understood as reflecting the belief that associative processes are among the basic mechanisms of thought, and that to understand associative processes it is necessary to understand the constituent associations of which they are formulated.

The idea that associative processes are basic to the understanding of thinking has a long tradition in our intellectual history. Both the philosophical and psychological antecedents of present-day association theory have been clearly traced by Boring (1950), Robinson (1932), Woodworth and Schlosberg (1954), and most recently, by Deese (1965), among others, and will not be repeated here. What we will attempt to do is to discuss the general question of why contemporary psychologists are interested in the study of word association. Again, Deese (1965) has written a clear and stimulating presentation of the implications of past and current word-association studies of psychological investigations of verbal behavior and thought, and the reader is referred to his

---

*For further discussion of this issue, the reader is referred to the reviews of Amster (1964), Cofer (1965), Deese (1962b), and J. J. Jenkins (1963).

excellent work for a more thorough treatment of this problem. Although a good part of the discussion which follows includes ideas presented by Deese, the present author is responsible for the way in which they are formulated.

As mentioned above, there is a long historical tradition for making the assumption that knowledge of overt verbal associations will tell us something about the nature and structure of the mind. The "laws of association" of the early Greek philosophers were developed out of an attempt to explain the sequence of ideas occurring in a train of thought. These laws—that associations between ideas are based on contiguity, similarity, or contrast—were taken over by the British empiricists during the eighteenth and nineteenth centuries, and were thought to be the basic principles which explained the way the mind functions. It was their belief that even the most complicated mental functions could be accounted for by the laws of association, or, to put it another way, that a thorough understanding of association would result in a complete understanding of thinking.

It was during this period that several additional, secondary laws of association were formulated. These took into account the influence on the formation of associative relationships of such varibles as stimulus intensity and duration, frequency, and recency of association. In addition to these factors—which might be considered to be task and environmental variables—the potential influences of certain subject variables—as constitutional differences, changes in emotional state, and differences in past experience—were also included in the secondary laws.

Interestingly enough, these two groupings of associative laws can be traced as resulting in two distinctive approaches to the study of association within psychology. Study of the primary laws of association—or attempts to determine the conditions under which associations are originally formed have, beginning with Ebbinghaus, typically been the problem of psychologists studying learning, and especially those studying verbal learning. Ebbinghaus, of course, used relatively meaningless material in his attempt to determine how associations are formed. It is in this connection that Woodworth and Schlosberg (1954) object to the use of natural language word associations in the study of learning, on the basis that such studies bypass the critical problem of how the associations were formed in the first place. Nevertheless, the clear parallel between the paired-associate paradigm used to study the experimental association of artificial material, and the stimulus-response pairs studied in word association investigations points to a basic congruence in the assumptions underlying the two methods. That is, in both cases it is assumed that understanding the simple S-R associative habit will be beneficial in understanding more complex cognitive processes.

In contrast to this approach to the study of association, those current investigations which are concerned with the conditions which modify *preexisting* associations basically involve studying the secondary laws of association. These systematic investigations of preexisting associations began with the psychometric, classificatory studies of F. Galton (1879–1880) and W. Wundt (in Boring, 1950), and continue today in studies grouped under the general heading of verbal behavior. In many of these studies, the veracity of the primary laws of association has been assumed, and the associations obtained have been classified according to categories based on these laws. As an offshoot of the early studies of Galton and Wundt—but including an additional concern about the role of subject variables in modifying association—came the early diagnostic studies of Jung and Ricklin in 1904, and the detective studies of Wertheimer in 1905 (both reported in Woodworth & Schlosberg, 1954). Both of these latter methods were based on the belief that either from the content of the associative response or in the emotional reaction accompanying the response, it would be possible to discern the central problem, or complex, which bothered the patient, in the former case, or to identify the criminal, in the latter case. The potential usefulness of the WAT as a psychodiagnostic technique received an additional boost from Bleuler's studies (1924) of schizophrenia, in which he identified as a primary symptom of schizophrenia a "loosening of association." Subsequently, the presence of an associative disorder has been the *sine qua non* for diagnosing schizophrenia. Presumably, then, a test such as the WAT, which focuses specifically on this aspect of behavior, should be ideally suited both for the practical problem of detecting associative abnormalities as well as for the theoretical problem of specifying the nature of the associative disorder which is manifest in schizophrenia. Both of these clinical methods have continued to be used as diagnostic techniques to the present day, although their popularity has diminished considerably. Part of this decline in popularity may well be the result of the ineffectiveness of the old *a priori* classificatory systems to make meaningful discriminations.

It was not difficult for psychology to adopt the associationistic position of the British philosophers, especially considering the emphasis on empiricism of the latter. However, following Watson's declaration (1913), it was some time before cognition was reinstated as a legitimate topic of interest within empirical, behavioristic psychology. The necessity for this move was manifest in Hull's postulating the pure stimulus act (Hull, 1930). The $r_G-s_G-r_G-s_G$ chains which Hull hypothesized to account for such cognitive behaviors as expectation, anticipation, and purpose, were conceived of as consisting of a series of subvocal, verbal reactions. In fact, Hull explicitly equated this chain of verbal associations with cognition (1952, p. 152), and by so doing brought thinking back into experimental psychology.

This approach to the study of cognitive processes has been continued by Osgood (1953) and others, by assuming that cognition consists of a series of implicit mediating responses between the initial overt stimulus and subsequent overt response. Whether or not these mediating responses are entirely verbal (as opposed to being, at least in part, physiological) has been a source of disagreement. Nevertheless, there have been a substantial number of investigators (e.g., Cofer & Foley, 1942; J. J. Jenkins, 1963; J. J. Jenkins & Russell, 1952) who have assumed that the chain of mediating responses follows the same pattern as that reflected in overt word associations. Again the study of word association would be expected to illuminate the nature of these mediating, cognitive processes.

Perhaps the clearest statement of this position is provided by Deese. He writes, "We study associations in order to make inferences about the nature of human thought, and these associations are cast in the language which embodies the thought.... To the extent that verbal behavior is the mediator of thought, modern association theory is a theory of thought. The whole of the current concern with associative mediators, as a matter of fact, is an effort to use the associative properties of *explicit* verbal behavior as a model for the implicit verbal processes of thought" (1965, p. 4). Deese, however, goes on to point out that the large part of work based on association theory has been concerned with the temporal sequence of associations—the process of getting from one idea to another—while relatively little attention has been given to the organization, or structure of associations. It is to this problem which Deese directs his book, in which he demonstrates that factor analysis may be meaningfully applied to word-association data to reveal the underlying patterns, or structures, of associative organization. This technique makes it possible to compare the basic structural similarity of different concepts, on the one hand, or of the cognitive structures of different subject groups, on the other. This latter comparison of the associative structures of different cultural and/or linguistic groups appears to have considerable promise as a means to study the broader question of whether there are constitutionally given principles which determine the way in which any individual structures his experience, or whether cognitive structures are primarily determined by the particular experiences which the individual encounters.

To recapitulate, then, there are two rather different lines of investigation within verbal learning and verbal behavior, both of which are based on association theory. One of these approaches can be seen as reflecting a concern about the primary laws of association, and the other is based on an interest in the secondary laws. To answer the question of how associations are formed in the first place, investigators typically have used relatively meaningless materials. To study the influence of secondary variables on the manifestation of associations, investigators have often made use of natural language, preexperimental associations, in which the associative connection is taken as a given. Whether or not these two types of associative habits will produce the same effects is open to some question, and it might be argued that if we want a theory of verbal learning which is relevant to the "real" verbal behavior of human beings, we should concentrate on the study of real language associations. On the other hand, as has been pointed out, it has also been argued that focusing on such natural language associations tells us nothing about the basic principles of association—i.e., does not explain how such associations are formed.* Recently, however, some attempts have been made to bridge this gap between the study of the formation of experimental, artificial associations and the manifestation of natural language associations. A number of developmental studies have investigated the changes in associative behavior which occur over time, and Ervin (1961) and McNeill (1963, 1966), in particular, have attempted to provide an explanation of how natural language associations are established in the first place.

As indicated, the criterion for the inclusion of a study in the present book is that a word association test was used as the measure of the dependent variable. More often than not, the word-association test *per se* was not the purpose of the study, but, rather, was used as a technique to investigate another problem. However, the studies often make the implicit assumption that the behavior observed in the responses given to a word-association test reflects the functioning of the underlying thought processes of the individual. This assumption corresponds to the author's point of view that thinking is at least partly associationistic, and that the discovery of the correlates, determinants, and constraints of association will aid us in understanding thinking. The present interest in the word-association test derives from the author's belief that stimulus-response word associations represent very simple units of thought, and that understanding these more simple units will aid us in understanding the enormously more complicated activity of "thinking."

In the material which follows, an attempt is made to present systematically the variables which influence the manifestation of natural language associative habits. The book is divided into two main parts. Part I includes those studies which demonstrate the effect of various task, or environmental variables on the responses given to a word-association test. The first

---

*The problem of natural language versus experimentally acquired associations has been discussed at some length by Russell (1961).

chapter in Part I considers the effect of different characteristics of the stimulus word itself on associative responses; for example, the rated emotionality of the stimulus, its familiarity, and the part of speech which it represents have all been found to influence associative responses. The second general topic to be considered in Part I is the effect on the responses obtained of the verbal context surrounding the association test. Context, here, may refer to the one word which precedes the (one) association test stimulus word. More generally, it may refer to the number and/or types of words which constitute the entire test, or to the verbal instructions provided by the experimenter. Investigations of priming, compound stimuli, and set, for example, are included in this section.

In Chapter 3, the effect of the repeated presentation of a stimulus word on associative responses is discussed. It has been suggested, on the one hand, that this procedure may result in verbal satiation—that is, may be responsible for that word's loss of meaning. On the other hand, it is interesting to note that this procedure has also been utilized to promote originality—or at least the giving of unusual responses. The findings of these different areas of study, which nevertheless utilize the same experimental procedure, are considered in this third section.

The fourth chapter is concerned with the effects of reinforcement on word association. Here, the customary problems of reinforcement studies are considered—variables of quantity, intensity, and schedule of reinforcement. However, as distinct from animal studies, reinforcement has often been found to have either an inconsistent effect or no effect on human verbal behavior or verbal learning. In these investigations, the effect of the subjects' awareness of the intent of the experimenter (e.g., the desire of the subject to please or to accommodate the experimenter) becomes a critical variable.

Finally, the effects of stress, or anxiety, in determining associative responses are considered in Chapter 5. In this section, stress is defined either in terms of being a subject variable, or in terms of being the result of the manipulation of some environmental variable. In the former case, subjects are selected for being anxious or nonanxious on the basis of their scores on some personality test—such as the Taylor Manifest Anxiety Scale—designed to measure anxiety. In the latter case, some manipulation of the physical environment—such as deprivation or application of a noxious stimulus—may be used as a stressor variable, or the environmentally induced stress may be psychological—e.g., the subject is told he is performing very poorly. These studies, which often vary both environmental and subject variables, provide a sort of bridge between the first and second parts of the book.

In Part II, those studies which have demonstrated the effect of subject variables on associative responses are presented. It is in this sense, of course, that the WAT is used as a clinical technique, under the assumption that different types of individuals give different types of associative responses. The "types" of individuals tested are generally suffering from some pathology, and part of the purpose of the testing is to help diagnose this condition.

Nevertheless, there are a number of other, less dramatic subject variables, which have been shown to influence associative responses. Chapter 6 discusses the relationship between several demographic variables—such as age, sex, educational level, and socioeconomic status—and word association responses. Chapter 7 presents the relationship between what are here termed organismic variables and associative responses. Included under this heading are the influences of such factors as intelligence, personal values, personality characteristics, and cognitive style—the more global aspects of the human organism. The consequences of pathology for association responses are treated in Chapter 8. The effects of both functional disorders—psychotic and neurotic—and of organic conditions are discussed here. Finally, the few investigations of the influence of social and cultural factors on word association are discussed in Chapter 9. In general, the variables discussed in Part II have been less systematically and less thoroughly investigated than those of Part I.

By and large, there has been little overlap between the studies of Part I and Part II. That is to say, relatively little attention has been paid to the interaction between task (or environmental) variables and subject variables. An exception to this generally valid assertion occurs both in those investigations which have studied the effects of therapeutic approaches (e.g., chemical, verbal) on subjects of different diagnostic categories, and in those studies which determine the effects of different types of environmental stress on subjects who differ as to preexperimental anxiety level. Also, an occasional study has investigated the relationship between particular stimulus words and the responses of subjects for whom those stimuli might be especially important (e.g., presenting to students of law stimulus words which are relevant to the concept "law").

However, on the whole, even though certain subject variables have been found to be correlated with consistent response effects, these variables have been little considered in the selection of subjects for the studies reported in Part I. Presumably, in these studies, possible subject effects are controlled for by random sampling. On the other hand, the importance of task or environmental variables has often been overlooked in the studies reported in Part II, or one finds a lag between the discovery of relevant variables in experimental studies and cognizance of these in clinical studies. This is not to suggest, however, that such is the case with all clinical studies. Certainly there are clinical investigations which show both ample awareness of "experimental" findings and considerable sophistication in the necessary controls and design required for this area of study, where so many small, seemingly insignificant variations in method or materials have been found to markedly influence results. One can only hope that, in the future, the two groups of investigators may make greater use of each other's findings.

In each of these chapters, studies will be reported in which one of several possible types of association tests were used. Also, different response measures have been used by different investigators. For those readers who may not be familiar with the differences among the several types of tests and response measures, as well as for those readers who find the comparison of test methods of intrinsic interest (and there are some critical theoretical questions involved in the choice of test format used to determine the nature of the associative domain),* a section on this topic has been placed just before Part I. This Prologue, which provides descriptions, definitions, and, where available, information contrasting the results of different test methods, may be found to be somewhat dull and of less interest than subsequent chapters. It is thus suggested that the reader may want to proceed immediately to Part I, and to refer back to the Prologue only when specific questions arise about test methods or response measures. At the end of this work, the author has attempted to formulate some general ideas about the functioning of associative processes, as revealed in these studies of word association. In addition, she has attempted to point out the relevance of these formulations to the more general issue of styles of cognition as a subject-determined variable.

One more word about the format of this book. Each of the chapters is organized in essentially the same way. The first part presents, in a concise version, the findings and conclusions of individual experimenters who have investigated the problem area of the chapter. These individual studies are grouped according to the aspect of associative response being studied—i.e., according to the response measure used. Following this factual presentation, an outline summary of the findings is provided, after which some summary statements, attempts at reconciliation of disparate findings, and other general comments by the present author are made.

---

*This issue is discussed further in Chapter 1, p. 53ff. and p. 64ff., and in Chapter 10, p. 229ff.

PROLOGUE

This section focuses on the methods and techniques of word association—the question of how association data are collected and what is done with the data, once obtained. As an initial problem, we will consider how the word-association test stimuli are chosen. Then we will consider various methods used for presenting the test stimuli and for eliciting associative responses. Finally, we will look at the variety of response measures which have been used to describe the results of the test. Where comparisons have been made among the various techniques, these are also included.

It seems appropriate to present these methodological issues at the beginning of this book, since subsequent chapters will present studies based on one or another of these procedures. Furthermore, the section on response measures will acquaint the reader with the notation which will be used throughout the book to designate these measures.

Choice of Stimuli

Although any set of words is, in theory, appropriate for use as word-association test (WAT) stimuli, in fact, experimenters ofter refer to a standard set of words, so as to be able to make use of normative data available for those words. For example, extensive information is available for the 100 stimulus words of the Kent-Rosanoff list (Palermo & Jenkins, 1964; Russell & Jenkins, 1954). Since these words are predominantly nouns and adjectives, Palermo and Jenkins (1964) have constructed a new list of stimuli of other grammatical classes and have gathered extensive normative data on these words. Bousfield, Cohen, Whitmarsh, and Kincaid (1961) also have compiled a frequently used stimulus list.

In clinical studies, the Menninger word list (Rapaport, Gill, & Schafer, 1946) has been a common source for stimulus words. Again, the availability of normative information as well as the classification of the stimuli into certain affective categories has enhanced the usefulness of this list.

Although these lists provide the most widely used sources for stimuli, there are a variety of other stimulus-word lists with normative information available. These have been listed toward the end of the references, under the heading "Normative Data." In addition, a number of experimenters will select idiosyncratic stimuli which are especially suited to the needs of their particular investigations.

There has also been some interest in obtaining verbal associations to random shapes (A. G. Goldstein, 1961; Vanderplas & Garvin, 1959), to pictures (Deterline, 1957), and to Bender-Gestalt figures (Greenbaum, 1955). In the latter technique, the verbal responses obtained are subsequently presented as stimuli, as part of the standard WAT, in an attempt to clarify the meaning which the figures have for the individual being tested.

Format of Association Test

Association tests may be divided into two general classes—free association and controlled association. In *free* association, the subject is free to give a response from any semantic or grammatical category. It is left unspecified as to what kind of response should be given. In *controlled* association, the subject is limited as to the type of response which is acceptable. The limitation may be in terms of instructions to choose a response from a particular category (e.g., antonyms), or it may be in terms of presenting a test in which the response alternatives are specified (e.g., as in a multiple-choice test).

FREE ASSOCIATION

Within the free-association method, there are several different procedures employed. Probably the more frequently used procedure is that in which the subject is given a single stimulus word and asked to respond as rapidly as possible with the first single word which comes to mind. This procedure is an example of a *discrete* free-association test (any single-word response is acceptable). Other types of free-association tests are used, however, and the resulting picture of the associative domain has been found to differ according to the format of the test. For example, in *continued* association, the subject is presented with the same stimulus word a number of times and must continue to give associative responses to the original stimulus. Sometimes he is instructed not to give the same responses; sometimes no instructions are given. The number of responses elicited may be determined by the number of times the stimulus is presented or by the interval of time allowed for the subject to make responses. In the method of *continuous association*, the stimulus term is presented only once; the subject uses this word as a point of departure for a chain of associative responses, only the first of which may be directly determined by the nominal stimulus. As before, the number of responses is determined, in part, by the length of the response interval allowed.

Discrete Association. A well-known study where the method of discrete free association was used is that of Russell and Jenkins (1954), in which the single responses of 1,008 subjects were used to establish the Minnesota norms to each stimulus of Kent-Rosanoff WAT. Subsequent normative studies (e.g., Palermo & Jenkins, 1964; Postman, in preparation) have also utilized this method. (For a more complete listing of normative data available, see Normative Data list, in the Reference section.)

Continued Association. The method of continued association is well exemplified in the work of Noble (e.g., 1952), in which the mean number of responses elicited by a stimulus during a 60-second interval was taken as an index of the "meaningfulness," m, of that stimulus. These m values have been found to be remarkably stable over time and consistent from one investigation to the next (e.g., cf. Cieutat, 1962; for a review of reliability studies of m, see Noble, 1963).

As a variant on this method of continued association to measure meaningfulness, Archer (1960) and Noble (1961) have asked subjects to *rate* stimuli in terms of their associative power. In Archer's study, association value, a, is based on the number of subjects who indicate the stimulus evokes at least one response; in Noble's study, the rated association value, m', is based on how many associations the stimulus evokes in the mind of the subject. The agreement between m, m', and a is high; Noble (1963) notes correlations of .90+ between m and m', the correlation between m and a is smaller, due to the fact that a is a very insensitive measure at the upper end of the associative scale. S. S. Shapiro (1964b), using nonsense and real word CVCs, also found a significant ($p < .01$) agreement between Noble's m^1 and the m values obtained from grade-school-aged subjects.

Successive Association. Another variant on the method of continued association is that of successive or intermittently repeated trials, in which the whole list of stimuli is presented several times, thereby separating each presentation of the stimulus by as many stimuli as there are in the total list. This is the standard method used for determining reproduction disturbances, in which case the subject is requested to repeat his response of the initial trial on a second trial. Appelbaum (1960a) has suggested expanding this technique to include a third trial on which the subject is requested to give a *new* response, the hypothesis being that by eliminating a highly overlearned response it may be possible to see to what extent this stereotyped response masks some underlying thought disturbance. Milgram (1961) also has suggested that the reliance on highly overlearned verbal habits may allow subjects to bypass idiosyncratic associative networks. The utility of this approach was borne out in a subsequent study (Appelbaum, 1960b) in which brain-damaged subjects, who were indistinguishable from nonbrain-damaged subjects on a reproduction test, showed more response disturbance and inability to produce a new response on the third trial. In a further study

(Appelbaum, 1963) involving emotional stimuli,* even though the subjects could be separated on the basis of second-trial reproduction responses, use of the third trial was a more effective differentiator.

A comparison of the standard reproduction test method with that proposed by Applebaum indicated that reaction time on the critical trial is longer for the Applebaum method, but that more errors are made when the standard method is used (Bodin & Geer, 1965).

The method of successive trials may be expanded to include studies in which there is a longer time interval between trials. Thus Weintraub, Silverstein, and Klee (1960), on retesting subjects after a 1-week interval, found the frequency of popular responses (responses which occurred with an absolute frequency of at least 10, in the Rapaport [Rapaport *et al.*, 1946] standardization data) to significantly increase on the second test, while both association disturbances and reaction time significantly decreased. This finding was interpreted as reflecting a tendency of normal subjects to try to make more appropriate, adaptive responses to stressful stimuli, a hypothesis which finds some support in the fact that LSD subjects did not show this corrective tendency. Shakow (1963) has also noted this increase in response commonality on a retest after a two-week interval, although 58% of the actual responses changed on the retest. However, as with LSD subjects, repeated testing of a group of schizophrenics over a 17-month period did not show any change in response commonality.

S. S. Shapiro (1965), retesting eighth-grade subjects on the same 30 stimuli 2 months later, similarly to Shakow, found that the number of Primary responses had increased, while 50% of the actual responses had changed on the retest. The Primary response increase was especially true for those subjects who learned, as a paired-associate task just prior to the second test, the Primary responses to eight of the WAT stimuli. However, it also occurred when the paired-associate responses were low-frequency associates of the stimuli, as well as when no paired-associate task was administered.

Continued Association, Successive Trials. Two studies have combined the method of continued association with that of repeated trials. Kanungo and Lambert (1963) retested subjects on the same stimulus list after a 1-day interval and on a new stimulus list after a 2-day interval. In both cases, the number of relevant continued-association responses increased and the number of irrelevant responses decreased on the second test—a finding which partially supports the Weintraub *et al.* hypothesis. In Jacobs' study, (1959), subjects were required to write 10 responses to each of 13 neutral and

*In general, the designation of a stimulus as emotional, or traumatic, has depended on the theoretical orientation of the investigator and/or on ratings made by independent judges, or by the subjects themselves.

emotional nouns, and were retested at an interval of 2 days, 1 week, or 2 months. For all time intervals, the proportion and rank of occurrence of identical responses on the second testing was significantly related to the order of elicitation of the response on the first presentation. Information on the absolute frequency of occurrence of Popular responses was not provided. Further studies of the effect of repeated trials on subsequent associative responses will be presented in the following section, in which *type* of preceding trial as a variable establishing psychological set will be discussed.

Continuous Association. The effect of continuous, or chain, association on subsequent associative responses has been studied by Osipow and Grooms (1965b), who found that with successive links in the chain, strength of Primary response decreases, while number of different responses increases. Furthermore, the authors cite these findings of increased idiosyncrasy of response with increasing response links as support for Appelbaum's suggestion (1960a) that investigating additional associative links might be clinically useful. Other continuous-association studies have been conducted by Cofer and Shevitz (1952) and Koen (1962), although the effect of the format of the test was not of concern in these investigations.

Additional Methods. Several other free-association methods have been proposed. One of these—that of discrete serial association—has been used by Fosmire (1965) to map the associative network of individual subjects. In this technique, the response to the first stimulus becomes the stimulus for the next trial; the second response, in turn, becomes the stimulus for the third trial; and so on. This technique is, then, similar to continuous association in that it elicits a chain of associative responses, but it differs in that there is more control over the actual stimulus for each link in the chain.

Another method of free association has been proposed by Robertson (1952). In this "time-limit version," the subject is instructed to write down as many words as possible within the time allotted. In addition, the subject is told that his responses must be phrases or sentences, and that one-word responses must be avoided. Twenty minutes is suggested as an optimal time limit.

CONTROLLED ASSOCIATION

The other general format used to present stimuli is that of the restricted, or controlled, association test. In this case, the subject must choose his response from a restricted domain of responses specified by the experimenter. This domain may be determined by a semantic category (e.g., the response must be supraordinate to the stimulus) or by a particular concept (e.g., the response must be the name of a color). Alternatively, the domain may be restricted to a small number of response alternatives provided by the experimenter. A variant on this latter, multiple-choice association test is the Remote Associates Test (RAT) (S. A. Mednick, 1962; Wilson, Guilford, & Christensen, 1953), in which multiple stimuli are presented and the subject is restricted to a response which is associatively related to all the stimuli. This response may be a forward or a reverse associate of the stimuli. In a related technique, Flaugher (1965) has made use of reverse association exclusively. Subjects are presented with an increasing number of associative responses and are requested to determine what stimulus word produced the given responses. In addition to the format of the RAT described above, Wilson *et al.* (1953) also have suggested an alternate form in which the stimulus word is presented, followed by five letters. The subject must indicate which of the five is the first letter of the correct associative response.

In other controlled-association studies, responses may be restricted to a particular semantic class. The results of two studies in which subjects were restricted to supra- or subordinate responses (Peters, 1952, 1958) will be discussed below. An investigation in which the subjects were restricted to synonyms of the stimuli (Hills, 1958) is presented in Part II.

A study by Underwood and Richardson (1956) provides an example of controlled association in which the response concept category was specified. In this investigation, the method of simultaneous visual and oral presentation was used, and subjects were instructed to give sensory-impression responses. With practice and discussion, subjects were able to adopt this set successfully within approximately ten trials.

In another investigation in which response category was specified (Beck, 1960), approximately 1,000 teenage subjects were asked to respond with one of 11 colors to 60 WAT stimuli. The results indicated that only five of the stimulus words were not significantly associated with some color, and that no significant change was apparent in a retest after 1 week. Lester (1960) also restricted subjects to "color" responses in a 10-minute continuous-association task and contrasted the performance on this production task with that on a task requiring the reproduction of a 40-item list of "food" words. The resulting responses were scored in terms of both a lenient and a rigid criterion. It was found that with increasing response restrictions (production versus reproduction; lenient versus rigid criterion) it was increasingly easy to differentiate among subject groups varying as to psychopathology (see p. 196). Bousfield and Barclay (1950) have also employed a continuous controlled-association task to determine the relationship between order and frequency of occurrence of a response. In this task, subjects were given 18 minutes to give as many "Bird," or "Carpenter's Tools," or "Heavenly Bodies" responses as they could.*

---

*For the relationship between the two response measures, see p. 17; for the effect of types of stimulus, see p. 73.

The use of the multiple-choice format, despite its expediency* has thus far remained a less popular method. In one such study (Buchwald, 1957), subjects were presented with the four response alternatives prior to being presented with the stimulus. Under these conditions, the obtained response frequencies were noted to differ (direction unspecified) from those obtained under discrete free-association conditions. The author hypothesizes that a recency effect may be responsible for this change. Priming studies to be reported subsequently would support this assumption. For example, Howes and Osgood (1954) found that the associative-response distributions to the same stimuli could be markedly altered by variations in the verbal context immediately preceding the stimulus word, and Storms (1958) noted that the presentation of an infrequent associative response just prior to the association test could increase significantly (that is, prime) the occurrence of that word as a response. These findings suggest that the overt presentation of response alternatives to the subject may produce a priming effect, whereby the usual distribution of associative responses is considerably changed.

It is clear that the use of a controlled-association test can substantially affect both the nature and frequency of the associative responses obtained. Although we have been considering this variable under the general heading of the format of the association test itself, the restriction of responses to particular semantic categories can as easily be considered as an instructional variable. Additional studies will be considered under this heading in Chapter 2.

Comparison of Association Methods

A comparison of the types of associative responses obtained from the different association test methods has been the topic of a number of studies. Most of these investigations have compared discrete, continued, and continuous responses given under free conditions, although an occasional study has looked at the effect of test format on controlled-association responses.

Continued versus Discrete Association

The differential effects of the methods of continued versus discrete association have been directly studied by Cofer (1958), Brody (1964), Garskof (1965), and Rosen and Russell (1957). In Cofer's study, each stimulus was listed repetitively; the subject was allowed 60 seconds to res-

---

*E.g., responses can be directly recorded on IBM cards, considerably facilitating data processing.

pond. These continued-association data were then compared with the discrete responses of the 1954 Minnesota norms to the same 25 stimuli. Although a close correspondence between the responses of the two methods was noted (e.g., 16 of the Primary responses of the continued method were also Minnesota Primaries), the agreement among the most frequent responses was not perfect, and the discrepancy was greatest when the high-frequency normative response was an antonym of the stimulus. Furthermore, Cofer found that the number of different responses elicited by the continued method, m, always exceeded those elicited by the discrete method, D. Noble (1963) has also noted that continued association always elicits more different responses than discrete. Howe (1965), on the other hand, found no relationship (either positive or negative) between the number of D and m responses elicited by 58 of the Kent-Rosanoff stimuli.*

Several studies have suggested that the response hierarchies obtained from discrete and from continued methods are quite similar. Brody (1964) tested 30 high-school boys with a discrete WAT and then presented the same stimuli to a new group of comparable subjects for continued associations over successive trials; on each trial the stimuli were presented in random order. In this study the number of different responses elicited by the stimuli under the two methods was quite similar (Kendall's tau $= .65$, $p < .01$). Furthermore, the results indicated that the probability of a word being given among the second to fifteenth continued-association responses was directly related to the frequency of that response in the discrete association data.

Garskof (1965) also found that continued association produced many more different responses than discrete. However, if only the responses which appeared in the single-word association hierarchies were considered for comparison purposes, then a correspondence between the frequencies of responses obtained under the discrete and (restricted) continued methods could be noted (product moment r ranged from .35 to .86). Furthermore, if in addition to response frequency, order of emission in the (restricted) continued-association data were taken into account, the correlations based on stimulus-response strength were increased in all cases ($r = .52$ to .94). These findings suggested to the investigator that the continued-association response hierarchies, when based on frequency plus order of emission of the responses, may closely approximate the response hierarchies based on the frequency of discrete responses.

*Clearly, the relationship between D and m depends, in addition to any intrinsic connection between the two measures, on the number of subjects in the sample used to determine the first measure, and the time allowed for determining the second. It should also be noted that in Howe's study, the stimuli were predominantly of high Thorndike-Lorge frequency (Howe, personal communication, 1965).

This similarity in associative hierarchies, at least among the dominant responses, was also noted by Rosen and Russell (1957). Subjects were asked to give two different responses to 50 Kent-Rosanoff stimuli; these responses were compared with the normative hierarchies based on discrete responses to those same stimuli (Russell & Jenkins, 1954). The results indicated that the average normative frequency of the second continued-associative response was lower than that of the first. (However, this trend was reversed for 29% of the subjects). In addition, of 15 selected stimuli, the most frequent second continued-associative response was identical with the normative secondary in eight cases; in the remaining cases, the most frequent second continued response was the same as the normative tertiary two times and the same as the normative Primary five times. Furthermore, when the frequency of the associations given as second responses was compared with the rankings of those same responses relative to each other in the discrete normative data, the resulting rank order correlations ranged from +.38 to +.98, with a median of +.75. The authors conclude that these results support the contention that normative data based on single discrete associations "may be taken as an index of the strength of the response" (p. 122). Furthermore, these results indicate a correspondence between response hierarchies obtained from discrete and from continued methods of association, at least among the dominant responses.

CONTINUOUS VERSUS DISCRETE ASSOCIATION

Continuous-association data also have been compared with the Minnesota discrete-association data (Laffal & Feldman, 1962). In this study, the continuous responses to each stimulus obtained during a 25-second interval, were assigned to one of several categories previously found useful in describing associative data, thereby making up a response profile for each stimulus.* Subsequently, each stimulus was paired with each other stimulus and the respective profiles were compared for degree of overlap. This procedure was repeated for the discrete normative data. Matrices of these overlap coefficients were then factor-analyzed separately for each kind of association data; the resulting factorial structure indicated that the associative-response profiles elicited by the two association methods were quite similar, but that continuous association involved an additional dimension—which might be described as secondary association, or chaining—not found in the associative structure based on discrete responses. Furthermore, the factor loadings were more extreme (both positive and negative) for the discrete data, a finding which led the authors to suggest that

---

*For the development and use of this method, see Laffal (1964).

restricting the subject to a single response results in a greater concentration of responses in a few categories—i.e., that "single word association screens out all but the most prominent categories of association" (p. 56).

Although this profile analysis of response categories suggested that responses obtained from discrete and continuous methods of association were highly similar, a comparison of the *actual* responses by Osipow and Grooms (1965a) did not find this similarity. On the contrary, the response hierarchies resulting from discrete free-associative responses were noted to be quite different from the response distributions based on continuous, or chain, responses.

However, in a study contrasting discrete and continuous responses to a *controlled*-association test (the stimuli were girls' names and responses were limited to other girls' names), Osgood and Anderson (1957) noted consistent positive correlations between the probability of A eliciting B as a discrete response and the probability that A would be followed by B in the continuous-association data.

Continuous versus Continued Association

Continuous (chain) association also has been compared with (successive) continued association by De Burger and Donahoe (1965); both methods involved controlled association, in which subjects were restricted to noun responses, and each response was only allowed once for each stimulus. Subsequently, subjects rated both stimuli and responses on three Semantic Differential scales. For both methods, it was found that the correspondence between the Semantic Differential meaning of the stimulus and response became progressively less similar with each successive response, and that the associative strength (as measured by response rank in the Russell-Jenkins 1954 norms) decreased with each response. Furthermore, both of these effects were more pronounced for the chain responses than for the continued associations.

In another study of continuous and continued association (Pollio, 1964b), subjects gave continuous associations to four stimuli for 4 minutes each. The interword reaction time between these continuous responses was used to select three types of associative clusters for each subject: those rapidly emitted (short interword latency), those emitted over a longer interval, and those emitted quite slowly (long interword latency). After a 4-week interval, the individual words comprising these clusters, as well as the four original words, were presented as stimuli for eight continued associative responses. Subjects also were asked to rate these stimuli on three Semantic Differential scales. A measure of "associative cohesiveness" was developed (see p. 34) from the continued-association data which reflected the number of potential interconnections among the items constituting each cluster. Analysis of the data indicated that there was a significant positive relationship between associative cohesiveness and speed of an associative cluster's emission. Furthermore, those clusters which were rapidly emitted were characterized by items which were significantly closer together in semantic space (i.e., had more similar Semantic Differential ratings) than were clusters emitted at a medium speed; items of slow clusters were semantically the most different.

Mode of Stimulus Presentation

The format of WATs may also vary in the mode of stimulus presentation. Stimuli may be presented visually—either printed on a page or projected on a screen—or aurally—generally accomplished by the experimenter pronouncing the stimulus word. Although both of these methods are used with substantial frequency, few investigations of their effect on associative responses have been made. Kintz (1964) presented Noble's 96 disyllables visually, aurally, and with both modes combined, and asked subjects to rate each stimulus on a 9-point scale in terms of the number of associations brought to mind. The correlations for the association values among the three methods of stimulus presentation were all quite high (.90+), leading the author to conclude that association values obtained from studies in which stimuli are presented visually can be used appropriately in subsequent studies when stimuli are presented aurally.

However, the fact that the rated *number* of associations closely corresponds does not necessarily imply similarity among the responses themselves, or among the frequency distributions obtained from these two modes of stimulus presentation. Thus when Palermo and Jenkins (1965b), using grade-school subjects, compared the written responses to stimuli presented either visually or aurally, they found the aural presentation to elicit a greater number of Primary and contrast responses but fewer supraordinate responses. Furthermore, the number of paradigmatic responses to noun stimuli was increased by aural presentation of the stimuli, while mode of stimulus presentation did not influence the number of paradigmatic responses to adjectives. Buchwald (1957) has compared the written responses to 10 Kent-Rosanoff stimuli presented both visually and aurally; he found three of the response frequency distributions to be significantly different (the direction of difference was not discussed). Furthermore, when these stimuli were presented as part of a multiple-choice WAT with four response alternatives, the frequency of response choice was dependent on the order of response presentation for the auditory stimuli, but not for the visual stimuli.

Visually presented stimuli may also vary in terms of the use of upper-case or lower-case letters. In a direct study of this issue, Anderson (1965), collecting discrete and continuous responses to single letters, found the Primary responses to both types of stimuli to be highly similar. However, upper-case stimuli elicited more proper-name responses, and more responses which, although not proper names, were written with the first letter capitalized.

Mode of Response Elicitation

Just as the mode of stimulus presentation may be an important variable, so the manner in which the response is given may affect the obtained associative responses. Unfortunately, studies of the effects of oral versus written responses are often confounded by the effects of the mode of stimulus presentation as well as of the social conditions obtaining in the testing situation—oral responses are obtained from situations in which the stimuli are presented aurally and the subject is tested individually, while written responses are frequently obtained under conditions in which the stimulus is printed and the subject is tested in a group setting—so that it is difficult to determine whether the response variable, the stimulus variable, or the social variable is responsible for the results. However, since many studies make use of normative data obtained under written-group conditions as a basis for subsequent studies involving oral-individual responses, it is important to evaluate the comparability of the two methods.

J. J. Jenkins and Russell (1960) were concerned with this issue and initially cited several studies which seemed to indicate that there was little difference among the responses obtained, especially if speed of response was stressed. The small differences that were noted indicated that the oral-individual method increased the frequency of Primary responses, which the authors interpreted as being a result of the greater obvious time pressure. Postman (1964) also found that the frequency of written and oral responses to stimuli of high, medium, and low Thorndike-Lorge (T-L) frequency (all of which were presented visually) were quite similar, although again the frequency of Primary responses was slightly higher in the oral individual situation. Subsequently, J. J. Jenkins and Palermo (1965) have found increasing evidence that the oral-individual method increases the frequency of the Primary response. In addition, in a study of fourth-grade children, Palermo (1964) found that oral-individual testing increased the frequency of the first five responses in the associative hierarchy, decreased by 20% the occurrence of supraordinate responses, increased by 100% the frequency of contrast responses, and increased the frequency of paradigmatic responses.

The importance of the mode of response has also been found in a study of fifth-grade subjects. Entwisle and Forsyth (1963) found that the frequency of the three most common responses was significantly greater under oral-

II. Controlled Association

As opposed to free association, this method restricts the type of acceptable response.

(1) The response may be chosen from a specified semantic or conceptual category, or

(2) the response alternatives may be provided by the experimenter (multiple-choice test).

(3) The Remote Associates Test, in which the subject is required to find a response in common to several stimuli, is another example of this type of test.

III. Comparison of Association Methods

(1) Comparisons of *discrete versus continued* association have found
   - (A) high agreement for the Primary response,* and
   - (B) high agreement for the response hierarchies obtained.†
   - (C) In addition, both methods have shown that the absolute value of m exceeds the absolute value of D, but that when stimuli are rank-ordered for values of m and D, rho is positive and significant.

(2) Comparisons of *discrete versus continuous* association have found that
   - (A) the *categories* of response are similar, but discrete responses are concentrated into fewer categories. However,
   - (B) the *actual* responses obtained from the two methods are quite different. Continuous association shows an additional factor of secondary association, or chaining—i.e., that aspect of the response process which depends on the effects of the preceding responses in the chain.
   - (C) It also has been found that the probability of B following A in continuous association is a function of the A-B associative strength in discrete association.

(3) Comparisons of *continued versus continuous* association have found
   - (A) a greater decrease in stimulus-response strength with each successive response for continuous association, and
   - (B) a greater decrease in agreement between the Semantic Differential ratings of the stimulus and response for continuous association. It has also been noted that
   - (C) the speed of emission of continuous-association response clusters is positively related to the degree of associative overlap obtained when these responses are presented as stimuli for a continued-association test.

---

*Except when the discrete response is an antonym.

†Especially when the discrete response frequency is used to predict the continued association hierarchy.

IV. MODE OF STIMULUS PRESENTATION

(1) Comparisons of *aural versus visual* presentation of stimuli have found that
- (A) the rated number of associations brought to mind is approximately equal for visual, aural, and visual plus aural presentation.
- (B) However, at least with children, the numbers of Primary responses and contrast responses are greater to aural than to visual stimuli, while the number of supraordinate responses is decreased. Also, the number of responses given by children to noun stimuli is greater for aural than for visual presentation, although no difference is found for adjective stimuli.
- (C) It also has been noted that the responses obtained from the two methods may differ, and that with a multiple-choice test, response frequency is dependent on the order of stimulus presentation for aural, but not for visual, stimuli.

(2) A comparison of *upper-case visual versus lower-case visual* stimuli has found that upper-case single letters elicit more proper name responses and more capitalized non-proper nouns than do lower-case letters.

V. MODE OF RESPONSE

(1) Comparisons of *oral versus written* responses have found the former mode to result in more Primary responses, more contrast responses, and greater response commonality. The oral response mode also elicits a greater number of supraordinate responses, when subjects are instructed to give either supra- or subordinate responses. However, without such instruction, children have been found to give more supraordinate responses when a written mode is used.

(2) It also was noted that these comparisons of response mode are often confounded with the variable of social interaction between the experimenter and subject. The *social presence of the experimenter* (versus his absence) has been found to increase reaction time and to increase the frequency of "human content" responses in a clinical situation of continuous free association. Also, measures of GSR have been found to be greater for first contacts between the experimenter and subject than for subsequent contacts, and to be greater toward a Negro than toward a white experimenter.

Response Measures

The associative responses which are elicited by any of the preceding methods must eventually be categorized in some way, if we are to be able to make some general statements about the results. A large variety of measures have been used to describe the findings of word-association studies. In some cases, the implications and/or referents of these different empirical measures have not been clearly differentiated; hence in this section some attempt is made to provide an interpretation of the response measures. The discussion is divided into two main sections. First those measures used to describe the responses to individual stimuli are presented; this is followed by a discussion of those measures used to describe the degree of similarity, or overlap, of responses given to two or more stimuli.

QUANTITATIVE MEASURES FOR INDIVIDUAL STIMULI

Associative-response Strength. The measures of responses to individual stimuli may be roughly grouped as either indicating the degree of organization of the associative-response domain—a quantitative characterization—or describing the nature of the responses which make up that domain—a qualitative characterization. Several quantitative measures have been used to indicate associative-response strength. Possibly the most frequent of these is a measure of the occurrence of Popular, or Primary, responses. The Primary is that response which occurs with the greatest frequency to any one stimulus. In some studies, this response measure is used in a dichotomous fashion. Here, the stimulus either does, or does not, elicit the Primary response, and the response measure indicates the number of stimuli which do elicit that response. In this case, the maximum number of Primaries is determined by the number of stimuli comprising the WAT. On the other hand, a measure of Primary response strength may indicate the actual frequency of the Primary response to each stimulus. Thus stimuli may have strong or weak Primaries, depending on the proportion of subjects who give that response.

An allied measure of Primary strength is that of response commonality. As used by some investigators (e.g., Horton, Marlowe, & Crowne, 1963; J. J. Jenkins, 1960) response commonality is simply a measure of the occurrence, or nonoccurrence, of the Primary response to a selected set of stimuli. However, "response commonality" has also been used to refer to the frequency of occurrence of any of the *three* most common responses to a stimulus. In addition, response commonality has been determined occasionally by scoring each response in terms of the absolute frequency of its occurrence among the responses of a group of subjects—i.e., its associative-response frequency—which could vary, theoretically, from zero to the total number of subjects tested.

The question of which of these techniques gives the best measure of associative-response strength has been discussed by J. J. Jenkins and

Palermo (1964). They attempted a number of weighting schemes to reflect the *frequency*, as well as occurrence, of a particular response—e.g., to differentiate between the occurrence of a Primary response with a frequency of 25% and a Primary response with a frequency of 65%. Due to the high correlations among the various scoring methods attempted, the authors concluded that a simple counting of the number of Primary responses is sufficient to approximate the weighted frequency score which would be obtained if each individual response were given a score based on its frequency of occurrence in the normative association data.

In all of the measures of response strength discussed thus far, the criteria for what constitutes a Primary, Secondary, or Tertiary response, as well as the associative frequency to assign to any response, may be based either on normative data gathered on some prior occasion, or it may be based on the sample currently being tested. The former method, provided the normative group is large enough and reasonably representative, has obvious advantages.

One final measure of response strength, which can be used only for individual testing, is that of associative reaction time. Here, either the absolute reaction time may be determined for each response, or, alternatively, the number of responses which exceed some standard time may be counted.

Size and Consistency of Associative-Response Domain. In addition to response strength, there are other quantitative measures which reflect the organization of the associative domain. Generally, these may be said to indicate the size of the associative domain, as well as the consistency, or redundancy, or—alternatively—entropy, of the responses given to any one stimulus. For example, a number of investigators have noted that different stimuli elicit varying numbers of associative responses. Although a clear distinction is not always made, "number of different responses" may refer to the number of different responses obtained across subjects based on one response per subject. This measure of discrete responses will be referred to by the symbol D in this book, and will be taken to be an indication of response heterogeneity. Alternatively, "number of different responses" may refer to the average number of continued associations given by each subject to each stimulus, usually within a 60-sec time limit. This measure of continued associative responses has been referred to as m,* and will be taken to be an indication of response availability.† Other measures strongly correlated with m are m^1 (based on subjects' ratings, on a five-point scale, of the relative number of associations elicited by a stimulus; Noble, 1963)

---

*Cf. Noble (1952).
†Underwood and Schulz (1960) have found m to be directly related to response availability.

and a (based on subjects' ratings of whether the stimulus does, or does not, elicit at least one response; Archer, 1960).

A measure allied to response heterogeneity is that of response idiosyncrasy, or originality. An idiosyncratic response is one which is given by only that subject—i.e., a response which, apart from that subject, does not occur in the normative (or group) data. Clearly, D and number of idiosyncratic responses are correlated, although D will always be larger.*

Occasionally the proclivity to give unusual or original responses has been inferred from the absence of Primary or common associative responses. That is, a measure of the number of original responses is estimated as the inverse of the number of Primary responses. Fosmire and Tryk (1963) have argued against this procedure on the grounds that one score places a constraint on the other—i.e., that the subject cannot give both a Primary and an original response to the same stimulus—and they have proposed a correction formula. However, as J. J. Jenkins and Palermo (1964) have clearly pointed out, the strategy to be adopted in determining commonality versus originality of response depends on the purpose of the investigation. If one wishes only a general estimation of originality scores, then counting the number of Primary responses should suffice, since the two measures correlate in the .80's. However, if the main purpose of the study is to investigate original responses, then clearly the most reasonable technique is to count their occurrence.

Measures of response entropy ($H = - p_i \log_2 p_i$) have also been used to describe the distribution of associative responses to a stimulus word. However, as Laffal (1955) has demonstrated, values of H and of D are highly correlated, and the relative ease of calculating the latter measure would appear to outweigh the slightly greater precision obtained by using the former.

Horvath (1963) has demonstrated that the Rule Distribution may be used to describe (statistically) the shape of the associative response hierarchy for any given stimulus word. This distribution is based on the number of different responses given to the stimulus, divided by the total number of responses. From the resulting parameter, α, it is possible to predict the number of responses which should occur, for example, with a frequency of one, the number which would occur with a frequency of two, or three, and so on. In other words, it is possible to predict the slope of the response gradient.

Variability of Associative Responses. Still another measure of response consistency is that of response reproduction. In this case, the stimuli are

---

*Except for the case where every subject gives an idiosyncratic response.

administered a second time and the subject is requested to give the same response as before. Errors in response reproduction are taken to reflect an unstable, or variable, stimulus-response connection.

Several variations on the response reproduction method have been employed. For example, the subject's response may be provided and he is asked to recall the stimulus. Flaugher (1965) has developed a technique to determine the degree of associative relationship between a stimulus and its responses, which he terms a Detection Value measure (DV). According to this technique, the subject is presented with the responses given to the stimulus—either in order of increasing or decreasing frequency—and has the task of identifying the stimulus word which produced them. The DV measure indicates the extent to which one response word serves as a clue in identifying another (i.e., the stimulus word).

Alternatively, the subject may be asked for recall or recognition of the stimuli without being given the response term. A technique of requesting the subject to give a different response than before has also been used. These measures also reflect the variability of associative connections, as well as depending more on memory functions than do the preceding measures.

QUALITATIVE MEASURES FOR INDIVIDUAL STIMULI

In addition to these quantitative measures of the organization of associative responses, there are also measures which characterize the qualitative nature of the responses. Thus responses may be described in terms of the part of speech they represent, whether they are the same part of speech as the stimulus (paradigmatic responses), or whether they occupy different grammatical positions in the language (syntagmatic responses) from the stimulus. They may also be described in terms of whether they are opposites, or contrasts, to the stimulus. These response characteristics, as well as Thorndike-Lorge frequency (T-L) and Semantic Differential (S.D.) polarization, may all be determined fairly objectively by reference to some standard criterion—as a dictionary,* the T-L word count (Thorndike & Lorge, 1944), or the S. D. Atlas (J. J. Jenkins, Russell, & Suci, 1958). Other qualitative response characteristics—such as emotionality, unusualness, degree of disturbance, conceptual closeness to, or distance from, the stimulus, degree of representing some concept, and classification as supra-, sub-, or co-ordinate responses with respect to the stimulus—are generally determined from ratings made either by the experimenter, the subject, or by

---

*E.g., C. L. Barnhart, *Thorndike-Barnhart Comprehensive Desk Dictionary* (Garden City, N.Y.: Doubleday, 1951) is useful, in that it lists the meanings of words in order of their frequency of usage.

an independent group of subjects (e.g., see J. J. Jenkins & Russell, 1960; Peters, 1952). A fairly large number of subcategories of response disturbance have been proposed, but the inconsistent and/or insignificant findings obtained when they have been used makes it somewhat doubtful if their use merits the amount of additional scoring effort required (e.g., Applebaum, 1963; Flavell, Draguns, Feinberg, & Budin, 1958).

PHYSIOLOGICAL MEASURES

Finally, a few studies have investigated the physiological reactions concomitant with making an associative response. Measures of GSR have been most frequent (e.g., Boyd & Valentine, 1953; Dixon, 1956, 1958; Epstein & Fenz, 1962; Jacobs, 1955), but also respiration (Boyd & Valentine, 1953), percentage of oxygen saturation in the blood (Doust & Schneider, 1955), and digital capillary dilation (Boyd & Valentine, 1953) have been used as measures of physiological stress and/or reactivity.

Measures of Associative Response Overlap

In addition to these measures, which describe the responses to individual stimulus words, there are also several measures which have been developed to characterize the degree of similarity among the responses given to two or more stimuli.* Several of such measures of associative overlap have been reviewed and discussed by Marshall and Cofer (1963), and will thus be presented only briefly here.

MEASURES OF ASSOCIATIVE OVERLAP BETWEEN TWO STIMULI

Techniques which have been suggested to compare the associative overlap of responses given to two stimuli include that of Mutual Relatedness (MR) (Bousfield, Whitmarsh, & Berkowitz, 1960) and of Mutual frequency (Mf) (Cofer, 1957; P. Jenkins & Cofer, 1957). Both of these measures are calculated by determining every response given in common to a pair of stimuli, summing the smaller response frequency values, and dividing by the total number of responses given to the two stimuli ($MR = \Sigma R_c/R_T$). Rothkopf (1960) also has proposed a measure of associative overlap for two stimuli, which is based on the sum of the products of the proportional occurrence of each response to each stimulus ($AO_{(A,B)} = \Sigma i P_{Ai} P_{Bi}$). All three of these approaches measure the intersection of the two response distributions. Since Rothkopf's is a multiplicative measure dealing with fractions, the

*Rothkopf and Coke (1961) have provided an empirical listing of the frequency with which each stimulus in the Kent-Rosanoff list elicits each other stimulus as a response.

proportional overlap will always be less than the proportional occurrence of that response to either of the individual stimuli. This is also true of *MR* (and of *Mf*), for although the actual frequency of the response to the less frequently eliciting stimulus is the value used to determine the overlap measure, that value is always divided by the total number of responses given to *both* stimuli—a total which will always exceed the number of responses given to the single stimulus.*

This relative decrease is not necessarily true when Deese's index of commonality† is used (1965), for here the denominator is the geometric mean of the number of responses occurring in the two distributions, while the numerator is determined in the same manner as that for *MR* or *Mf* ($IC = \Sigma R_C / \sqrt{N_A \cdot N_B}$).

Thus, for both *AO* and for *MR* (or *Mf*) the proportional frequency of any one response in the area of overlap, or intersection, between two response distributions will always be less than the proportional frequency of that response in either of the response distributions considered separately. However, there is also a consistent difference between these two measures in the overlap values obtained. This can be seen most clearly in the case where the two response distributions have an equal number of entries (equal *Ns*), and where the response in question occurs an equal number of times in each response distribution. In that case, when the *MR* (or *Mf*) measure is used to determine associative overlap, the proportional frequency of the response in the overlap measure will be exactly one-half of the proportional frequency of the response in either of the separate response distributions. However, when the *AO* measure is used, the proportional frequency of the response in the overlap measure will equal one-half of the proportional frequency in either of the separate distributions only when that latter frequency equals .50. When that frequency is greater than .50, the proportional frequency in the *AO* measure will *exceed* one-half of the proportional frequency in the separate distributions, while a separate distribution frequency of less than .50 will result in an *AO* measure of *less* than one-half its value.‡

A concrete example may illustrate this point. Let us say that each response distribution consists of 100 responses, and that the response in question occurs 50 times in the first distribution and 50 times in the second.

---

*We are omitting from consideration the frequency of the implicit representational response, just as this frequency is omitted in the determination of the total number of responses given to the two stimuli.

†Also referred to as an intersection coefficient ($S_A \cap S_B$).

‡It may be noted that under these conditions of distributions with equal Ns and equal response frequencies, *IC* will always *equal* the proportional frequency of each separate distribution.

Using *MR* (or *Mf*) to calculate associative overlap (disregarding, for this example, the possibility of other responses which the two stimuli might share) we would take 50 (the "smaller" frequency of occurrence) and divide by the total number of responses in the two distributions; thus $MR = 50/200 = .25$. Applying *AO* to this example, we obtain a value of $.50 \times .50 = .25$, which is identical to the result obtained with *MR*.

Let us now consider the case where the proportional response frequency in the separate distribution is greater than .50. For *MR*, if there are 100 responses in each distribution and the response in question occurs 90 times in each, this measure of associative overlap would give us a value of $90/200 = .45$, again equal to one-half the proportional frequency in the separate distribution. On the other hand, if *AO* is used as a measure, we would obtain a value of $.90 \times .90 = .81$, which clearly exceeds one-half of .90. For the case where the proportional response frequency in the separate distributions is less than .50, *MR* will again give an overlap value of one-half the proportional value of the separate distributions (e.g., $30 \div 200 = .15$), while *AO* will give a value less than one-half (e.g., $.30 \times .30 = .09$).

A slightly different approach to measuring the degree of associative relationship between two stimuli has been taken by Bousfield, Whitmarsh, and Danick (1958) in their Index of Generalization. Unlike the intersection measures discussed above, this measure is based on the sum of the percentage frequency values for one stimulus only (the test stimulus)* of all responses given in common to a pair of stimuli, divided by the total number of responses given to that stimulus. That is, this measure determines the extent to which a second stimulus shares in the meaning of the first— and it is the first stimulus which determines the associative meaning.

Garskof and Houston (1963) have suggested, as a measure of associative overlap, the Relatedness Coefficient (*RC*). This ratio of obtained to maximum possible overlap takes into account the number of associates which two stimuli have in common (irrespective of frequency) plus the congruence of the order in which these associates are emitted.† That is, *RC* is based on the ratio of the product of the rank of occurrence of associates in common to two stimuli (obtained overlap) to the maximum possible overlap, $RC = \bar{A} \cdot \bar{B}/(A \cdot B) - [n^p - (n-1)^p]^2$. In this formula, p is a fixed number ≥ 0, based on the slope of the associative hierarchy. Garskof and Houston have suggested that p may differ for different individuals, but Deese (1965) has argued that differentially weighting responses and correlating these measures with ratings of word relatedness does not produce results

---

*Regardless of whether this percentage is larger or smaller than that for the other stimulus.

†Houston and Garskof (1963) also have shown that associative overlap is related to the frequency with which each word elicits the other as a response.

much different from simply weighting responses in terms of linear rank order of emission.

Garskof and Marshall (1965) have compared the *RC* values obtained from continuous association with *MR* values obtained from discrete association, for the same stimuli. Two types of stimulus pairs were used: those for which there was some direct association between the two members of the pair, and those for which there was none. For the direct-association pairs, the correlation between *RC* and *MR* was .54; for the nondirect-association pairs, $r = .40$; the difference between these correlation coefficients was not significant, indicating that direct association did not influence the relationship between the two measures. However, the relationship of these measures to degree of direct association was quite different; for *MR* the correlation was .88, while for *RC* the correlation was only .43. As the authors point out, this suggests that associative overlap cannot be meaningfully differentiated from measures of direct association if *MR* is the overlap measure; however, *RC* does appear to be measuring aspects of associative relationship different from those tapped by the strength of the simple stimulus-response bond.

Measures of Associative Overlap Among More Than Two Stimuli

In addition to these measures of the degree of associative overlap between two stimuli, several methods have been suggested for determining the associative relatedness among a set of stimuli. These measures can be differentiated on the basis of whether the *frequency* of the responses which occur in common among the several stimuli is important, or simply whether the occurrence or nonoccurrence of common responses is the important factor.

An example of the first method is Deese's (1959) measure of inter-item associative strength (*IIAS*). This measure is based on the percentage frequency with which each item in the set elicits each other item in the set as a direct (actual) associative response, divided by the number of items in the set ($IIAS = \Sigma_1^n \% \, DR/n$). Similarly, Marshall and Cofer's index (1963) of total association depends on the percentage frequency of response, both for the direct associations among the words of the set and for their nondirect associations (e.g., A may elicit B and B may elicit C, but A does not elicit C; A and C are thus nondirectly associated), $ITA = \Sigma_1^n (\% \, DR + \% \, ND)/R_T (n)$. Marshall and Cofer's index (1963) of concept cohesiveness also depends on response frequency, although in this case frequency is based on those responses which occur to *all* the stimuli in the set, divided by the frequency of occurrence of responses which are common to any two or more stimuli in the set ($ICC = \Sigma_1^n \% R$ common to all n $Ss/\Sigma_1^n \% Rs$ common to 2 or more Ss).

Deese (1962b, 1965) also has proposed a factor analytic approach for determining the underlying relationships among a set of words. In this method, the intersection coefficients (see p. 31) for each pair of stimuli in the set of n words are entered into an $n \times n$ matrix. These intersection coefficients are then subjected to a centroid factor analysis, from which, by a simple rotation of pairs of factors through the main clusters of stimulus words, it is possible to establish orthogonal factors which describe the dimensions underlying the associative intersections, and to determine the loading of each stimulus on each factor. This method for determining the associative structure of a set of words has been used by Deese to investigate both the semantic and grammatical patterns of relationships among stimuli.

As described earlier, Laffal and Feldman (1962) also have used a factor analytic approach to discern the associative overlap among a set of stimuli. However, the overlap measures which they enter into the matrix depend in turn on scores based on a prior classifiction of responses into conceptual categories, while Deese's overlap measure (IC) directly reflects the frequency of occurrence of common responses. Three other studies have used factor analytic techniques to study categories and styles of associative response (Mandler & Parnes, 1957; Moran, Mefferd, & Kimble, 1964; Nunnaly, Flaugher, & Hodges, 1963). These will be discussed in Chapter 8.

An example of a measure of associative relatedness which does not depend on the frequency of response is Bousfield, Steward, and Cowan's (1961) technique for determining Stimulus Equivalence. Here, stimulus equivalence is based on a count of the number of different responses which two or more of the stimuli in a set elicit in common; however, the frequency of occurence of those common responses is not important.*

Pollio (1963b) has suggested a measure similar to Deese's $IIAA$, but rather than basing the extent of overlap on associative-response frequency, the entries in the cells of the $n \times n$ matrix are either zero or one, depending solely on whether the coordinates do or do not elicit each other as a response; such a matrix is called a W matrix. Pollio (1964b) also has expanded this measure to include the *potential* relationships among stimuli (Marshall and Cofer's nondirect associations). That is, although A may not directly elicit C as a response, they may be indirectly linked by B, if A → B, and B → C; this would be an example of a potential relationship. To account for these mediated connections, Pollio (1964b) suggests raising the original W^1 matrix to its various powers ($W^2, W^3, \ldots W^n$, where n is the size of the initial

---

*Except that the responses must be given by at least 3% of the subjects to be considered.

matrix W^1), using rules of binary addition; by then performing a cell-wise summation of matrices W^1 through W^n, an A matrix is obtained. This A matrix indicates all the potential mediated relationships possible among the original group of stimulus words. To express these potential connections, Pollio suggests the term, Measure of Total Cohesiveness ($MC = \Sigma_i \Sigma_k a_{ij}$). When this MC measure is divided by the number of connections possible for that group of words (number of stimuli)² one obtains a Measure of Relative Cohesiveness (MC_R) which takes into account the fact that not all matrices will consist of the same number of stimuli.

MEASURES OF ASSOCIATIVE OVERLAP AMONG INDIVIDUALS

The final measure to be considered in this section is that proposed by Postman and Adams (1960). This Index of Communality (C) provides a way of assessing the degree of similarity among the associative responses of a group of *individuals*. This is accomplished by comparing the responses to each stimulus of every subject with those of every other subject, tabulating the number of agreements, and then dividing by the number of comparisons made, $C = A/N(N - 1)/2$. Different groups of subjects may then be compared and characterized as having more or less associative communality. Like Garskof and Houston's measure of RC, this measure is also at least partly independent of response frequency. However, just as the use of response rank makes RC partially independent on response frequency, so Rosenzweig (1964) has pointed out that each associative response contributes to the measure of C in proportion to the frequency of its occurrence, and thus the frequency of the Primary response largely determines the value of the index. To illustrate this point, Rosenzweig demonstrated that, when the frequency values of the Primary responses were squared, they correlated .9894 with the communality index; when the frequency values of the secondary and tertiary responses were squared and added to those of the Primary, the correlation increased to .9998. Rosenzweig concludes from this that the summed squared frequencies of the three most common responses provides as satisfactory a measure of the associative communality of a group of subjects as does the complete index.

Summary

I. ORGANIZATION OF THE ASSOCIATIVE-RESPONSE DOMAIN

(1) This may be reflected in measures of
    (A) associative response strength, such as
        (a) the Primary response,
        (b) response commonality, and

(c) reaction time.
(B) This organization is also indicated by measures of the *size and consistency of the associative response domain*, as seen in
  (a) response heterogeneity (D),
  (b) response availability (m), (m'), (a),
  (c) response idiosyncrasy, and
  (d) response entropy (H)
(C) as well as in the *variability of associative responses*, which can be measured by
  (a) response reproduction errors, and by
  (b) modifications of the response reproduction method.

II. QUALITATIVE NATURE OF ASSOCIATIVE RESPONSES
 (1) These can be determined by
  (A) reference to some *objective criterion*, as
   (a) grammatical category,
   (b) dictionary meaning,
   (c) Thorndike-Lorge frequency, or
   (d) Semantic Differential polarization (D_4)
  (B) or by *ratings*, as of
   (a) the emotionality of the response,
   (b) indications of response disturbance, and/or
   (c) semantic classifications of the response.

III. RESPONSIVENESS TO WORD-ASSOCIATION STIMULI
 (1) This has also been determined by *physiological reactions*, such as
  (A) GSR, and
  (B) measures of respiratory and circulatory changes.

IV. MEASURES OF *ASSOCIATIVE RESPONSE OVERLAP BETWEEN TWO STIMULI*
 (1) These include
  (A) Mutual Relatedness (MR) (Bousfield, Whitmarsh, & Berkowitz, 1960)* and Mutual frequency (Mf) (Cofer, 1957)*,
  (B) Associative Overlap (AO) (Rothkopf, 1960)*,
  (C) Index of Generalization (Bousfield, Whitmarsh, & Danick, 1958)*, and
  (D) Relatedness Coefficient (RC) (Garskof & Houston, 1963).

V. MEASURES OF *ASSOCIATIVE RESPONSE OVERLAP AMONG MORE THAN TWO STIMULI*
 (1) These are of two general types.

(A) Those *dependent on response frequency* include
   (a) Inter-Item Associative Strength (*IIAS*) (Deese, 1959)*,
   (b) Index of Total Association (*ITA*) (Marshall & Cofer, 1963)*, and
   (c) Index of Concept Cohesiveness (*ICC*) (Marshall & Cofer, 1963)*.
(B) Those *not dependent on response frequency* include
   (a) Stimulus Equivalence (Bousfield, Steward, & Cowan, 1961)*,
   (b) Measure of Total Cohesiveness (*MC*) (Pollio, 1963b), and
   (c) Measure of Relative Cohesiveness (MC_R) (Pollio, 1964b).

VI. MEASURES OF *OVERLAP OF ASSOCIATIVE RESPONSES AMONG INDIVIDUALS*
 (1) These include
   (A) Index of Communality (*C*) (Postman & Adams, 1960), and
   (B) a revision of this approach (Rosenzweig, 1964) based on Primary, Secondary, and Tertiary response frequency.

*Those starred are reviewed by Marshall and Cofer (1963).

/ PART I

TASK AND ENVIRONMENTAL VARIABLES

Chapter 1

THE STIMULUS WORD

In the previous sections we have considered the various types of procedures which may be used for studies of word association. We have also reviewed a variety of response measures which may be employed to characterize the results. In the following sections, we shall examine how the particular stimulus words which constitute the WAT affect the associative-response results.

It has been suggested (e.g., Deering, 1963; Laffal, 1955) that stimulus variables, rather than subject variables, are the critical determinants of WAT responses. While this may be too strong a statement, it is clear that there are identifiable stimulus variables which have consistent effects on the associative process. Such variables—emotionality or affectivity, familiarity, grammatical form class, semantic level, and response characteristics—are the topics of the following sections.

Stimulus Affectivity

The largest number of investigations of the effect of the stimulus word have studied the response consequences of the relative emotionality, or affectivity, of the stimulus, where emotionality has been determined by ratings made by the experimenter, by independent judges, or by the subjects themselves. In some investigations, the comparison has been between a heterogeneous group of emotional stimuli and a set of nonemotional or neutral stimuli. Other studies have compared specific types of emotional stimuli. Also to be discussed in this section are those studies in which the affective or evaluative weight of stimulus words was determined by their polarization on Semantic Differential scales.

AFFECTIVE VERSUS NEUTRAL STIMULI

Studies comparing the general categories of affective versus neutral stimuli may be conveniently discussed in terms of their effect on several aspects of the associative-response process. In this section, associative-response variability, associative disturbance, response latency, and physiological responses concomitant with the associative response will be considered.

The relationship between stimulus emotionality and response variability has been investigated in a number of studies, which have made use of a variety of methods for measuring variability. For example, taking the number of associative responses elicited by a stimulus as the measure of response variability, Terwilliger (1964) found that stimuli rated by subjects as "less pleasant" elicited more responses than "pleasant" stimuli. Cramer (1965b) found emotional stimuli to elicit more different responses than neutral stimuli, for both normal and schizophrenic subjects; Bodin and Geer (1965) found hostile stimuli to elicit more different responses than neutral stimuli (for hospitalized psychiatric patients); and Veness (1962) found an insignificant tendency for the number of responses to emotional stimuli to exceed that to neutral stimuli. On the other hand, Koen (1962) found no difference between emotional and neutral stimuli on this variable, and R. C. Johnson and Lim (1964) found "good" stimuli to elicit more responses than "bad." These inconsistent results cannot be explained in terms of differences in stimulus familiarity, because studies demonstrating both a positive relationship between affectivity and response variability (Veness) and a negative relationship (Johnson & Lim) used stimuli matched for Thorndike-Lorge (T-L) frequency. Furthermore, in Cramer's study, T-L frequency was unrelated to the number of different responses. (In addition, as will be indicated in the following section, since familiarity is positively related to the number of continued associative responses, and neutral stimuli would be expected to be more familiar, even if stimulus familiarity were an important variable in these studies, it would work against the finding of emotionality producing response variability.) Thus, we must look elsewhere for an explanation of the inconsistent findings.

Another variable which may account for the inconsistent response variability results is that of the type of association test used to establish the response distribution on which the conclusions are based. Each of the studies in which emotional stimuli were found to produce greater response variability used a WAT calling for a single, discrete response; on the other hand, the two inconsistent studies used a continued-association task. It is suggested that variability based on number of different single, discrete responses across subjects, D, does not necessarily reflect the same underlying process as that which is reflected by the number of responses elicited from subjects on a continued association task, m. In the case of emotional and neutral stimuli, what these discrepant D and *m* findings indicate is that emotional stimuli elicit more different first responses across individual subjects, but that the total *pool* of associative responses available within any one subject is smaller for emotional than for neutral stimuli.* It is also sugested that the increased *D* is due to the large number of idiosyncratic reactions to the emotional stimuli.

Support for this last notion is found in several sources. A study by Deering (1963), using stimuli matched for T-L frequency, found emotional stimuli to elicit more idiosyncratic responses (responses given by only one subject) than did neutral stimuli (although the author did not discuss or test this finding). Jacobs (1959), in a study of continuous association, found emotional stimuli to elicit a greater variety of words among the initial responses, while neutral stimuli produced more identical initial responses. A related finding comes from a study of bilingualism by Kolers (1963), in which a WAT was presented in both the subject's native language and in English. The number of responses similar in the two languages was found to be less for emotional stimuli than for neutral, concrete nouns.

It appears, then, that the initial response to emotional stimuli is likely to be highly individualistic, with a resulting distribution of first responses which shows great heterogeniety. However, this diverse associative-response distribution may not accurately reflect the associative repertory of any one individual subject. Rather, the above findings suggest that for any individual subject, neutral stimuli may in fact be associated with more different responses than are emotional stimuli.

Another way of investigating associative variability is to utilize a second association trial to test for response recall. If the assumption is made that the ability to reproduce a response reflects the stability of that response habit, then failure to reproduce an associative response may be taken as an indication of response variability. The experimental findings on this issue have been quite consistent. Bodin and Geer (1965), W. P. Brown (1965), Deering (1963), and M. J. Goldstein and Jones (1964), using stimuli matched for T-L frequency, found more response reproduction errors for emotional than for neutral stimuli, for both psychiatric patients and normal subjects. Using unmatched lists, the same results were found by Levinger and Clark (1961) for normal subjects and by Appelbaum (1963) for brain-damaged subjects, nonpsychotic psychiatric patients, and normal individuals.

Modifications for the response reproduction method have also demonstrated that variability is a function of the emotionality of the stimulus. R. M. Jones (1958), for example, gave subjects their previous responses and asked them to recall the stimuli which elicited these;

*It is further suggested that Koen's failure to find a significant difference in the *m* values of emotional and neutral stimuli is due to the fact that the latter words were more familiar ($t = 1.73, p < .10$). This point will be discussed in the following section.

emotional stimuli were more difficult to recall than neutral. This finding may be interpreted as evidence that the backward associative connection between emotional stimuli and their responses is less reliable (more variable) than that for neutral stimuli.* However, clear proof of this interpretation would require a demonstration that emotional and neutral stimuli are equally *available* for recall, regardless of the associative connection.

Evidence supporting the variable associative connection interpretation is provided by Deering's study (1963). After the standard association and reproduction test procedure, a recognition test, consisting of the stimulus words plus additional filler words, was administered; subjects were asked to circle those words which had been WAT stimuli. Despite matching for T-L frequency, emotional stimuli were not recognized correctly as often as neutral ones, indicating that even when emotional and neutral stimuli were made equally available, the associative connections to emotional stimuli (in this case between the stimuli and the entire WAT) were less reliable.

Finally, Appelbaum (1963) has demonstrated that while the responses evoked by emotional stimuli show greater variability, they can also be characterized as being more restricted. Thus, when asked on a third association test trial to give a second, *different* response, both psychiatric and normal subjects were less successful with emotional than with neutral stimuli.

This finding would suggest that there are *fewer* responses available to emotional stimuli for individual subjects—an hypothesis made earlier to explain the difference in results of discrete- versus continuous-association studies. However true this general hypothesis may be, it seems unlikely that unavailability of responses can explain the findings when only two responses are called for. Furthermore, the consistent finding of greater response reproduction errors for emotional stimuli indicates the ready availability of at least one other response.†

When one considers the fact that emotional stimuli are both harder to give the same response to, when this is requested, and harder to give a different response to, when requested, it appears that, in addition to the issue of response variability, what we may be dealing with is the problem of the ability to maintain a response set. Whether the set is to give the same or different responses, it is more difficult to maintain for emotional stimuli.

---

*The problem of backward association—the fact that although a subject learns to associate two stimuli in an $A \rightarrow B$ sequence, he also may develop a $B \rightarrow A$ association—has been of considerable interest in recent verbal learning studies (cf., e.g., Ekstrand, 1966).

†Whether these errors are due to less reliable associative connections or to response unavailability has not yet been investigated.

If this is a valid assumption, a further hypothesis might be formulated to account for the greater initial response variability found for emotional stimuli. That is, if emotional stimuli result in a disruption in the ability to maintain a set, the greater D variability in response to these stimuli may be due to a disruption of the implicit set ordinarily adopted by subjects, which produces a certain communality in the responses given to neutral stimuli.*

An issue related to response variability is that of association disturbance as seen in "unusual," "distant," or "autistic" responses, or in a variety of response faults (e.g., blocking, stimulus repetition, clang response). M. J. Goldstein and Jones (1964), in a study of schizophrenic subjects using emotional and neutral words which were carefully matched for familiarity, length, and first letter, found emotional stimuli to elicit more (although not qualitatively different) associative disturbances. Similar associative response disturbances to emotional stimuli have been found for normal subjects (Jacobs, 1959; Veness, 1962; Weintraub, Silverstein, & Klee, 1959) and to stimuli selected to be emotionally relevant for particular groups of subjects (Boyd & Valentine, 1953; Epstein & Fenz, 1962). Similar findings were obtained by W. P. Brown (1965), who also used stimuli matched for similarity, length, and for number of idiosyncratic responses elicited.†

Studies of the effect of stimulus emotionality on response latency have consistently reached the same finding: emotional words are responded to more slowly than are neutral words. This is true for normal college students (W. P. Brown, 1965; Epstein and Fenz, 1962; Jacobs, 1955; Powell, 1955; Smock & Thompson, 1954; Weintraub, et al., 1959, 1960), children (Doris, Sarason & Berkowitz, 1963), adolescents (Powell, 1955), parachutists (Epstein & Fenz, 1962), LSD subjects (Weintraub et al., 1959), dysmennorheac patients (Boyd & Valentine, 1953), and psychiatric patients (Bodin & Geer, 1965).

In a study which further refines this relationship, Epstein and Fenz (1962), testing parachutists, determined the effect on reaction time of stimuli with four degrees of relevance to parachuting. They found that reaction time was a direct function of the degree of stimulus relevance—i.e., the more relevant, the longer the reaction time. Similarly, in the Bodin and Geer study (1965), stimuli which were highly hostile had longer reaction times than did moderately hostile stimuli, which in turn were responded to more slowly than were neutral stimuli.

These findings of increased response latency are most obviously

---

*For a discussion of this implicit set to give popular response in the absence of instructions to do so, see Moran et al. (1964). This work is discussed in Part II, p. 176.

†Although emotional words did elicit (insignificantly) more idiosyncratic responses ($t = 1.39$).

interpreted as reflecting weak associative connections between emotional stimuli and responses. However, an alternative interpretation is offered by Geer and Mollenauer (1964), based on a study utilizing a restricted WAT. In this procedure, subjects were given five hostile and five neutral words as stimuli, and were restricted to using ten hostile and ten neutral words as responses. The results indicated that when the stimulus and response were of the same class (i.e., both hostile or both neutral), the reaction time was shorter than when the stimulus and response were of different classes. Furthermore, when the stimulus and response were of the same class, the reaction time to hostile stimuli was actually faster than to neutral stimuli. On the basis of these findings, the authors suggest that the slower reaction time usually found for negative, or traumatic, stimuli may be due to the subject's seeking for a response word which is socially desirable, and hence from a different class. In this case, then, the reaction time represents not so much a weak stimulus-response habit, but rather the process of searching for a particular kind of response. Subsequently we shall return to this point.

A few studies have been concerned with the effect of stimulus emotionality on physiological responses. Epstein and Fenz (1962), in their study of parachutists, found measures of GSR consistent with those of reaction time; that is, the magnitude of GSR was a function of the relevance of the stimulus word to parachuting, for the experimental subjects, and was greater for anxiety stimuli than for neutral ones, for all subjects. This consistency of GSR findings with those of response latency was also found by Boyd and Valentine (1953), and Dixon (1956, 1958) in a pilot study which appeared to offer some evidence that, for both aural and visual subliminal presentation, affective stimuli elicit a larger GSR than neutral stimuli.* On the other hand, Jacobs (1955), while finding significant reaction time differences between emotional and neutral stimuli, did not find GSR to be an effective discriminator.

Respiratory functions have also been shown to be affected by the emotionality of the stimulus word. Boyd and Valentine (1953) found pneumographic responses to differentiate between the reactions of dysmenorrheac patients and control subjects to significant affective stimuli. Finally, Doust and Schneider (1955) used a technique of spectroscopic oximetry to determine the percentage of oxygen saturation in the blood (a measure shown to be related to emotional change). They found that while the oximetric values did not change from a resting level following the WAT presentation of neutral stimuli, emotional stimuli (as compared

---

*However, few subjects were studied, and a serious problem in experimental design—see p. 205—make it difficult to accept these findings with confidence.

to neutral) produced significant anoxemia in all subject groups (normals and a variety of pathologies) except constitutional schizophrenics.

Types of Affective Stimuli

Thus far we have been concerned primarily with the effect of the *general* class of affective stimuli as compared to neutral stimuli. The present section focuses on the effect of specific types of affective stimuli—e.g., hostile—as compared, first to neutral stimuli, and then as compared to other classes of affective stimuli.

Several studies have investigated the interaction between associative responses to oral stimuli and experiences of food deprivation. Kollar, Slater, Palmer, Docter, and Mandell (1964) compared subjects deprived of food for 0, 4, or 6 days, administering a different WAT each day. The reaction time to oral stimuli increased with increasing deprivation for the fasting subjects, while no change was noted for the control subjects. In a more extensive study (Brozek, Guetzkow, & Baldwin, 1951), subjects underwent a semistarvation procedure over a period of several months. As compared to a control group, the food-deprived subjects gave a significantly greater number of infrequent responses (frequency less than 1% on the Kent-Rosanoff or O'Connor norms) to "Food" stimuli. Furthermore, when asked to recall the stimuli and responses of the WAT, "Hungry" was among the first 10 items recalled for 26% of the fasting subjects but for none of the control subjects. In another investigation, Wispé (1954) matched neutral, food-related, and water-related stimuli for T-L frequency, and administered these to subjects deprived of food and water. To a large extent, the type of response elicited depended on the type of stimulus; food stimuli elicited food responses, water stimuli elicited water responses, neutral stimuli elicited neutral responses. However, "object" stimuli (those which could be classified as "satisfiers" of both affective categories), elicited more food responses, while "act" stimuli (those referring to "taking into the body" elicited more water responses.

This tendency of affective stimuli to elicit as responses items from the same affective category to which they belong was well demonstrated in a study by Pollio (1963a). In this investigation, the affective connotation of three CVCs was experimentally established via paired-associate learning. Each of the CVCs was learned as a paired-associate stimulus for one of three sets of nine words chosen from the Semantic Differential Atlas (J. J. Jenkins *et al.*, 1958); the nine response words paired with any one CVC were either all positive, all neutral, or all negative. The CVCs were subsequently administered for a continued association test of six successive trials. The results indicated that the CVC to which positive words had been learned as paired-associate responses continued to elicit positive responses, both from within the original set of nine positive words (accounting for some 50% of the responses) and from other new positive responses selected from outside the set; this transfer of the same evaluative set was found also in the responses to CVCs originally paired with neutral or with negative words. (A subsequent study demonstrating the effect of increasing affective context on modifying associative responses toward becoming affectively more like the context will be discussed subsequently (cf. Pollio & Lore, 1965, p. 90).

This study demonstrated that affective connotations can be conditioned to CVCs, and, more important for the purposes of the present essay, that this (conditioned) connotation will then be used as the basis for determining the class from which to select an associative response.

Geer and Mollenauer (1964) also have pointed out the tendency of subjects to choose responses from the same affective class as that of the stimulus, and that stimuli and responses from the same class had faster reaction times than when the class of the stimulus and response differed. Furthermore, the reaction time for hostile stimuli eliciting hostile responses was shorter than for neutral stimuli eliciting neutral responses. The authors suggest this latter finding is due to the greater specificity of the "hostile" class than of the "neutral" (i.e., fewer response alternatives result in less response competition). However, considering the fact that the experimental procedure required the subject to choose responses from a *restricted* set of 10 hostile and 10 neutral words, this interpretation would not seem to apply. An alternative explanation, suggested earlier, would interpret the faster reaction time as an indication of a stronger associative connection between hostile stimuli and responses, when the subject does not feel compelled to find a socially acceptable response. When the stimulus and response must be of different affective classes, reaction time is increased.

The findings of increased reaction time to stimuli of increasing hostility in the Bodin and Geer study (1965) mentioned earlier led those authors also to propose, as a possible explanation, an hypothesis consistent with the present suggestion. That is, they suggest that the increased reaction time may be due to the tendency to inhibit negatively toned responses. This hypothesis gains even more credence when it is noted that the increased reaction time related to increased hostility levels could not be accounted for on the basis of increased response entropy.

The choosing of responses from an affective category different from that of the stimulus was used by Hinze (1961) to measure the amount of conflict engendered by stimuli dealing with school and with parent-child relationships. After the WAT, subjects rated the stimuli and their own continuous associations as positive or negative. A stimulus was considered a "conflict" word when most of the responses were given a rating opposite from that given to the stimulus. The data indicated that in this college-aged population, parent-child stimuli provided more conflict words than school stimuli.

A series of studies have used reaction time to differentiate between responses to stimuli representing various affective categories. Eriksen and Lazarus (1952), in a study of associative reactions to succourant, homosexual, and aggressive stimuli, noted that increased reaction time to one stimulus category was related to increased reaction time in the other areas ($r_{s.h} = .53$; $r_{s.a} = .41$; both $p < .01$; $r_{h.a} = .26$; $.05 < p < .10$). However, the number of need-related response words was unrelated to indications of reaction time disturbance in any of the three need areas, a finding which supports the thesis that the content of an association, viewed independently of the reaction time required to arrive at that response, may fail to represent adequately the associative response process. Studying third-graders, Doris *et al.*, (1963) found school stimuli to have a significantly longer reaction time than aggressive or body-image stimuli, and a slightly longer reaction time than dependent stimuli. Smock and Thompson (1954), using the difference between reaction time to affective and to neutral stimuli as a measure, found the greatest response latency for culturally taboo stimuli, with sibling rivalry, oedipal, anal, and oral stimuli following, in descending order.

It is possible to consider these studies in terms of the correspondence between response latency and levels of psychosocial development (cf. Erikson, 1950). From this point of view, it can be noted that stimuli from the earlier developmental levels generally elicited more rapid responses, while there was a longer delay between the stimulus and response representing the relatively later psychosocial levels. If we assumed that these latter, chronologically more recent psychosocial levels are emotionally more potent, then it makes sense that they should have longer reaction times, since it is a consistent finding that degree of emotionality and reaction time are positively related (cf. p. 47).

Another study which appears to support the hypothesis that reaction time to stimuli of different conflict areas may be related to changing stages of emotional development is that of Powell (1955). In this instance, subjects representing three age levels between 10 and 30 years were tested with stimuli representing seven potential "conflict" areas. Conflict, as measured by the difference in reaction time between these critical stimuli and neutral stimuli, was found, over all age groups, to be greatest for stimuli concerning social acceptability, heterosexual relationships, and "emotional tendencies" (stimuli representing unpleasant emotional states). However, examination of the data reveals that there are some striking changes in the conflictfulness of other areas, and that these changes are related to age group. For example, the *most* conflicted area for preadolescents is that of Religion, while this is of relatively less concern to the adolescents and even less to the young adults. On the other hand, Vocational Outlook, of relatively less concern to either of the younger age groups, becomes the most conflicted area for the young adult group. Here again, the different rank orderings of psychological areas by response latencies at different developmental levels appear to depend on the psychosocial concerns of the corresponding developmental stages. Further evidence for this hypothesis will be discussed later (pp. 75–6), in connection with the finding that reaction time to pictorial, as opposed to verbal, stimuli varies with the developmental level of the subject.

Polarization on the Semantic Differential

A third group of studies to be considered in this section are those which have used Semantic Differential (S.D.) scales (Osgood, Suci, & Tannenbaum, 1957) to select highly polarized, evaluative or affectively loaded stimuli. For example, Pollio (1964b), using a continued association task, found that stimuli rated on the positive evaluative pole of the S.D. elicited more responses than stimuli rated on the negative pole.* R. C. Johnson, Weiss, and Zelhart (1964) also compared "good" and "bad" stimulus words matched for T-L frequency. For both normal and schizophrenic subjects, "good" words elicited significantly more m responses, fewer idiosyncratic associations, and stronger Primaries. Koen's study (1962), reported earlier, also used a continued-association task, and compared emotional and neutral stimuli which had been rated on 12 S.D. scales; neutral stimuli which were also highly polarized were found to elicit more associative responses than neutral nonpolarized stimuli; however, response availability was unrelated to degree of polarization for emotional stimuli. J. J. Jenkins and Russell (1956) also found degree of polarization, D_4, of neutral stimuli to be positively related to response availability ($r = +.71$).

In an extensive study of the relationship between polarization, D_4, "good" and "bad" affect, and associative response variables, Howe (1965) demonstrated that for "bad" words, and for highly polarized "good" words, degree of polarization is positively related to entropy, H, response variability, D, and number of idiosyncratic responses, and negatively related to Primary response strength. Rather surprisingly, "bad" and "good" words *per se* did not differ from each other for these four variables; that is, extent of polarization, but not direction, was a significant variable in determining

---

*Although an interaction with the abstract-concrete stimulus dimension is also apparent in the data (see p. 75).

these measures of associative response. However, the two affective types of words did differ as to response availability, m, such that significantly fewer responses were available to "bad" words than to "good" words. Furthermore, it was demonstrated that the positive correlation between "good" words and m depended on the "good" words being of low polarization and/or high T-L frequency. Howe also notes that the correlations between m and D are insignificant, indicating that "the two measures are not interchangeable" (p. 503)—a point being made in the present essay to explain the apparently discrepant "number-of-associative-responses" results (cf. p. 42).

Consistent with the findings on response variability, Pollio and Lore (1965) have found that Semantic Differential "unpleasant" stimuli have a longer reaction time than do "pleasant" ones. This reaction time was further increased as a function of the number of "unpleasant" context words which immediately preceded the "unpleasant" stimulus word, while the reaction time to "pleasant" stimuli was unrelated to the number of "pleasant" context words presented. Furthermore, similar to Weiss, Goldfried, and Bayoff (1965), they found that while the responses to both types of stimuli were less polarized than the stimuli themselves, this was significantly more true for unpleasant than for pleasant; that is, the responses to unpleasant stimuli were more different in evaluative meaning from their stimuli than were the responses to pleasant stimuli. On the other hand, the two types of stimuli did not differ as to the familiarity (T-L frequency) of the responses they evoked. Weiss *et al.*, (1965) also found that the relationship between affectivity and polarization is not a direct one. In this study, stimuli were individually selected for each subject in terms of being "loaded" (i.e., resulting in response disturbances); the S.D. ratings of the stimulus word by subjects for whom it was "loaded" were then compared with those of subjects for whom it was not "loaded." Similar to Howe's finding (1965), measures of response disturbance were unrelated to negative S.D. ratings. Rather, those subjects for whom the stimulus was "loaded" were more likely to rate it as neutral or positive on the S.D. scales, than were subjects for whom the stimulus was neutral. This attempt to make a disturbing stimulus less negative is an important point in the discussion which follows (see pp. 54–5). Bodin and Geer (1965) also have found that responses to hostile stimuli are less negative (on the S.D. Evaluative dimension) than are responses by the same subjects to neutral stimuli.

Pollio and Lore (1965) have used their data as the basis for a theoretical explanation of the consistent finding of increased reaction time to stimulus words of unpleasant affect. Dismissing either response frequency or semantic distance between the stimulus and response as an explanation of reaction time, they focus instead on the nature of the representational mediation response (r_m), as postulated by Osgood. According to Osgood's conceptualization, this r_m consists, in part, of the response originally made to the significate for which the stimulus word (sign) stands. Thus an unpleasant stimulus word must evoke implicit avoidance responses, and it is the occurrence of these responses which the authors propose to account for the increased latency of overt response.*

Pollio (1964a) also has examined the 52 Kent-Rosanoff stimuli which, along with their Primary responses, appeared in the Semantic Differential Atlas (J. J. Jenkins et al., 1958), and noted significant product-moment correlations between the S.D. ratings of S and R on the evaluative ($r = .52$), potency ($r = .26$), and activity ($r = .36$) scales. When the stimuli were ordered according to strength of Primary response, and the top third responses were compared with the bottom third (mean associative strength of 65% versus 26%), the correlations between the S.D. ratings for the strong stimulus-response pairs, while still positive, were not significantly different from zero, while the correlations for the low strength pairs were all significantly greater than zero. From these findings the author concludes that two distinct types of relations may exist between word associates—a relation based on word-word habits (as found in the strongest pairs), or a relation based on connotative similarity (more characteristic of the weak pairs).

This study also investigated the difference in semantic distance between a stimulus and the responses of its hierarchy as a function of the initial semantic location of the stimulus word. The results indicated that for the evaluative dimension only, the S.D. ratings of associative responses were a function of the position of the initial stimulus word, such that negatively evaluated stimulus words produce responses which are semantically more distant from the stimulus (i.e., less negative), as was found by Pollio and Lore above.

Finally, Staats and Staats (1959) compared the S.D. rating of 10 stimuli with the mean S.D. rating of the first 20 associative responses given to those stimuli (as determined from the Russell-Jenkins norms). The resulting rank order correlation of .90 led the authors to conclude that "the meaning of the associates of a stimulus word tends to be the same as the meaning of the word" (p. 140). Although not discussed by the authors, the data also indicate that the associates are less polarized than their respective stimuli, (consistent with the finding of Pollio & Lore, 1965, and Pollio, 1964a, reported above).

---

*Howe (1965) also has hypothesized that it is "affect arousal," as a consequence of evaluative directionality, rather than degree of polarization, which accounts for those associative effects which differentiate "bad" from "good" stimulus words; just how this works is left unspecified.

Summary and Discussion

In summary, let us review the findings of the effects of stimulus emotionality on associative responses, and then consider a possible explanation.

Stimulus emotionality (negative) has been shown to have the following effects:
(1) reaction time is increased,
(2) response availability, m, is decreased,
(3) response heterogeneity, D, is increased,
(4) association disturbances (blocking, clang, unusual responses) are increased, and
(5) number of emotional responses is increased.

It has also been found that responses to emotional stimuli
(1) are drawn from same affective category or semantic space as the stimulus; however, the responses are less polarized than their respective stimuli,
(2) in addition, psychophysiological disturbances (GSR, respiration) are increased,
(3) response reproduction errors are increased,
(4) "errors" in giving a different response on request are increased, and, finally,
(5) errors on a modified reproduction test (response provided, subject is to recall the stimulus) are increased.

In the preceding text, the following interpretations have been advanced in an attempt to explain and reconcile certain apparently discrepant results:

(1) The question of whether (negative) affective stimuli elicit greater or fewer associative responses than neutral stimuli depends on the measure of number of associative responses. Affective stimuli elicit more responses when the number of different discrete responses across subjects is used as a measure, and fewer responses when the average number of continued associative responses within each subject is used as a measure. Put another way, affective stimuli elicit many idiosyncratic first responses but have a small pool of additional associative responses available. The converse is true for neutral stimuli.

(2) The greater number of errors in reproducing the original response, as well as in producing a new response when requested, was interpreted as reflecting, at least in part, difficulty in maintaining a response set. It was further suggested that this disruption of the implicit response set adopted by the subject for the association task may account for the large number of idiosyncratic associative responses obtained to affective stimuli.

negative, or avoidance characteristics are determined, at least in part, by the developmental level of the subject.

Stimulus Familiarity

A second large group of studies have investigated the effect of stimulus familiarity on associative responses. Familiarity is generally determined by reference to the Thorndike-Lorge word count, although occasionally subject ratings of familiarity have been used. In discussing the influence of this stimulus variable on the associative process, an outline similar to that of the preceding section will be followed; the effect of familiarity on response availability, heterogeneity, and variability, on response strength, and on reaction time will be considered, and then a smaller number of studies of type of associative response will be presented.

Investigations of the relationship of stimulus familiarity to response availability, m, have not yielded consistent results. A number of studies have found a positive relationship between familiarity and number of associative responses, m, regardless of whether the stimuli are emotional or neutral (Koen, 1962), adjectives or nouns (Cofer & Shevitz, 1952; M. T. Mednick, Mednick, & Jung, 1964a) or letters (Anderson, 1965). This relationship holds regardless of whether the words are measured for familiarity by the T-L count (as in the above-mentioned studies) or rated by the subject (Noble, 1953; Terwilliger, 1964), and it is true for tasks of continued (M. T. Mednick *et al.*, 1964a; Noble, 1952, 1953; Schulz & Thysell, 1965; Underwood, 1959) and continuous (Cofer & Shevitz, 1952; Koen, 1962) association. Within this group of studies, not only have stimuli with high T-L frequency values (HF) been found to elicit more responses than stimuli with low T-L values (LF), but also a continuous relationship has been demonstrated; thus Noble (1953) demonstrated that a negatively accelerated positive function best described the relationship between m (the number of associations elicited by selected disyllables) and stimulus familiarity (as rated by the subject), and Underwood (1959) has shown this same relationship to hold between m and T-L measures of familiarity. On the other hand, Davids (1956), selecting stimuli relevant to alienation from five levels of T-L frequency, and Wispé (1954), using oral and neutral stimuli matched for T-L frequency, found no relationship between familiarity and number of responses, m. Furthermore, Matthews (1965), making a direct comparison of his results with those of Noble and Underwood, failed to find a relationship between m and T-L frequency.* Matthews attempts to explain this discrepancy in terms of the

*It is not clear why the data for only 59 of the 89 stimuli used in this study are reported.

different stimuli used. In his study, there were more HF words, and the LF words used were of greater familiarity. Further characteristics of the LF words which are used to explain the finding that these stimuli elicited as many m responses as HF stimuli will be discussed below.

Studies of the role of stimulus familiarity in determining the number of different responses in a *discrete* association task, D, have found either no relationship or that familiarity and D are inversely related. For example, an insignificant bi-serial correlation between the two variables was found by Cramer (1965b) (+ .06 for normal subjects and − .22 for schizophrenic subjects) and by Veness (1962) ($r = +$ .095, normal subjects). Moreover, Hall and Ugelow (1957), using a ratio measure of number of different responses, D, to total number of responses, found HF stimuli to elicit proportionally *fewer* different responses. However, this measure is difficult to interpret, since the total number of responses varied from stimulus to stimulus, depending on the frequency of blocking to that stimulus. Since blocking occurred significantly more often to LF stimuli (suggesting, incidentally, that more emotional words may have been included among the LF stimuli), we can infer that the dividend for LF stimuli was smaller, and hence the range of different responses was spuriously inflated. Nevertheless, Postman's data (1964), based on 1,000 college subjects, also suggest an inverse relationship between D and T-L frequency of noun stimuli.

Since the latter four studies used a discrete-association task, one might be tempted to interpret the discrepant results as another example of how association norms based on data pooled across subjects differ from norms based on within-subject data. It might be, as suggested by Veness (1962), that although associative responses are readily available to familiar stimuli, the initial response is quite likely to be the same across subjects, and hence in any response distribution based on single response, familiar stimuli will appear to evoke few different responses.

However appealing this interpretation may be—and despite its analogy with the previous discussion of the response heterogeneity, D,-response availability, m, issue for emotional and neutral words—it does not account for the absence of relationship between familiarity and number of responses found by Davids, Matthews, and Wispé, all of whom used a continuous-association task.* A more likely explanation may lie in the fact that, with the exception of Matthews, all the studies in which there was no relation-

---

*It is interesting to note that the experimental analogue of natural language familiarity—i.e., stimulus familiarization—has also been unsuccessful in this regard. Thus neither familiarization of CVC trigrams (Riley & Phillips, 1959; Winnick & Ellner, 1965) nor of disyllabic words and paralogs (Schulz & Thysell, 1965) increased the number of associative responses elicited in a continued-association task.

ship between familiarity and number of associative responses, D or m, used a stimulus list which was made up, in part or entirety, of stimuli which differed on an additional, second stimulus dimension—in this case, on the dimension of emotionality. It may be that the emotional-neutral dimension interacted with the familiarity dimension in such a way as to obliterate any effect of the latter. Matthews (1965) points out another factor which he believes may account for his LF' stimuli eliciting as many m responses as did HF stimuli. Of Matthews' 32 LF words, 24 were selected to have HF associates, while this was judged to be true for only 9 of Noble's 46 LF words. Matthews suggests that when a LF stimulus has a HF associate which is also a member of the same conceptual class, then the HF word may serve as a mediator, such that the responses usually given to that HF word are now given to the LF word. Matthews provides some *post hoc* evidence to support this contention, and theoretically it is a feasible explanation. Further work would help establish its validity.

In other words, it is being suggested that familiarity, considered independently from other stimulus variables, is inversely related to the number of different responses, D, elicited in a discrete association task; in terms of D, HF < LF. However, when a second stimulus dimension is added, the effect will depend, in part, on the relationship between that dimension and D. It also is hypothesized that the effect will depend on whether the possible combinations of the two variables are equally represented among the stimuli—that is, whether there are an equal number of words in each of the cells of the 2×2 table. If such equating is not done, it is likely that one value of the first variable will be overly represented among the stimuli representing the second variable.

A concrete example of this type of interaction affecting m comes from the study of Koen (1962) reported earlier. In this investigation of continuous association, both familiarity and emotionality of the stimulus words were varied. Unlike the Davids (1956) and Wispé (1954) findings, and despite the presence of emotional stimuli, a positive relationship was found between familiarity and m. However, as pointed out before there were clearly more neutral stimuli among the HF words and more emotional stimuli among the LF words. Since we know that neutral stimuli elicit more m responses than emotional stimuli, we can assume that both neutrality and familiarity were contributing to the increased m value for the HF stimuli.

Let us consider, now, what would be the effect on number of D responses when the stimuli vary on two dimensions, and the four possible combinations are not equally represented. Since the HF stimuli are more likely to include the neutral words and the LF stimuli are more likely to include the emotional words, the cumulative effects of HF plus neutrality and of LF plus emotionality must be determined. With regard to D, these effects should be cooperative. That is, HF decreases and LF increases the number of different responses (Hall & Ugelow, 1957; Postman, 1964); similarly, neutrality decreases and emotionality increases the number of different responses, D, elicited (cf. preceding section). Thus both variables should contribute to an inverse relationship between familiarity and D. This inverse relationship between familiarity and D is exactly what was found by Terwilliger (1964). In this study, the stimulus words varied as to emotionality, balance (slope of the response gradient), and rated familiarity. In this case, the negative correlation between familiarity and D ($r = -.27$) was significant at the .01 level.

If this negative relationship is being determined by the addition of the effects of emotionality to those of familiarity, we should expect that if the emotionality effects were eliminated, the LF stimuli would then show relatively* fewer responses (lower D), and the HF stimuli would show relatively more responses (higher D). In other words, removal of the emotionality factor should decrease the negative correlation. Again, the data support the hypothesis. When Terwilliger (1964) statistically partialed out the effects of emotionality and, in this case, of balance as well, the correlation between familiarity and D changed from $-.27$ to $+.36$. This notable change was largely determined by eliminating the effect of balance; if only the effects of emotionality had been ruled out, the change in the correlation would have been much less marked, although in the same direction. This study, then, provides some evidence that eliminating the effects of emotionality decreases the negative correlation between D and familiarity which is found when HF and LF stimuli are not matched on the emotionality dimension.

On the other hand, when the stimuli are matched on both stimulus dimensions, we find a situation in which the two variables should work cooperatively for the HF-neutral stimuli and for the LF-emotional stimuli, as indicated above, but should have conflicting effects for the HF-emotional stimuli and the LF-neutral ones (e.g., HF decreases D, emotionality increases it). It is suggested that in studies in which the stimuli are matched for familiarity and emotionality, the addition of stimuli with conflicting effects on D should eliminate the relationship between familiarity and D. Again, the data support this hypothesis. Using stimuli matched in terms of familiarity and emotionality, studies by Cramer (1965b) and by Veness (1962) found no relationship between familiarity and D.

---

* Relative to the number obtained when emotionality was contributing to the effect.

The same reasoning can be applied to continued association studies in which the stimuli are equated for familiarity and emotionality. Again, the two dimensions should work cooperatively for HF-neutral stimuli and LF-emotional stimuli, but should result in conflict for HF-emotional stimuli and LF-neutral stimuli (e.g., HF increases m, emotionality decreases m). As in the case of the conflicting effect of these latter stimuli on D, we would expect that their addition to the stimulus list would result in findings which indicate that m appears unrelated to familiarity.* In fact, this is the result obtained when equated stimulus lists are used; both Davids (1956) and Wispé (1954) found no relationship between familiarity and m.

Further support for the hypothesis of a second stimulus dimension masking the effect of stimulus familiarity is found in a continued-association study by Winnick and Kressel (1965), in which abstract and concrete stimuli were used. While there was no difference between the number of associative responses, m, given to HF and LF words, when the data were further analyzed in terms of the degree of abstractness of the stimuli, the number of responses was significantly related to familiarity for concrete stimuli ($r = .737$) but not for abstract stimuli ($r = .03$). It is this type of interaction effect which is suggested may account for the apparently discrepant findings reported above. Further discussion of this point will follow.

It would appear, then, that there is a positive relationship between familiarity and response availability, m, and a slight negative relationship with response heterogeneity, D, except when some other stimulus variable—as emotionality or abstractness—interacts in such a way as to mask the effect of familiarity. The hypothesis that stimulus familiarity is positively related to response availability finds further support in studies using reproduction techniques as measures of stimulus-response variability. Carlson (1954) found a significant positive correlation between T-L frequency and number of errors on a response reproduction test. This relationship between stimulus familiarity and stimulus-response variability also has been clearly demonstrated in the study by Postman (1964) in which subjects were requested to give the *same* response on successive association trials; the results indicated that the number of response changes to HF stimuli exceeded those to MF or LF stimuli. Similarly, Jacobs (1959), retesting subjects on a continuous-association task, found greater variation among the first two responses for HF stimuli than for LF words. Thus it does appear that there is greater within-subject variability among

---

*Whereas in Koen's (1962) study using HF and LF stimuli not matched for emotionality, familiarity and m were positively related.

stimulus-response connections where the stimuli are familiar than where they are less familiar.

Since this latter study involved emotional as well as neutral words, we must assume that emotionality and familiarity both contributed positively to the number of reproduction errors. In this instance, emotionality and familiarity worked cooperatively to increase stimulus-response variability. However, the overriding aspect of the emotionality variable, as hypothesized above, is well demonstrated in a study by R. M. Jones (1958). Using HF and LF emotional stimulus words and HF neutral words, a standard WAT was administered; subjects were then given their responses and asked to recall the stimulus terms. Supporting the above hypothesis, familiarity was not a discriminating variable for emotional stimuli; there was no difference between HF and LF emotional words in the number of reproduction errors, and both of these categories showed more response-stimulus variability (i.e., more modified reproduction errors) than HF neutral stimulus words. (Unfortunately, LF neutral words, which we would hypothesize to have fewer errors than HF neutral, were not included in the study.) Again, as discussed in the preceding section (see p. 44), it is difficult to determine if these results are due to variability in the stimulus-response associative connection or whether instead they reflect a differential availability of the stimulus for recall—i.e., that emotional stimuli are more difficult to recall than neutral stimuli. Nevertheless, it seems justified to conclude that within the category of affective stimuli, emotionality is a stronger variable than familiarity and tends to mask the usual effects of the latter variable.

While one of the consequences of stimulus familiarity appears to be to increase stimulus-response variability and availability, at the same time there is evidence to support the paradoxical hypothesis that stimulus familiarity is positively related to response strength. In a study by Postman (1964) based on 1,000 college subjects, the frequency of the primary response to HF stimuli (26.6%) exceeds that of the Primary response to MF stimuli (25.3%), which in turn exceeds that to LF stimuli (23.8%). Entwisle and Forsyth (1963), defining commonality as the frequency of the three most common responses, found that for fifth-grade subjects HF words elicited the highest commonality scores, MF words elicited the next highest, and LF words elicited the lowest scores. Hall and Ugelow (1957) also found greater commonality for HF words than for LF words.

While this relationship between stimulus familiarity and response commonality may generally hold, it is possible it may not apply to particular stimulus categories. For example, although Entwisle and Forsyth (1963) found a positive relationship between T-L frequency and commonality of responses for adjective and verb stimuli, and Terwilliger (1964) found the response gradient for stimuli rated "familiar" to be steeper than the gradient for less familiar adjectives, a somewhat different relationship may apply to noun stimuli. In the Entwisle-Forsyth study, noun stimuli rank-ordered (in terms of greatest to least commonality) MF > LF > HF. The author did not analyze the data for separate form classes, and it is doubtful that these differences are significant. Nevertheless, it is noteworthy that if this measure of commonality (frequency of the three most common responses) is applied to Postman's data for noun stimuli, the differences, although small, follow the same rank order: i.e., MF > LF > HF.

Findings on response latency might also suggest that familiarity is positively related to response strength; Jacobs (1955), Veness (1962), and Wallenhorst (1965) found a *tendency* for HF stimuli to have a shorter reaction time than LF stimuli, and both for Eriksen (1952) and for Hall and Ugelow (1957) this difference was significant. However, a study by DeLucia and Stagner (1954) raises some question in the mind of the present author as to the interpretation of the reaction time results. In the latter study, the stimuli were projected on a screen; subjects were first tested for recognition time (time required to name the stimulus correctly) and then for association time (time from the activation of the projector until the verbal association of the subject stopped a voice-key controlled clock). Using five levels of T-L frequency, the authors found no relationship between familiarity and associative-response latency; on the other hand, stimulus-recognition time was related (inversely) to familiarity. These findings raise the question, then, of whether the inverse relationship observed between stimulus familiarity and reaction time represents a longer *association* interval between an unfamiliar stimulus and its response, and hence is indicative of a weaker stimulus-response bond for unfamiliar stimuli, or whether the reaction time measure actually reflects an increase in the time required for *recognition* of unfamiliar stimuli.*

Two further studies which raise some doubt about the relationship between stimulus familiarity and reaction time are those by Riley and Phillips (1959) and by Gillhooly (1965), in which CVC trigrams were "familiarized" and subsequently given as WAT stimuli. Contrary to expectation, the reaction time to familiarized CVCs did not differ from that to unfamiliar CVCs. In a second study, Gillhooly was able to produce a difference in reaction time by having subjects pronounce, as well as spell, the CVC. If his interpretation of these results as being a function of

---

*As has been demonstrated, e.g., by Howes and Solomon (1951) and Eriksen (1952). In this light, it is interesting to reconsider Veness' study (1962) which found that, of the various types of response faults occurring, mistaken perceptions of the stimulus term are more likely to occur to emotional stimuli, while mistakes involving the response term are more likely to occur to neutral stimuli.

pronouncing is accurate (although this variable was confounded with increased frequency of exposure), and if we can assume that being able to pronounce a stimulus aids in its recognition, then the decreased response latency in this study may provide further evidence for the hypothesis that stimulus familiarity is related to stimulus-recognition time, but not necessarily to strength of the stimulus-response bond. At this point, then, the findings regarding stimulus familiarity and reaction time are somewhat equivocal.

Three studies have focused on the type of associative response as a function of stimulus familiarity. In one (Deese, 1962a), the number of paradigmatic and syntagmatic responses given to various grammatical form classes was determined. With the exception of adjective stimuli, the occurrence of either type of response was unrelated to the T-L frequency of the stimulus; for adjectives, LF stimuli elicited more syntagmatic responses and HF stimuli elicited more paradigmatic ones. In the second (T. J. Johnson, Meinke, Van Mondfrans, & Finn, 1965), subjects were restricted to synonym responses in a continued association test. The T-L frequency of the resulting associative responses was found to be directly related to the frequency of the stimuli. Finally, Schulz and Thysell (1965), also using a continued-association test, varied the number of familiarization trials of selected disyllables. The results indicated that while degree of familiarization was ineffective in determining response familiarity, natural language familiarity (as determined by T-L frequency) was positively related to T-L frequency of response.

Summary and Discussion

Stimulus familiarity has been shown to have the following effects*
(1) a tendency for reaction time to be decreased, [b]
(2) response availability, m, is increased, [a], [b]
(3) response heterogeneity, D is decreased[a]; furthermore,
(4) the strength of the Primary response is increased,
(5) response commonality (the frequency of the first three responses) is increased, except perhaps for noun stimuli, and
(6) the T-L frequency of the responses is increased.[b]
(7) The frequency of paradigmatic or syntagmatic responses is not affected except for adjective stimuli, where LF stimuli result in syntagmatic responses, and HF stimuli result in paradigmatic responses.
(8) Finally, there is an increase in response reproduction errors.

As was found in the preceding section on stimulus affectivity, measures of response availability, m, and response heterogeneity, D, as a function

*(a) except when the presence of a second stimulus dimension (e.g., emotionality, abstractness) masks the effect; (b) except when familiarity is based on experimental familiarization rather than natural language (T-L) frequency.

of stimulus familiarity are inversely related. However, as opposed to the effect of emotionality, stimulus familiarity increases response availability and decreases response heterogeneity. Also as contrasted with emotionality, the degree of familiarity of the stimulus determines the degree of familiarity of the response. That is, while with emotional stimuli the responses appear to reflect an avoidance of the affective category which defines the stimulus, with familiar stimuli the responses are *chosen* from the category which defines the stimulus; thus HF stimuli elicit HF responses, and LF stimuli elicit LF responses.

We also have seen that the effects of familiarity on associative responses may be masked by the effects of a second stimulus dimension and that this is even more likely when the stimuli are experimentally matched on the two dimensions in a way which does not reflect the frequency of natural occurrence of these types of stimuli. For example, unselected emotional stimuli are more likely to be of lower familiarity and neutral stimuli are more likely to be of higher familiarity; when stimuli are equated via selection procedures on these two variables, the usual relationships between familiarity and response heterogeneity or response availability are not found. This implies the obvious, but sometimes overlooked, point that whenever stimuli can be classified along more than one dimension, the possibility of associative responses being determined by an interaction between the two dimensions should be considered.

The conclusions at which we arrive about the relationship between stimulus familiarity and strength of associative response vary, depending on the measure of habit strength being considered. Thus the shorter reaction time found for more familiar stimuli suggests a stronger associative bond; yet there is some evidence to suggest that the reaction time reflects stimulus recognition time rather than stimulus-response association time. Even more important, however, is the fact that while both response commonality and frequency of the Primary response are shown to increase with increasing familiarity, response variability (i.e., number of reproduction errors) also increases. Thus we are faced with an apparent paradox in that the associative response appears to become both stronger (more predictable) and weaker (less predictable) with increasing stimulus familiarity.*

However, it appears that this paradox may depend in large part on the choice of the model used to determine associative strength. That is,

---

*This paradox also has been discussed by Postman (1964), who notes "... the absolute strength of pre-experimental associations increases with word frequency but so does the amount of competition among alternative responses." (p. 189). These conflicting effects of associative habits have been described as the "interference paradox of associative probability" (Underwood & Schulz, 1960, p. 46).

it derives from a model which assumes that unity, or 100%, is the fixed maximum for the sum of all the associative-response strengths to any one stimulus. This model has developed from the use of norms based on a fixed N, such that if 70% of the subjects give the first response, R_1, the maximum possible strength for any second response R_2 is 30%. It is conceivable, however, that another model might better describe the associative response characteristics of a stimulus. It might be, for example, that the total associative response strength is greater to some stimuli than to others; in a sense, Noble's m findings support this viewpoint. In this case, the overall associative strength for one stimulus might be 40% while for another it might be 200 or 300%; the associative strength for any one response would be relatively independent of the strength of the other responses to that stimulus. The failure to assume independence of response strengths derives, it seems, from two circumstances. First, as mentioned above, it is based on a model which assumes a fixed number of items in the associative-response repertory, each of which may stand for the same or different words; then, the more items which stand for the same words, the fewer available to stand for different words—i.e., the total number of available responses (items) must equal unity. This will be referred to as the fixed maximum strength (FMS) model. Secondly, this model, in which the value of unity depends on the number of subjects tested, is based on the data from a situation in which the subject is allowed only one response, a fact which may distort the associative-response strength values obtained. Suppose, for example, that 70% of the subjects tested gave the same first response to a stimulus word. Using the FMS model, the associative strength of R_1 would equal 70%. Now suppose these same subjects were asked to give a second response to the same stimulus, and that all of the above 70% gave the same R_2. What associative-response strength value should be assigned to R_2? R_2 is given by 70% of the subjects, but, since it was not the first emitted response, we must assume it is somewhat weaker than R_1. One way to decide upon the R_2 value, of course, would be to determine the frequency of its occurrence as a *first* response. In this case, the maximum *possible* value for R_2 as a first response is 30%. Let us say, for the moment, that despite the fact that 70% of the subjects gave R_2 as a second response, we accept this 30% as an estimate of the R_2 value; however, we recognize that, although within this model this is the maximum value we can assign to R_2, in terms of its actual frequency of occurrence, 30% appears to be a rather low estimate. If we now ask our subjects to give a *third* response, and if again all of them gave the same word, we are faced with a real dilemma; what associative strength value can we assign to R_3? If we assume a universe with a fixed number of items, these have been totally expended by R_1 and R_2; i.e., there is no room in this universe for R_3. Should it then be assigned an associative value of zero? Yet clearly R_3 is a strong associate of the stimulus, since so many subjects gave it as a response, once the two most dominant responses were emitted. While it might be argued that if R_3 is truly a strong associate, it should have been given by at least some of the subjects as a first response—i.e., of the 30% who did not give R_1, some should have given R_2, some R_3, and some R_x; thus R_3 would not, using the FMS model, receive an associative value of zero. Nevertheless it would appear that this FMS approach may greatly underestimate the associative strength of certain responses.

While the example given makes use of extremes (70, 30, and 0%), the problem is fairly clear; the FMS model does not adequately account for cases where there are several relatively strong associative responses to the same stimulus. What is being suggested is that associative-response strength should, perhaps, be determined by having subjects give several responses to a stimulus (as in continued-association tests) and that the associative strength of any one response should be based on the frequency of its occurrence within, say, the first five responses. Thus in the example above, R_1, R_2, and R_3 would all have an associative strength value of 70%. (It is possible, however, that some subjects might give R_2 or R_3 as first, fourth, or fifth responses, or that some subjects might give R_1 as second, third, fourth, or fifth responses; if this were true, the response strengths of R_1, R_2, and R_3 would depend on the total frequency of occurrence of the response over the five trials. It is conceivable, for example, that the associative value of R_2 might exceed that of R_1, if the *total* number of R_2 responses over the five trials markedly exceeded that of R_1 responses.) However, *order* of response emission probably should be given some weight in determining the value assigned to each response (cf. e.g., the formula proposed by Garskof, 1965).

This variable maximum strength (VMS) model, then, postulates an associative universe which may vary in size from stimulus to stimulus and in which each stimulus may thus have a total associative response strength of greater or lesser value. Using the VMS model, it is possible to reconcile the apparent paradox that both associative-response strength and response variability (as determined from reproduction errors) can be positively related to a third variable (as stimulus familiarity), whereas response strength and response variablity are customarily thought of as being inversely related. According to this model, the greater the number of elements, the greater the possibility that any one word can be represented more frequently—and since strong responses are more likely to be represented than weak ones, the absolute associative strength of strong responses should be increased in a universe of many elements. In this case, more responses should exceed the overt response threshold, and hence there should be greater variability in responses over several trials. That is, a model which allows for a variable total maximum response strength allows for the possibility of several responses exceeding threshold, and thus it allows for the possibility of response competition. From this point of view, it is not paradoxical that response strength and response variability should be positively related.

Part of Speech of Stimulus

A third stimulus characteristic which has been shown to influence associative responses is that of the grammatical form class of the stimulus. As was found true for the stimulus variables of emotionality and familiarity, form class is related to the number of responses elicited by the stimulus in a continued or continuous association task. Thus M. T. Mednick *et al.* (1964a) found nouns to elicit more responses, m, than adjectives; Cofer and Shevitz (1952) found this relationship to hold for HF stimuli but for LF stimuli there was no difference in the number of responses, m, elicited by nouns and adjectives. (However, since each category—e.g., HF noun—was represented by only one stimulus word, generalization to the *class* of nouns or of adjectives must be made with caution.) The role of nouns in determining response availability has also been shown to depend on the type of noun being used. Thus Lambert (1955) found, for both French and English, that more responses, m, were available to concrete nouns than to abstract ones which did not differ appreciably from adjectives.

The range of form classes investigated has been extended in several studies, with the result that nouns generally are found to elicit *fewer* responses, D or m, than most other grammatical categories. For example, Palermo (1963) found that a WAT consisting of stimuli which sampled the various form classes elicited more different responses, D, than the standard Kent-Rosanoff list, which consists of nouns and adjectives only. Glanzer (1962), using a four-trial successive WAT, found that the number of *different* responses elicited and the reaction time data both supported the assertion that stimulus-response bonds are strongest (fewest different responses and fastest reaction time) for nouns, next strongest for adjectives, and weakest (most different responses and slowest reaction time) for conjunctions, with prepositions, pronouns, adverbs, and verbs falling somewhere in between.

Fillenbaum and Jones (1965) have found a similar rank order based on the strength of the Primary response. Adjectives and then nouns elicit the strongest Primaries, while conjunctions elicit the weakest Primaries; pronouns, adverbs, prepositions, and verbs are, respectively, intermediate in Primary response strength. Finally, Entwisle and Forsyth (1963), using fifth-grade subjects, found response commonality (frequency of the three most common responses) to be greatest for adjectives, less for nouns, and least for verbs.

These findings, then, consistently demonstrate that adjectives and nouns have stronger stimulus-response bonds and elicit fewer different responses than do other grammatical forms of stimuli. Whether nouns and adjectives differ as to the availability and heterogeneity of responses is less clear-cut. Furthermore, when stimuli are categorized for number of possible grammatical usages (i.e., the word can be used as a noun and/or an adjective and/or a verb), it was found that those words which could be used as both a noun and an adjective elicited more m responses than words which could be used both as a noun and a verb, and more than those words which had only a single usage (Matthews, 1965).

The influence of stimulus form class on the *type* of response elicited has been demonstrated in several studies. Deese (1964), in a factor analytic study of the responses to 278 adjectives, found 80 (40 pairs) of these stimuli to be polar opposites, in the sense that their responses defined the extremes of 40 orthogonal factors. Siipola, Walker, and Kolb (1955) found that, when subjects are encouraged to respond quickly (as in the standard WAT procedure), adjective stimuli elicit more adjective responses than noun responses. However, when subjects are encouraged to take their time, the response frequencies are reversed. On the other hand, regardless of time pressure conditions, noun stimuli consistently elicit more noun responses than adjective responses.

Other studies which have investigated the correspondence between form class of the stimulus and the form class of the response have resulted in consistent findings. Thus Glanzer (1962) noted that responses tend to be of the same grammatical category as the stimulus (i.e., tend to be paradigmatic) and when this is not so, the stimuli and responses generally correspond in terms of both belonging to the broader category of content words (nouns, adjectives, verbs, adverbs) or of function words (pronouns, prepositions, or conjunctions).

Furthermore, it has been noted that certain grammatical categories elicit a higher proportion of paradigmatic responses than do other categories. Over an age span from first grade to adult, R. W. Brown and Berko (1960) found paradigmatic responses to be greatest for count nouns, and then to decrease for adjectives, intransitive verbs, adverbs, and mass nouns. Kagan, Rosman, Day, Albert, and Phillips (1964) also have found this rank order of nouns, adjectives, and verbs for the number of paradigmatic responses obtained from first- through fourth-grade children. Also, Deese (1962a) has found paradigmatic responses to be greatest for noun and HF adjective stimuli, and Palermo (1964), using fourth- to twelfth-grade subjects, noted that these responses are less likely to be elicited by prepositions, conjunctions, or interjections. Deese (1965), in further investigations, found that the paradigmatic responses to adjectives are generally either antonyms (opposite responses) or synonyms. In addition, he found that the occurrence of antonym responses is highly correlated with the T-L frequency of the stimulus. More familiar adjectives are likely to elicit antonym paradigmatic responses, while less familiar adjectives elicit synonym paradigmatic responses; unfamiliar adjectives, as implied above, elicit syntagmatic responses.

Further evidence for this rank order between type of stimulus and number of paradigmatic responses comes from a study by Fillenbaum and Jones (1965). In addition to finding that the largest percentage of responses came from the same grammatical class as that of the stimulus,* they also found the percentage of paradigmatic responses to be greatest for nouns, followed by pronouns and adjectives, then adverbs, verbs, and prepositions, and least for conjunctions. On the other hand, syntagmatic responses have been found to be most often elicited by adverbs, followed by adjectives and verbs, and then by nouns (Deese, 1962a).

Osgood and Sebeok (1954) have used this paradigmatic-syntagmatic distinction in an attempt to explain the preponderance of coordinate and contrast responses among the associations of adults. According to their analysis, if both the paradigmatic and syntagmatic variables are factors which determine association, then the strongest associations should be for pairs of words which can be both paradigmatic and syntagmatic. Such strongly associated words as *Table-Chair* (83.3%) and *Black-White* (74.5%) are pairs of this type.

McNeill (1963), prompted by earlier suggestions by R. W. Brown and Berko (1960) and Ervin (1961), attempted to explain how these two types of associations are established. Pursuing the hypothesis that paradigmatic associations result from the use of words in *identical* speech contexts,† while syntagmatic associations are learned by contiguity due to the sequential arrangement of speech, sentence frames were constructed such that CVCs occurred either in a noun or an adjective position. Subsequently, these CVCs were given as WAT stimuli, and subjects were instructed to respond with other CVCs from the original set. The number of paradigmatic responses—e.g., "noun" CVC eliciting "noun" CVC as a response—was shown to be a function of the degree to which the initial sentence-frame contexts were learned—a finding which the author took to support his initial hypotheses. Furthermore, such paradigmatic responses increased with learning only when the two same-class CVCs had been learned in the

---

*With the exception of "article" stimuli.
†And hence these paradigmatic associates tend to occur contiguously through implicit erroneous anticipations.

same sentence context. When they had occupied the same grammatical position in *different* sentences, their occurrence as paradigmatic responses did not increase with learning.

Further evidence for the origin of paradigmatic responses comes from a similar study by Glucksberg and Cohen (1965). The number of noun responses to CVCs previously occurring in a noun position (78%) exceeded the number of noun responses to CVCs not presented previously (56%) and approximated the number of noun responses to noun stimuli (77%) (associative strengths from Palermo, 1963). Similarly, the number of verb responses to CVCs occurring in a verb position (47%) exceeded verb responses to new CVCs (10%) and again approximated the frequency of verb responses to verb stimuli (44%) (Palermo, 1963). Thus the embedding of CVCs in a sentence frame resulted in their acquiring a stimulus property of functioning like a noun or a verb on a WAT, which suggested to the authors that paradigmatic responses are due to substitution processes based on grammatical category rather than to the stimulus having frequently occurred in the context of identical other stimuli.

Ervin (1963) has also investigated this problem within a similar frame of reference. A large number of high-school and college subjects, subsequent to taking a WAT, were asked to use each of the WAT stimuli in a sentence, and then to provide four words which would substitute for the stimuli in those sentences. For most stimuli, it was found that the best predictor of the frequency of a particular associative response was the frequency with which that response was substituted for the stimulus in the constructed sentences. Furthermore, the greater the variety of sentences in which the stimulus word was used, the greater the likelihood that the associative responses would be paradigmatic. In addition, contextual contiguity (syntagmatic association) was found to be a predictor of associative frequency, if the response followed the stimulus in the constructed sentences. Associative responses which were drawn from the context preceding the stimulus occurred primarily with noun and adjective stimuli; such responses tended to be of the same form class as the stimulus, making it questionable as to whether they represented reverse syntagmatic associations or, rather, the more common paradigmatic responses found to such stimuli.

Summary and Discussion

To summarize the findings of the effect of grammatical class on associative responses, we have noted that stimuli can be rank-ordered by class in terms of their consequences for several response measures.*

---

*[a]The relative response availability to adjectives and nouns may be reversed when more than four responses are allowed, when the stimuli are of high T-L frequency, or when concrete noun stimuli are used. [b]Fifth-grade subjects. [c]Count (as opposed to mass) nouns.

(1) For reaction time, conjunctions > adverbs > prepositions > verbs > pronouns > adjectives > nouns.
(2) For response availability, m, conjunctions > prepositions > pronouns > adverbs > verbs > adjectives > nouns.[a]
(3) For response heterogeneity, D, other grammatical classes > adjective + noun.
(4) For the strength of the Primary response, adjective > noun > pronoun > adverb > preposition > verb > conjunction.
(5) For response commonality (strength of first three responses),[b] adjectives > nouns > verbs.
(6) It has also been noted that paradigmatic responses are the modal response, and that in terms of the frequency of paradigmatic responses,
  (A) nouns[c] > pronouns > adjectives > adverbs, verbs, prepositions > conjunctions, interjections,
  (B) and for adjectives: HF > MF > LF.
(7) In terms of the frequency of syntagmatic responses, adverbs > adjectives, verbs > nouns.

We may note that, in the case of stimulus grammatical class, reaction time, response availability, and possibly response heterogeneity are all positively related—i.e., the more responses available to the stimuli of a particular grammatical class, the longer the reaction time. On the other hand, strength of the Primary response, and possibly of the first three responses, is inversely related to the first three variables; thus the stronger the stimulus-first response association, the fewer available responses and the shorter the reaction time.

Furthermore, if the rank order of grammatical classes of stimuli is examined first for associative reaction time, and then for frequency of paradigmatic responses (or, conversely, number of syntagmatic responses), an interesting correspondence may be noted; stimuli from those grammatical categories with the shortest reaction time are most likely to elicit responses from the same grammatical class, while stimuli with long reaction times are most likely to elicit responses from other classes. These findings lend support to the previous interpretation of the increased reaction time to emotional stimuli as being the result of the response being chosen from a different affective class (cf. p. 55).

Finally, some discussion of the two studies dealing with the origin of paradigmatic associations is in order. Both McNeill and Glucksberg agree that paradigmatic associative responses are due to substitution processes based on the CVC item's having occupied the same grammatical position within a sentence context, rather than to the item having occurred in the context of other stimuli of the same grammatical class.* However, Glucksberg and Cohen's main conclusion—that the embedding of CVCs in a sentence frame results in their acquiring a stimulus property of functioning like a noun or verb on a WAT—is specifically rejected by McNeill. In his study, increasing paradigmatic association was based on the learning of CVCs which occurred in the same grammatical position *in identical sentence contexts*. CVCs occupying the same grammatical position in *different* sentences did not show the same pattern of increased paradigmatic associations as a function of learning.

Since Glucksberg and Cohen *did* find paradigmatic associations to depend on the CVCs having occupied the same grammatical position in *different* sentences, some attempt should be made to reconcile the two studies. McNeill studied noun and adjective grammatical categories, while the Glucksberg and Cohen CVCs occupied noun or verb positions. Whether or not this is an important difference cannot be assessed, since McNeill used only the "noun" CVCs as WAT stimuli, and the Glucksberg-Cohen study did not differentiate between the two stimulus classes in reporting the association test results. Also difficult to assess is the fact that McNeill restricted subjects to CVC responses from within the set used in the learning task, while subjects in the other study were free to respond with any word they wished. Perhaps a more critical difference between the two studies, however, is that McNeill presented the sentence frames for 20, 40, or 60 learning trials, while in the Glucksberg-Cohen study each frame was presented only once, for rating on S.D. scales. Since McNeill bases his conclusion on the fact that same-category CVCs from *different* sentences show a curvilinear relationship between amount of learning and number of paradigmatic responses (while same-category CVCs from the *same* sentence context show a monotonic increase), it is possible that the Glucksberg-Cohen findings (based on minimal learning) represent a point very early on the McNeill continuum. In this case, we might be able to conclude that, at least within certain limits, CVCs can acquire the stimulus property of functioning as a member of a particular grammatical class. However, to increase the functional strength of this property beyond a certain level requires additional support from shared contextual associations.

If this were true, it would suggest that paradigmatic associations may

---

*It should be noted that McNeill has more recently abandoned the point of view that "erroneous anticipation" of the substitute response is the cause of the development of paradigmatic associations. Instead, he suggests that paradigmatic associations result from the individual choosing that response word which shares with the stimulus the maximum number of defining features. As McNeill puts it, "The paradigmatic response thus forms a *minimal contrast* with the stimulus" (1966, p. 555).

originally develop from words occupying the same grammatical position in a variety of different sentences, but that further increase in the associative frequency of paradigmatic responses depends on their occurrence in the same grammatical position in the *same* sentences. This suggestion may help explain the grammatical class rank order for frequency of paradigmatic responses. That is, conjunctions have a very low incidence of paradigmatic responses (although these are still the most frequent class of response), since the number of different sentence contexts in which *and*, *but*, *nor*, or *for* may function as conjunctions is virtually limitless. On the other hand, nouns can occupy the same position in fewer different sentences, due to contextual constraints. This relatively higher probability of nouns occupying the same grammatical position in the same sentence context may thus account for the higher incidence of paradigmatic responses to noun stimuli.

Semantic Level of Stimulus

A fourth set of studies may be grouped under the heading of the effect of different semantic levels of the stimulus on associative responses. Under this heading will be included investigations of stimuli chosen to represent a particular (nonaffective) concept, of single- versus multiple-meaning stimuli, of the concrete-abstract stimulus dimension, and of pictorial versus lexical stimuli.

A small number of studies have investigated the associative-response effects of stimuli which represent a particular (nonaffective) concept, or meaning class. For example, Bousfield and Barclay (1950), in a continuous, controlled-association task, had subjects give as many "Bird," or "Carpenter's Tools," or "Heavenly Bodies" responses as possible, within an 18-minute time interval. The mean number of responses per subject was greatest for "Birds" (36.97), next greatest for "Tools" (24.60), and least for "Heavenly Bodies" (17.32).

In another type of study of the relationship between conceptual classes and word association, Cofer (1957) chose sets of stimuli consisting of a "standard" word and five synonyms, and found that the proportion of responses which two stimuli had in common (Mf) was a function of the degree of rated similarity between the two stimulus words. Put another way, these findings can be interpreted to indicate that the degree of associative response overlap is a function of the extent to which one stimulus belongs to the meaning class of the other stimulus. In a similar line, Tresselt and Mayzner (1964b), using stimuli representing the concept "Economic," found that a subject's initial response to each stimulus was rated higher for belonging to the concept than was his second response. In another study, Epstein and Fenz (1962) found the number of "parachute" content responses to be a function of the degree of relevance of the stimuli to parachuting. In two studies, Kimbrough and Cofer used stimuli which were closely, moderately, or only slightly relevant (far) to the concept "Law." In one of these (Kimbrough & Cofer, 1958), the authors found that "close" stimuli elicited more responses with law content than did "far" stimuli while the results for "moderate" stimuli depended on the subject's attitude (subjects favorable to the law giving more law responses). In the other study (Kimbrough & Cofer, 1957), three groups of subjects were given stimuli either closely, or moderately, or distantly related to law. The responses of the three groups were evaluated for their degree of reference to the concept "Law." Taking into account both frequency and order of emission of the resulting responses, each response word was assigned a weight; these weighted scores were then assigned to the responses of the initial three groups of subjects. The results indicated that the mean weighted response score (indicating saturation of law-relevant responses) for the group of subjects given stimuli highly relevant to law was significantly greater than for those subjects given stimuli of moderate relevance, who in turn gave significantly more law-relevant responses than subjects given low-relevant stimuli. As a further test of the role of stimulus conceptual category in determining the conceptual category of the response, the stimuli were rank-ordered according to their weighted associative-response scores; this rank-ordering then was compared with a second ranking of the stimuli, based on an independent assessment of their "belongingness" to the concept "Law." The rank order correlation between associative value score rank and conceptual ranking was .71 (or .59, when 13 of the 29 stimuli which had zero associative value scores were removed).

In general, then, these studies support the assertion that the greater the belongingness of a stimulus to a particular concept, the more likely it will elicit a response which belongs to the concept.

In one additional study of the relationship between concepts and word association (Messick & Solley, 1957), two artificial concepts were constructed. These concepts (Tribe A and Tribe B) consisted of 20 instances of various combinations of four bipolar attributes (tall-short, fat-skinny, happy-sad, and black-white). The frequency of occurrence of any individual attribute value was the same for both concepts, but they differed in terms of the joint occurrence of combinations of attributes (e.g., concept A had twelve "skinny-happy" instances, while concept B included only eight such instances). The twenty instances of each concept were represented as line drawings and were presented in two successive probability learning trials. Subsequently, the eight attributes were presented as verbal WAT stimuli. The associative responses obtained reflected the frequency of joint occurrence of two attributes within each concept—i.e., the WAT responses differentiated between the two concepts.

Four investigations of single- versus multiple-meaning stimuli are relevant in this section, in the sense that they are concerned with the effect of level or complexity of stimulus meaning on associative responses. Faibish (1961), matching stimuli for T-L frequency and difficulty in defining, found multi-meaning stimuli to have a shorter response latency and fewer unusual responses for normal subjects, while single-meaning stimuli had shorter reaction times (but produced as many unusual responses) for schizophrenic subjects. In this instance, the availability of alternative response meanings facilitated associative responding, for normal subjects, but produced competition and/or confusion in schizophrenics. On the other hand when stimuli were matched both for the number of possible grammatical usages (e.g., the stimulus could be used as a noun, and/or an adjective, or a verb, as compared to stimuli which could be used only as two or as one of these), as well as for T-L frequency, the results indicated that having more than one conceptual referent was unrelated to the number of responses, m, available (Matthews, 1965).

The third study to be reported here, like that of Faibish, also demonstrated the interaction of the subject variable in determining the effect of multi-meaning stimuli. Using homonyms which had both a "body-meaning" and a "nonbody-meaning" (e.g., colon, tablet), Secord (1953) found the number of "body" responses to correlate with the amount of body concern demonstrated by the subject on other psychological tests. On the other hand, a word-association study using numeral homonyms (e.g., eight-ate) as stimuli (Cook, Mefferd, & Wieland, 1965; cf. p. 91), indicated that the meaning to which the subject responded was strongly determined by the context surrounding the stimulus.

The results of comparisons of concrete and abstract nouns have been consistent in demonstrating that concrete nouns elicit more associative responses than abstract nouns in a continued- or continuous-association task (Lambert, 1955; M. T. Mednick *et al.*, 1964a; Pollio, 1964b; Winnick & Kressel, 1965). However, although concrete stimuli have more available associative connections, there is also some evidence that they are more consistent in the responses they evoke. Thus Kolers (1963), testing bilingual subjects, presented stimuli both in English and in the native language of the subjects, and found that the number of associative responses which were similar in both languages was greater for concrete than for abstract nouns.

Comparisons of pictorial and lexical stimuli offer tentative support for the hypothesis that the effect of the abstract-concrete verbal dimension may be extended downward to include pictorial concrete stimuli. For example, Davidon and Longo (1960) presented as stimuli either a picture of an object or the name of the object. Using the method of discrete association, both types of stimuli elicited approximately an equal number of different responses; however, the response latency for picture stimuli was shorter than for name stimuli for 10-year-old and junior-high subjects, suggesting that responses to picture stimuli are more readily available for the younger age groups. However, by the time the subjects reached college age, this differential reaction time was not observed, suggesting that the predominance of strong associative connections for concrete pictorial stimuli had been replaced by a developmentally linked increase in the strength of associations to concrete verbal stimuli.

Further evidence for the hypothesis that both availability and consistency of associative responses are a function of stimulus concreteness and clarity of meaning comes from a study by Mandler and Parnes (1957). Using a continuous-association task, they found the greatest number of associative responses to be elicited by line drawings, then by adjectives, then by Rorschach stimuli, and then by nonsense syllables, while the percentage of idiosyncratic responses was greatest for Rorschach cards and nonsense syllables, and least for adjectives and drawings. Noble (1952) and Schulz and Thysell (1965) also have found a greater number of associative responses to disyllabic words as compared to disyllabic paralogs; in addition, the latter study found a higher proportion of idiosyncratic responses to the paralogs. Thus the effect of concrete and less ambiguous stimuli is to elicit both a greater number of and more consistent responses.*

A corresponding preference for concrete *responses* has also been noted (Deterline, 1957). Subjects were presented with pictorial stimuli chosen to represent three concept categories—concrete objects, form, and number—and were asked to write the first word suggested by each picture. Regardless of the stimulus category, the most frequent responses were object names ($\bar{X} = 38.50$), followed by form responses ($\bar{X} = 4.08$) and number responses ($\bar{X} = .40$), again suggesting the greater availability of associations from the concrete, as opposed to the abstract, domain of associative meaning.

Summary and Discussion

Semantic level of the stimulus has been shown to be related to the following associative-response effects:

*Investigations of associative responses to CVC trigrams (nonsense syllables) have been reviewed by Noble (1963). Neither these studies, nor those of associations to random shapes (e.g., A. G. Goldstein, 1961; Vanderplas & Garvin, 1959) will be discussed here, since the intent of these studies has not been to explain why the stimuli differ, for example, in number of associations elicited, but rather to demonstrate their consistency in doing so. One additional study which does focus on the association process itself is that by R. C. Johnson (1964a, 1964b), in which he found that CVC association value, a, is negatively related to reaction time—i.e., the higher the association value, the more quickly a response is given.

(1) The greater the belongingness of the stimulus to a concept, the greater the probability that the response will belong to that concept.
(2) For multi-meaning stimuli (versus single-meaning stimuli):
  (A) Reaction time is decreased for normal subjects, but is increased for schizophrenics.
  (B) Response availability, m, is not affected when familiarity and grammatical usage are equated.
  (C) The meaning which is responded to may be a function of subject variables, and/or of
  (D) the stimulus context
(3) For concrete verbal stimuli (versus abstract):
  (A) response availablity m, is increased, and the
  (B) bilingual consistency of the response is increased.
(4) For pictorial stimuli versus lexical:
  (A) response heterogeneity, D, is unaffected
  (B) reaction time is decreased for 10-year-old and junior-high subjects, but is unaffected for college subjects.
(5) Stimulus clarity and meaningfulness (versus ambiguity and meaninglessness) result in
  (A) an increase in response availability, m,
  (B) a decrease in the proportion of idiosyncratic responses, and
  (C) a decrease in reaction time.

While relatively fewer investigations have studied the effects of semantic level on associative responses, as opposed to the effects of emotionality or familiarity, it does seem possible to draw a few tentative conclusions. Thus while the semantic category of a stimulus word is likely to determine the category from which the response is selected, when a stimulus belongs to more than one semantic class, the choice of meaning responded to is determined both by the context surrounding the stimulus and by intrasubject variables—both of which topics will be discussed in subsequent sections of this book.

There also appears to be some evidence that availability and consistency of associative responses is, at least in part, a function of the concreteness and lack of ambiguity of the stimulus. Furthermore, the data suggest that the relative meaningfulness of stimuli from different semantic levels may vary at different stages of development and that, barring the presence of thought pathology, the stimulus from the semantic class which is most meaningful for that developmental period will be responded to most rapidly.

The Stimulus Defined in Terms of the Responses Evoked

The final group of studies to be considered in this section on the effect of the stimulus variable consists of several investigations where the stimulus has been defined in terms of the responses it evokes. For example, Carroll, Kjeldergaard, and Carton (1962) noted from the Minnesota data (Russell & Jenkins, 1954) that certain stimuli (OES) tend to evoke opposites as Primary responses, while other stimuli (non-OES) regularly evoke synonym or other coordinate responses. The OES were found to have stronger Primaries than the non-OES. Furthermore, the number of (opposite) Primaries given to OES and the number of Primaries given to non-OES were not significantly correlated. Subsequently, the responses to OES were found to be more stable over a 16-month period than the responses to non-OES in a high-school population. This study, then, demonstrates that a stimulus dimension, initially defined in terms of the responses evoked, can be subsequently used to identify other effects of associative responses. (Parenthetically, it may be noted that Kjeldergaard & Carroll [1963] have discussed the tendency to give opposite or nonopposite Primaries as a response trait, rather than as a stimulus characteristic.)

Another group of studies have defined the stimulus dimension in terms of the number of different responses evoked, D or m, by the stimulus; Primary response strength, response latency, variability, and disturbance have all been found to be related to this dimension. Thus Howe (1965) found stimuli which elicit many responses (high D stimuli) to have significantly weaker Primary responses than low D stimuli. High D stimuli also have been found to have a longer reaction time than low D stimuli (M. J. Goldstein, 1961; Wiggens, 1957), and to elicit proportionately fewer idiosyncratic responses than low D stimuli (Schulz & Thysell, 1965) or low m stimuli (Mandler & Mandler, 1962).

The number of responses evoked by a stimulus also has been shown to be related to other measures of response variability. Thus M. J. Goldstein (1961) and Laffal (1952, 1955) found high D stimuli to elicit more response faults, Veness (1962) noted a significant positive correlation between these two variables, and Levinger and Clark (1961) found D to be positively related to the number of reproduction errors. The Mandler and Mandler (1962) study also provides GSR evidence which fits with the general finding that high D stimuli result in greater associative-response disturbance.

Stimulus m value has also been shown to affect associative responses. Rau (1958) found high m stimuli to elicit relatively fewer different responses (D/total number responses) than medium or low m stimuli, and Mandler and Mandler (1962) found high m stimuli to elicit a relatively smaller percentage of idiosyncratic responses that did low m stimuli.* Schulz and Thysell

---

*They also found high m stimuli to have a shorter reaction time than low m stimuli, but here the measures of m and of reaction time appeared to be confounded.

(1965), using a continued-association task, found high m stimuli to elicit more HF than LF responses, while low m stimuli elicited more LF than HF ones. Furthermore, the associative responses to the low m disyllabic stimuli tended to begin with the same letter as the first letter of either the first or second syllable of the stimulus—a phenomenon not true of the high m stimuli.

Finally, and related to the high D-low D stimulus dimension, there are several studies which considered the associative-response effects of stimuli differing in the slope of the response hierarchy gradient. M. T. Mednick et al. (1964a), in a continued-association task, found stimuli with flat associative gradients to elicit more associative responses, m, than stimuli with steep gradients. Similarly, Tecce and Glassco (1965) found stimuli with flat associative gradients (high response competition) to have a longer response latency than stimuli with low response competition (i.e., strong Primary). This same finding has also been demonstrated by Wiggens (1957), who used nonsense syllables to establish experimentally the slope of the associative-response gradient.

Osgood and Anderson (1957) also experimentally controlled the slope of the response gradient by varying the number of presentations of paired associates. The pairs consisted of girls' names; each name was paired with one other six times, with a second name three times, and with a third name once. Subsequently, each stimulus was presented in a WAT and the subject was instructed to write the first other response which occurred. Either prior to, or following this association test, the subjects also gave continuous associations (restricted to girls' names), writing one name per notebook page (transitional test). The correlations between the frequency of initial stimulus-response pairing and the frequency of that response as a discrete associative response to the WAT stimulus were consistently positive, with some decrease noted as a result of interpolation of the transitional test (mean $r = .49$ versus $.37$). However, these correlations were due primarily to the stimuli and responses which had been paired six times; the difference between one and three pairings was not significant.

Furthermore, the transitional probabilities were consistently found to be positively correlated with discrete associative-response probabilities, although the former were not related in any consistent way to the initial input stimulus-response frequency. These findings were taken to support the initial hypothesis that the development of stimulus-response associative structures depends on the frequency of the contiguous occurrence of the stimulus and response in the subject's experience, and that the patterning of the sequential output of the subject depends directly on his associative structures, but only indirectly on his past experience.

In two related investigations, Wallenhorst (1965) found a strong inverse relationship between strength of Primary response and response latency, and Schlosberg and Heineman (1950), considering the entire associative-response hierarchy, noted that the log response latency varied inversely with the strength of the response.

Summary and Discussion

Stimuli defined in terms of the responses they evoke have been found to have certain consequences for other measures of associative response.
 (1) Opposite-Evoking Stimuli (OES)
  (A) have stronger Primary responses, and
  (B) produce more stable responses than non-OES.
 (2) High *D* stimuli show
  (A) a decrease in Primary response strength,
  (B) an increase in reaction time,
  (C) a decrease in the proportion of idiosyncratic responses,
  (D) an increase in the number of response faults,
  (E) an increase in the number of response reproduction errors, and
  (F) an increase in GSR.
 (3) High *m* stimuli show
  (A) a decrease in the proportion of idiosyncratic responses, and
  (B) an increase in the T-L frequency of the responses.
 (4) Low *m* stimuli show an increased probability that the response begins with the same letter as the initial letter of the first or second syllable of the stimulus.
 (5) Stimuli with a flat response gradient (versus steep gradient) show
  (A) an increase in response availability, *m*, and
  (B) an increase in reaction time.
 (6) Stimuli with strong responses (Primary or other) show a decrease in reaction time.

Again, relatively few investigations have been made in which the stimuli were selected on the basis of their relationship to some measure of associative-response effects. From these studies, however, it may be concluded that stimuli selected on the basis of producing heterogeneous associative responses also produce a number of other associative-response effects. Thus an increase in reaction time, response faults, GSR, and response reproduction errors have all been found for high *D* stimuli. Furthermore, these findings appear to be due to an increased number of responses of moderate strength rather than to a proliferation of idiosyncratic associations—i.e., they appear to reflect the results of response competition, rather than of highly unusual and/or weak stimulus-response associations.

The relationship between response availability, *m*, and type of response word bears some further comment. Although high m stimuli were found to elicit HF responses and low m stimuli to elicit LF responses, it has been pointed out previously that stimulus m value is also positively related to stimulus familiarity. Thus the present relationship between m and response familiarity may actually be due to stimulus familiarity rather than to m. At any rate, as was found with other stimulus dimensions, there appears to be a "matching" of stimulus and response either on the basis of familiarity or, if a weak variable, on the basis of other stimulus cues, such as the initial letter of the word and/or of the syllables constituting the word.

Chapter 2

VERBAL CONTEXT

Associative responses also have been shown to be affected by the nature of the preceding verbal context. This chapter reviews studies in which context is established by manipulation of the associative environment surrounding the association test stimuli, or, more generally, by control of the verbal context preceding the association test. Also to be considered are the effects of the interpolation of verbal tasks prior to the association test, as well as investigations of the effects of examples and of instructions in determining associative responses. Each of these variables may be considered as establishing an increasingly direct, or explicit set. As will be seen, each variable is a powerful determinant of associative responses.

Manipulation of the Associative Environment

DIRECT PRIMING

One way in which an implicit associative set is established is via the technique of priming. Most generally, priming may be defined as a change in antecedent conditions which is specifically designed to increase the probability of a particular response, B, being given to a particular stimulus, A. In *direct* priming, this is accomplished by presenting the B term itself, prior to the association test. The first experiment demonstrating the influence of direct priming on associative responses was performed by Storms (1958). In this study, the A-B normative frequency of 1% was increased to 19% in a situation in which B terms were presented (for one-trial learning) immediately prior to the association test. Furthermore, some specificity of the priming effect was demonstrated in the finding that the frequency of B as a response to its appropriate A exceeded the frequency of its occurrence as a response to any other A, in 13 out of 14 cases; in other words, priming is effective only on habits of some nonzero strength. Storms further suggested that since the effect is situational and transitory, it should be classified as a "performance" effect, as distinguished from a change in habit strength. Segal and Cofer (1960) replicated Storms's findings and extended the method of presentation of the *B* terms from an intentional learning task to several incidental tasks. In all cases, priming increased response frequency; however, increasing the number of presentations of the priming words did not further increase the priming effect.

J. G. Martin (1964) has also demonstrated the effects of direct priming by constructing a WAT in which Kent-Rosanoff response terms, *B*, were presented as stimulus items prior to the presentation of their appropriate stimuli, *A*. The results indicated that when either 5 or 10 items intervened between *B* and the subsequent *A*, the *A-B* frequency was significantly increased; however, when 20 items occurred between *B* and *A*, the *A-B* frequency did not differ from that obtained under standard, normative conditions.

M. T. Mednick, Mednick, and Mednick (1964b) adapted this direct priming technique to increase the probability of solving Remote Associates Test (RAT) items. Priming was accomplished by giving subjects a simple analogies test. The subject's task was to discover the missing term needed to solve the analogy; in this way, he provided his own priming, *B*, word. This word, in turn, was the response required on the RAT. The results indicated that priming was successful in increasing the number of correct RAT responses, and that this was true regardless of the presence or absence of a 24-hour interval between priming and test. This finding would appear to be markedly at odds with that of Martin; perhaps the explanation lies in the fact that in Mednick's study the subject produced his own priming word, while in the previous study the priming word was but one of many being presented to the subject.*

It is possible, as suggested by Storms, that priming may not produce any real change in associative strength. Rather, the priming effect may reflect a temporary change in the *availability* of a particular response. An interesting investigation by Horowitz *et al.* (1964) is relevant to this issue. In this study, an associative structure was established experimentally, such that each of three items in the set of seven was learned as a paired-associate response to two of the items in the set; the resulting structure could then be represented as

$$\begin{array}{ccc} B & D & F \\ \downarrow & \downarrow & \downarrow \\ A \to C \to & E \to & G. \end{array}$$

The authors define the "availability" of an item as a function of its having been produced as a response from memory during practice; in this structure, *C*, *E*, and *G* are "available" items. Furthermore, of these three "available"

---

*Studies by Horowitz, Brown, and Weissbluth (1964) and by Freedman (1965), discussed below, would support this notion.

items, C and E are double function terms; i.e., C and E are the only "available" stimuli. Subsequent to paired-associate learning, the seven items were administered as WAT stimuli; the subject was limited in response to other items included in the set. Under these conditions, the Primary response to each item was the learned paired-associate response (C or E or G); however, the next most frequent responses, for nearly every item, were the two remaining "available" items. Furthermore, backward associative responses (e.g., $E \to D$) and mediated associative responses (e.g., $E \to F$) were rare if that associative response was not an "available" item, as it was not in these examples. However, if the associative response was an "available" item, backward associations (e.g., $E \to C$) occurred as often as the learned forward association ($C \to E$), and mediated associations (e.g., $F \to E$) occurred more often than other random stimulus-response combinations (e.g., $F \to D$), indicating that both contiguity and context are relevant variables in establishing an associative response.

To test further the hypothesis that the availability of the item, rather than the associative link, determines the overt manifestation of an associative response, the authors repeated the experiment, this time eliminating the associative link between C and E. As predicted, the frequency of occurrence of C, E, and G in the associative response hierarchies to A and B, and of C and E in the response hierarchies to F and G, were unchanged. These findings, considered *in toto*, led the authors to conclude that while contiguity and context determine which items will associate, the availability of an item determines which associations are manifest.

INDIRECT PRIMING

In contrast with direct priming, indirect or mediated priming is a technique in which the priming words are associatively related to the desired response, but the response word is not itself presented. Howes and Osgood (1954) were the first to demonstrate that this type of priming could increase the frequency of a *class* of responses; furthermore, they found that the magnitude of the priming effect was a function of the number of priming words used, of the proximity of these primers to the association test stimulus, and of the Thorndike-Lorge frequency of the stimulus.

Cramer (1963, 1965a) has attempted by mediated priming to increase the probability of a *specific* response. In an initial study (Cramer, 1962, 1963), a series of associative clusters (words related either by forward or reverse associative connections to a specific word) were presented for one-trial learning. This was followed by an association test and subsequently by a recall test of the initial list of words. Under these conditions, the A-B associative frequency was unchanged; however, the primed-for B term was imported into recall significantly often, suggesting that mediated priming was having *some* effect. In an attempt to obtain this effect on the association test, a subsequent study was conducted in which each set of priming words immediately preceded the cue-stimulus of the association test (Cramer, 1964a). In this instance, the A-B frequency was increased for every stimulus (as compared to normative data), when forward associative bonds connected the priming words and the desired response; the effect was not obtained when reverse associative connections were involved.

The success of this latter investigation suggested that the failure of the earlier study should be reexamined. Accordingly, an experiment was designed in which it was possible to determine whether the priming effect was disrupted by the interpolation of verbal material for learning between priming and test (the learning list of the initial study consisted of more than 20 items), by the interpolation of activity *per se*, or by the brief time lapse between priming and test (Cramer, 1964b). The results indicated that only the first variable was significant in decreasing the priming effect, while all other conditions showed mediated priming to be effective in increasing the A-B frequency.

Coleman (1964) has also been successful in producing mediated priming effects. A varying number of noun stimuli known to elicit common adjective responses (from Underwood & Richardson, 1956) were presented just prior to the association test cue-stimulus. The frequency of occurrence of the primed-for adjective response was a direct function of the number of priming words (0, 1, 3, or 5) which preceded the cue-stimulus. Musgrave (1958) has shown that in order for a priming word to increase the frequency of an associative Primary response, that word must be associatively related to the desired response; where there was no association between primer and response, the effect of having such words precede the cue-stimulus was to *de*crease the frequency of the Primary response. Furthermore, this decrease in Primary frequency, as well as the increase in response variability, was found to be directly related to the number of such words preceding the cue-stimulus. However, it should be emphasized that these "priming" words were not associatively connected with the desired response, but rather formed an A-B-C associative chain, and the desired response was a further link, D, in the chain.

The RAT (S. A. Mednick, 1962) itself may be thought of as a type of indirect priming study, in that the probability of a particular response to any one of the cue-stimuli is presumably enhanced by the presence of the other two. The influence of certain subject variables on the effectiveness of this type of priming will be discussed in the second part of this book.

A related technique is that of Flaugher (1965), in which the subject is given an increasing number of B responses and is asked to identify the A stimulus which could have produced those B's. Accurate identification was found to be a function of the number of B clues, of the sequence in which they were provided (presenting the associates in the order strongest to weakest was more effective than weakest to strongest), of the associative strength of the response, and of the Thorndike-Lorge frequency of the A term ($AA > A > $ 5-50/million).

Backward associative relationships also have been used by Maltzman, Belloni, and Fishbein (1964) in an attempt to prime the association which correctly solves RAT problems. In these experiments, priming was accomplished by presenting an associate of the desired RAT word as a stimulus for a WAT. This stimulus (actually the Primary response to the desired word) was presented zero (control group), two, four, or six times; the subject was asked to give a different response on each presentation. The number of correct RAT responses was found to be a significant function of the number of presentations of the priming stimulus word. Subsequently, this facilitation was also found if the priming word was simply included as the first word among the other three words which formed each RAT item. It was also found in these two conditions when the priming word was chosen from lower in the response hierarchy (although the effects appear to be limited to the first 10 responses in the hierarchy). When words which were not associatively related to the desired response were used in these conditions, no priming (facilitation) occurred. Interestingly enough, this nonassociative (control) training, like the associative training (priming), reduced the number of failures to respond, as compared to a second control group which received no additional training in giving associative responses. However, facilitation of the *correct* response required associative priming. That is, it was determined that it was the presence of the associative priming word, rather than the giving of associative responses, which was responsible for the facilitation of correct RAT responses.

Manipulation of Other Aspects of the Verbal Environment

Changes in associative responses may also result from variations in the preceding verbal context other than priming. The effects of verbal context have been studied by the use of compound stimuli, by the choice of the stimuli used to construct the association test, by the presentation of the association test in the context of other association tests, by the interpolation of verbal material prior to the critical association test, and by the use of examples or instructions.

Compound Stimuli

The use of compound verbal stimuli to elicit associative responses is a technique which is similar to priming but differs in at least two important ways. In priming, the subject is instructed to associate to the last stimulus only (as opposed to responding to the entire stimulus compound); furthermore, the hypothesis is made that the frequency of a specific associative response will be increased (as opposed to noting a general change in commonality or overlap of associative responses). These differences, and perhaps especially the choice of priming words, each of which is known to elicit one particular response, may account for the fact that while priming has been shown to increase response predictability, the effects of compound stimuli have been to decrease response consistency.

In one of the earlier studies of compound stimuli, Cofer and Ford (1957) chose stimuli of equal preexperimental reaction times. These stimuli were then presented alone, or they were preceded by one of two types of context words. Although not significant, the reaction time to either type of compound stimulus was greater than to single stimuli; further, a synonym context word produced a greater response delay than did an unrelated context word. P. Jenkins and Cofer (1957) also found compound stimuli to result in greater response variability (D) and weaker Primary responses than single stimuli. Using adjective-noun pairs, they compared the responses to these compounds with the Minnesota (1954) normative responses to each separate item. The resulting response distributions for compound and single items were quite different, but it was noted that the responses to nouns were less affected by the addition of adjectives than were the responses to adjectives changed by the addition of nouns. In other words, it appeared that noun stimuli carried more weight than adjectives in determining the associative response to an adjective-noun compound stimulus.

Cofer (1960) has investigated in more detail the relative importance of part of speech and, in addition, has studied the role of semantic category in determining compound stimulus effects. After first noting that the degree of associative overlap of responses to single noun stimuli chosen from the same meaning category exceeded that to adjective-noun compounds made up of the same noun stimuli, Cofer went on to demonstrate that categorized nouns impose constraints on uncategorized adjectives (the degree of associative response overlap is greater, in this case, for the compounds than for the adjectives alone). Furthermore, categorized adjectives impose constraints on uncategorized nouns (the associative response overlap to the compounds is greater than to the nouns alone). When both the adjectives and nouns used in the compound belong to distinct meaning categories, the effect on associative responses is inconsistent; in some instances, the associative-response overlap of the compound exceeds that of nouns alone, and in some instances the overlap is decreased.

Based on a similar rationale to that used by Musgrave in the study cited on page 85, Grooms and Osipow (1963) constructed stimulus compounds from Kent-Rosanoff stimuli and their Primary responses in order to see if these *A-B* compounds would elicit a consistent response, *C*, thereby demonstrating an *A-B-C* associative chain. The frequency of the most common *C* response varied from 7 to 70%, indicating considerable variability among compounds. When the five most frequent responses to each compound were compared with the five most frequent responses to the first stimulus, *A*, in the compound (exclusive of *B*, the most common response), slightly more than one-third of the responses of the two samples were found to overlap, suggesting to the authors that these responses were being determined by *A*, rather than by the compound *AB*. Furthermore, although some compounds elicited a consistent *C* response, the suggestion that this is a demonstration of an associative chain in action is additionally countermanded by the finding that when the order of stimuli in the compound was reversed, *BA*, little change in responses was noted. For eight of the ten compounds, the most common response remained the same; for the other two compounds, the primary and secondary responses were interchanged. Furthermore, there was an overlap of 92% of the five most common responses to *AB* and *BA* compounds. In light of their failure to find evidence for *A-B-C* chains via the use of *AB* compounds, the authors then raised the question if *B*, as a single stimulus, elicited any consistent *C* response (Osipow & Grooms, 1964). The results of this study indicated that *B* elicited *A* as a response in 44 out of 100 cases, that *B* elicited the secondary response of *A* as a response in 10 out of 100 cases, and that for 16 out of 100 cases the Primary response to *B* was the same as that to the *AB* compound. (In a subsequently reported study, 28 out of 100 Primaries to *B* were identical to those given to the *AB* compound [Osipow & Grooms, 1965a].) The remaining 38 responses did not fit any category. The results of this experiment suggested that the *A-B* pairs used in the first study (Grooms & Osipow, 1963) were unlikely to demonstrate an *A-B-C* chain, since the majority of responses to *B* referred back to *A*.

Further evidence for compound stimuli increasing response variability and decreasing Primary response strength comes from one of the studies by Musgrave (1958). In this experiment, the stimuli were eight nouns of high Thorndike-Lorge frequency, presented individually as well as in all pair combinations. In addition to compound stimuli resulting in weaker Primary responses than single stimuli, it was also found that the number of Primary responses to compound stimuli depended on the strength of the Primary response to the stimuli considered singly. Furthermore, stimuli in the second position of the compound were more likely to elicit *their* Primary response than were stimuli in the first position.* Although compounding

*D. S. Palermo (personal communication, 1966) has pointed out that this finding appears to be in contrast with that of Grooms and Osipow (1963), in which the responses obtained to the compound were determined by the stimulus in the first position, *A*. The explanation

stimuli decreased the Primary response frequency (as determined from single stimuli), it is important to note that where the associative hierarchies of the two stimuli overlapped, for 10 of the 20 compounds it was possible to predict the word which would occur as the most frequent response by considering the product of the probabilities of that response to each individual stimulus.* Furthermore, in four additional cases, the most frequent response to the compound stimulus came from the intersection of the response hierarchies of the single words.

These findings, then, are congruent with the priming results which show that there is a summation of associative effects which increases the probability of occurrence of those associative responses which are shared by the stimuli which constitute the compound. On the other hand, the probability of occurrence of nonoverlapping, disjunctive responses is decreased. However, the choice of stimuli in compound stimulus studies without regard for the existence of shared associative responses is unlikely to reveal these associative constraint effects.

In a study by Podell (1963), each of the stimulus items in the compound also was known to elicit a particular *associative* response, which was not the Primary response of any individual item. In this study, like that of S. A. Mednick (1962), the subjects were requested to associate to the entire compound (which consisted either of two or of four items). While Mednick's RAT calls for a single, discrete response, Podell's study required continued association for a specified time interval. A comparison of four-item compounds with two-item compounds concurred with the findings reported above. Increasing stimulus complexity resulted in greater response variability; that is, the frequency of occurrence of a common response to four-item compounds was less than the frequency to two-item ones. However, the frequency of occurrence of the specified response, common to all members of the compound, exceeded that which would be expected on the

---

of this apparent discrepancy would seem to lie in the nature of the components of the compounds used in the two studies. In the Grooms and Osipow study, it was subsequently discovered that 70% of the second-position stimuli, B, when presented individually, elicited responses which referred back to A. It will be recalled that the conclusion that this first-position stimulus, A, was the main determinant of the response was based on the finding that slightly more than a third of the responses to the AB compound were the same as those given to A alone. However, since it was found that B elicits many of the same responses as does A, it is not really possible to determine whether it was A or B (first-position or second-position stimulus) which was in fact determining the response.

*The formula for this calculation, suggested by J. J. Jenkins, and reported in Musgrave (1958), states that the probability of any response to a compound stimulus is the product of the probability of that response to each individual stimulus divided by the sum of such products for all responses occurring in common to the stimulus words.

basis of the summed frequencies of that response to each individual stimulus. Furthermore, in at least one experiment, the frequency of occurrence of the common response to two-item stimuli exceeded the product of the probabilities of that response to each individual stimulus. Both of these findings indicate that there is a summation of excitatory potential which converges via associative pathways at a common response.

Further evidence for the assertion that the effect of compound stimuli depends on the existence of shared associative responses comes from a study by Rouse and Verinis (1965). In this investigation, the second term of the AB compound stimulus was always a Kent-Rosanoff stimulus word; the first term, A, was chosen because it both defined the Primary response to B and it showed high A-B-C transitional probability (List 1); alternatively, the first term, A', was chosen such that neither of these criteria was true (List 2). The association test results indicated that the frequency of Primary responses to List 1 compound stimuli, AB, exceeded that to List 2 compounds, $A'B$. Furthermore, List 1 had a greater, and List 2 a smaller, frequency of Primary responses, as compared to the normative frequency of Primary responses to B stimuli. In addition, List 2 showed greater response variability (a greater number of different responses) and required a longer time to complete the test. Although the authors attribute the facilitative effects of the List 1 compounds to the two variables stated above (response defining and transitional probability), examination of their stimuli reveals that for the majority of the compounds the first term is also *associatively* linked to the desired response—a factor which the present author would hold to be the critical variable.*

An allied study showing the effects of context on associative responses is that of Pollio and Lore (1965), discussed in Chapter 1. In this investigation, the number of affectively congruent context words (0, 1, 2, or 3) preceding pleasant or unpleasant stimuli was varied; the results indicated that the reaction time to unpleasant stimuli increased as the number of unpleasant context words was increased. (Reaction time and context were unrelated for pleasant words.) Also, increasing context produced a slight tendency ($p < .20$) for associative responses to become affectively more similar to their stimuli, but was unrelated to the Thorndike-Lorge frequency of the responses.

OTHER STIMULI IN THE ASSOCIATION TEST

It is also possible to consider the association test itself as providing a context for each individual stimulus word. As has been shown by J. G. Martin (1964; cf. p. 83), the context provided by the (noncritical) stimulus words

---

*This point will be considered further in the discussion.

can influence the associative responses given to the critical stimuli. The influence of association test context has been demonstrated in several additional studies. Amster and Battig (1965) presented 15 CVC words in the context of 15 other stimuli of high-, medium-, or low-rated meaningfulness, m'; subjects were allowed 45 seconds for continued associations to each of the 30 stimuli. The results indicated that response m increased and response m' decreased as a function of increasing context m'. Wynne, Gerjuoy, and Schiffman (1965) also found the stimulus list to produce an important context effect. In this study, Opposite Evoking Stimuli were placed either early or late in the list of association test stimuli. The results indicated that the overall number of antonym Primary responses given to the entire list was decreased by late presentation of the OES, while neither the number of nonantonym Primaries nor of non-Primary antonyms was affected.

Finally, Cook *et al.* (1965) have shown that the responses to numeral homonyms (e.g., eight-ate) are determined by the number of nonnumeral stimuli to intervene between the critical stimuli. When no stimuli from a nonnumeral class intervened, the majority of responses to the numeral homonyms were numerals. When two or six nonnumeral stimuli intervened, there was a decrease in numeral responses to the critical stimuli; these changed responses were about equally distributed between numeral-related responses (e.g., eight → cylinder) and nonnumeral responses (e.g., ate → food). When 18 nonnumeral stimuli intervened, there was a further decrease in the number of numeral-related responses, as compared to the number of nonnumeral responses. Furthermore, if a numeral stimulus (three) was introduced at the beginning of the "two-intervening-word" list, the number of numeral responses showed a 50% increase.

Examples and Instructions

The use of associative-response examples at the beginning of a WAT is another way in which the items constituting the stimulus list have been shown to influence subsequent responses. Boyer and Elton (1958) prefaced a WAT with five examples, which consisted of either very common responses or of very uncommon responses; a control group was given no examples. When the percentage of Primary responses in each group was compared, it was found that subjects given examples of uncommon responses had the fewest Primary responses. However, the effect of the "common response" set dissipated after the first stimulus in the WAT, and the effect of the "uncommon response" was not noticeable after the third stimulus.

In a certain sense, considering the use of instructions as a context variable used to establish a psychological set cannot be differentiated from the use of instructions to change a *free*-association test into a controlled test. Thus the studies included in this section might have been considered in the Prologue discussion of various test formats. Instead, they have been included in the present discussion of set, for it seems to this author that there is a distinction between the controlled association technique which asks a subject to respond with a color, a number, or a specific part of speech—all limited and clearly defined categories—and requesting the subject to give a "different" response, or the response "most people" would give—categories which are both broader and vaguer. Nevertheless, these latter types of instructions consistently have been shown to modify associative responses. For example, it has been clearly demonstrated that "most people" instructions will, in fact, increase the associative-response frequency (Horton *et al.*, 1963) and the number of Primary responses obtained (J. J. Jenkins, 1959; Wynne, 1964), as compared to the performance of the same subjects under conditions of standard instructions or under conditions where speed of response is stressed (Horton *et al.*, 1963). Furthermore, if a multiple-choice WAT is used, "most-people" instructions increase the number of Primary responses even further (Wynne, 1964). Similarly, Wynne *et al.* (1965) found "most people" instructions to increase the number of nonantonym Primary responses, and this effect was increased when a multiple-choice WAT was used. However, instructions had no significant effect on the frequency of antonym Primary responses.* J. J. Jenkins (1959), while noting a positive intra-subject correlation between number of Primary responses obtained with and without instructions, also found that "most people" instructions produced a relatively greater increase in number of Primary responses for subjects initially low on this dimension.

Other types of instructions have also been found to be effective in modifying associative responses. Kjeldergaard (1962) has noted that instructions to give "opposite" responses increases the number of Primary responses obtained (since many Primaries are opposites), and that "opposite" instructions are even more effective than "most people" instructions for subjects initially low on the Primary-response-giving dimension (while they slightly decrease Primary responses in subjects initially high on this dimension). R. M. Jones (1958) gave subjects instructions to respond to neutral and emotional stimulus words with a word which "never wants to go with" the stimulus. This condition of negated instructions increased the number of errors on a reproduction test for both types of stimuli. Maltzman, Bogartz, and Breger (1958) found that instructions to

---

*This finding is not due to a ceiling effect. The obtained means of 11.5 and 15.8 are well below the maximum possible of 24.

give original responses on the test list significantly decreased response commonality (as measured by associative-response frequency in this group of subjects), regardless of whether the subject was practiced (with or without reinforcement) or not practiced in giving different associative responses.

Milgram and Goodglass (1961), instructing children to respond to a multiple-choice WAT as adults, as younger children, or as themselves, found instructions were ineffective in increasing either number of abstract responses (adult response), or number of concrete response choices (child response) until children reach the fourth grade. After that age, they were able to discriminate among associative styles, and hence the type of instruction given determined the choice of associative response.

Wild (1965) used a prose passage descriptive of a "regulated" (conventional) person and an "unregulated" (original) person as a basis for asking subjects to respond as each of these described individuals would do. The results provided some evidence for an increase in original responses* following the "unregulated" condition; however, instructions to give "regulated" responses, rather than increasing the conventionality of the associative responses, slightly *de*creased the response conventionality.

Summary and Discussion

The following aspects of verbal context have been found to affect associative responses.

I. DIRECT PRIMING (PRIOR PRESENTATION OF THE DESIRED ASSOCIATIVE RESPONSE)

(1) This method
    (A) increases the frequency of the (desired) primed response,
    (B) but is effective only for associative habits of nonzero strength.
(2) The effect occurs
    (A) whether priming is accomplished via an intentional or an incidental task, and whether the priming word is provided by the experimenter or produced by the subject, and
    (B) when 5, 10, or 14, but not 20, words intervene between primer and test.†

---

*Responses which did not appear on the Kent-Rosanoff (1910) norms, or which had a frequency of less than 10% on the Rapaport *et al.* norms (1946).

†An exception to this was found in a study by M. T. Mednick *et al.* (1964b) which used a subject-produced primer, and found priming effective after 24 hours.

(3) There is some evidence that increased response availability, rather than increased associative strength, may best explain (direct) priming effects.

II. MEDIATED PRIMING (PRIOR PRESENTATION OF *ASSOCIATES* OF THE DESIRED RESPONSE)

(1) This method
    (A) increases the frequency of a class of responses
        (a) as a function of the number and proximity of primers, and
        (b) as a function of the Thorndike-Lorge frequency of the stimulus.

(2) It also increases the frequency of a particular (primed) response, when no meaningful verbal material is interpolated between priming and test.

(3) It appears that this technique may be effective only when the desired response is an *associative response* to the priming words. That is,
    (A) priming is not effective when the desired response is associatively unrelated to the priming words, and
    (B) there is some evidence that priming may not be effective when a reverse associative relationship exists between the desired response and the priming words.

III. THE USE OF COMPOUND STIMULI (AS OPPOSED TO SINGLE-WORD STIMULI)

(1) This approach
    (A) increases associative reaction time, and synonym compounds result in a longer increase than compounds of unrelated words;
    (B) increases response heterogeneity, D,* and
    (C) decreases Primary response strength.*

(2) Those stimuli
    (A) which consist of a noun and an adjective indicate that nouns are more important than adjectives in determining the Primary response;
    (B) which are noun-noun, AB, compounds indicate that B is more important in determining the Primary response;
    (C) in which B is an associative response to A indicate that the probability of eliciting C as a response, thereby demonstrating an A-B-C associative chain, is low.

(3) The best prediction of the most frequent response to a compound stimulus is based on the extent of associative response overlap of the individual items.

*Exception: Rouse and Verinis (1965).

(4) The degree of associative overlap between semantically unrelated nouns or adjectives is increased when these unrelated stimuli are compounded with a second set of semantically related stimuli.

(5) Increasing the number of affectively congruent stimuli which precede the critical affective stimulus.
- (A) increases the reaction time to unpleasant stimuli but does not affect pleasant stimuli;
- (B) results in responses being chosen with increasing frequency from the same affective class as that of the stimulus.

IV. THE EFFECT OF THE OTHER STIMULI CONSTITUTING THE ASSOCIATION TEST

(1) This effect has been noted on several dimensions:
- (A) Increasing the rated meaningfulness, m', of the noncritical stimuli
  - (a) increased response availability, m, and
  - (b) decreased the rating of response meaningfulness, m', of the critical stimuli.
- (B) Presentation of OES early in the stimulus list
  - (a) increased the number of antonym Primary responses, but
  - (b) left the number of nonantonym Primary responses unchanged, and
  - (c) also left the number of non-Primary antonym responses unchanged.
- (C) Increasing the number of numeral, versus nonnumeral, stimuli in the stimulus list increased the number of numeral and numeral-related responses to numeral homonym stimuli.

V. THE USE OF COMMON (OR UNCOMMON) EXAMPLES AT THE BEGINNING OF A WAT

This has the effect of momentarily increasing the number of common (or uncommon) responses.

VI. THE USE OF INSTRUCTIONS TO MARKEDLY MODIFY ASSOCIATIVE RESPONSES

(1) Instructions to give the response "most people" would
- (A) increases the frequency of Primary responses;
- (B) increases response commonality (associative-response frequency).

(2) Instructions to give "opposite" responses results in an increase in Primary response frequency.

(3) "Original" instructions decreases response commonality.

(4) The use of a character description, with the subjects instructed to

make the response the individual described would make, results in a decrease in response commonality. This was true regardless of whether the character was described as being original or conventional.

As long as the response is part of the associative hierarchy of the stimulus—that is, as long as some minimal associative connection exists between the stimulus and response word, then priming can increase the probability of that word being emitted as a response. It is further suggested that this is a transitory effect which depends on temporarily increasing the *availability* of a particular response, rather than effecting any change in associative strength. Although the temporal limits of the phenomenon are not known at this time, we do know that interpolated activity involving meaningful verbal material between priming and test can disrupt the priming effect. Furthermore, there is some evidence to suggest that the interpolation of only one such item can cause some diminution in the priming effect, and that somewhere between 14 and 20 items is the critical limit, beyond which the effects of priming will no longer be manifest. However, the relative effectiveness of priming versus the inhibitory effects resulting from the interpolation of other material may depend on additional variables, such as whether the subject had to *produce* the priming word (as opposed to having it presented to him by the experimenter).

There also is plentiful evidence to suggest that modification of associative responses, in the absence of specific instructions to do so, depends on the convergent *associative* connections between the verbal context and the desired response. Thus, for example, presenting several links of an associative chain does not set off a serial reaction which activates subsequent links in the chain. Rather, the effects of verbal context appear to depend on convergent associative pathways by which a response common to the several stimuli is activated.

It is further suggested that priming works by the arousal of implicit associative responses (either the implicit representational response, in the case of direct priming, or implicit associative responses, in the case of mediated priming), and that it is this arousal which accounts for the temporary increase in response availability. In the absence of converging associative effects, the general effect of increasing the verbal context preceding the stimulus word is rather different. Rather than providing constraints and thereby limiting the range of associative responses, when contextual stimuli are chosen without regard for the existence of shared associative responses, the effect is to increase response variability and, correspondingly, to decrease response predictability. These effects may also be interpreted as due to the arousal of implicit associative responses. That is, when context stimuli are chosen without regard for associative connections, a greater number of *different* implicit associative responses are aroused, since the stimuli do not have overlapping associative hierarchies.

It should be pointed out, however, that there is some evidence which appears to demonstrate that context selected on the basis of nonassociative criteria—as semantic, affective, or degree of meaningfulness—may influence associative responses. However, it does not seem unreasonable to suggest that these effects also depend, at least in part, on associative connections, although the context words were not specifically selected on this basis. For example, the study by Rouse and Verinis (1965) demonstrated that an AB compound in which the A term was selected to define and to provide high transitional probability for producing the desired response could increase the probability of that response, while AB compounds in which the A term did not meet these criteria showed the more usual decrease in response predictability. However, as mentioned earlier, examination of the stimuli used in this study revealed that for the majority of the compounds the A term also was associatively linked to the desired response—a factor which the present author suggests was the critical variable.

Another example of context selected on a nonassociative basis, which the present author would suggest was actually functioning via associative connections, is the study by Amster and Battig (1965). They found that presenting CVCs in the context of increasing rated meaningfulness, m', increased the number of responses, m, emitted in continued association. Since meaningfulness is positively related to stimulus familiarity (Noble, 1953), this suggests that as m' was increased, the context also came to consist of words of higher Thorndike-Lorge frequency. In turn, the probability of words of high Thorndike-Lorge frequency being associatively related (i.e., direct or indirect associative responses) to the critical stimuli would be greater than that of words of low Thorndike-Lorge frequency (cf., e.g., Howes' demonstration [1957] that Thorndike-Lorge frequency and probability of associative response occurrence are positively related). Viewed in this way, the increase in number of associative responses, m, found in connection with increased m' is interpreted as a result of increasing the number of context words which are associatively related to the critical stimuli.

In addition to associative effects, it is undoubtedly true that set—or the establishment of a response strategy—plays some role in understanding the effects of context. Thus the finding that a higher proportion of numeral homonyms in a stimulus list produces a greater number of numeral responses can be explained in associative terms as the result of the convergence of excitation on implicit associative responses which are numbers. However, when we find that the majority of implicit associative responses can be characterized as belonging to a common semantic group, it is likely that we are moving from the arousal of specific implicit associative responses to the activation of a *category* of responses—and that the manifestation of the arousal of this semantically defined domain is what is customarily termed the effect of response set, or of response strategy.

The effects of OES on increasing the number of antonym responses and of stimulus-response examples on influencing the number of Primary responses can be understood as the result of the arousal of this type of response set, which the subject may or may not be able to verbalize.

This shift from the contextual arousal of individual responses to the arousal of a semantic category can, of course, be accomplished explicitly by instructions, whereby the subject is told to choose his response from a particular class of responses. What is being suggested, then, is that context may affect associative responses on a discrete, word-word basis, but that this may, under certain circumstances, cause the activation of a semantic category which will determine the nature of the overt response, without the subject necessarily being aware of the set. On the other hand, the semantic category may be activated by explicit instructions, in which case the subject is more fully aware of the set, or strategy, determining his response.

The converse of this heightened arousal of a subset of responses was well formulated by Osgood and Sebeok (1954). Noting that the effect of set and/or instructions on associative responses was to decrease response variability, to increase the frequency of a few responses, and to reduce response latency, they stated, "It is as if a major portion of the response hierarchy were removed and only the specific subportion designated by dual class membership—[i.e., the intersect of responses which belong both to that stimulus word and which satisfy the stipulations of the instructions] . . . were available." (p. 113)

In summary, then, it is suggested that it is the associative connections between the contextual stimuli and the implicit associative responses which are responsible for the overt associative-response effects of context. When these connections converge on a common response, the probability of occurrence of that response will increase. When there are no common associative responses—when the associative pathways are divergent—the context will cause increasing heterogeneity of responses. It was also suggested that the experimental arousal of a response "set"—of which the individual may be unaware—may be understood as the result of the convergent associative activation of a particular response category.

Chapter 3

REPEATED STIMULUS PRESENTATION
Originality or Satiation?

In the Prologue, we cited several systematic changes in associative responses which occur as a function of the WAT being administered a second time (cf. the discussion of successive trials, pp. 12–13). Most often, these studies were concerned with the response changes which occur over varying intervals of time. In the present chapter, the effects of such repeated stimulus presentation will be discussed in connection with two other areas of investigation—that of originality training and that of stimulus satiation. Although these two problems initially may seem quite different, the methodological approach to both is similar, in that both make use of repeated presentation of the stimulus. In addition, it will be suggested subsequently that the meaning of the effects obtained from originality training must be evaluated in connection with the meaning of the satiation results.

Studies of Originality Training

In their attempt to increase the originality of associative responses, Maltzman *et al.* (1958) early noted the potential influence of a preceding WAT on subsequent tests. Including this initial study, ten Experiments have been conducted by Maltzman and his associates and by Gallup in an attempt to specify the variables which are responsible for increasing the uncommonness of associative responses. The standard procedure for these experiments generally includes a control group, in which an initial WAT is immediately followed by a second WAT, and an experimental group, in which the initial list is repeated several times and the subject is instructed to give a different response on each repeated trial. In addition to these two standard conditions, the effects of a variety of other variables have been investigated, and will be reported below.

Training in Giving Different Responses

With the exception of one negative finding by Gallup (1963), it has been found consistently that repetition of the intitial list with instructions to make a different response each time produces increasing originality (idiosyncrasy) of responses over the course of the training trials. For example, in the Maltzman *et al.* (1958) study cited above, by the fifth list repetition, 75% of the responses were idiosyncratic, and this was true whether or not the subjects were verbally reinforced for giving a different response. This increasing originality during training was also found by Maltzman, Simon, Raskin, and Licht (1960), and by Rosenbaum, Arenson, and Panman (1964), although in the latter study the frequency of idiosyncratic responses was less than that obtained by Maltzman (29% versus 75%). These findings are consistent with those of De Burger and Donahoe (1965), cited in the Prologue. In a controlled-association test, in which subjects were instructed to give a different response to each successive presentation of the stimulus, it was found that both associative strength and S.D. correspondence between the stimulus and response decreased with each successive response.

Secondly, the effect of repeated trials with instructions to give a different response has been shown in five separate experiments to increase the originality of responses to a second test list of *different* stimuli (Maltzman *et al.*, 1958, 1960; Rosenbaum *et al.*, 1964). This has been found to be true regardless of reinforcement during training or of instructions to be original on the test trial; furthermore, it has been found to hold both for intervals of 1 and 48 hours between training and test. Finally, the number or original responses evoked has been shown to increase as the number of training trials preceding the test list increases (Maltzman *et al.*, 1960).

From these findings, Maltzman concluded that it is practice in giving *different* responses to one WAT which increases the originality of responses on a subsequent WAT—an assumption which is further supported by his finding that practice in giving the *same* response over repeated trials does not produce such an increase (Maltzman *et al.*, 1960). Gallup, however, calls this assumption into question. Rather than seeing training in giving different responses as the critical variable, Gallup has found in three separate experiments that the second WAT always elicited more original responses than the first, while the presence or absence of repeated trials or of training had no effect on the number of original responses produced on the test list. This latter discrepancy in findings between the two experimenters is discussed in a joint paper (Maltzman & Gallup, 1964) and attributed as possibly due to Gallup's smaller and all-male subject population. However, Gallup's findings—that the prior presentation of a different set of stimulus words may in itself increase the originality of test responses—is a point to be considered.

On the other hand, Moran et al, (1964) found no change in response commonality over a period of four successive days on which a different WAT was administered each day. In addition, it has been found that presentation of a second stimulus list after a 48-hour interval increases the number of *relevant* responses and decreases the number of irrelevant (or unusual) responses in a continued association task (Kanungo & Lambert, 1963). Neither of these findings supports Gallup's position.

Furthermore, Rosenbaum et al. (1964), in the study mentioned above, have independently found supporting evidence for Maltzman's results. In a carefully controlled study, Rosenbaum equated subjects for initial proclivity to give idiosyncratic responses and then held this factor constant in the comparison of test list responses by using an analysis of covariance. The findings clearly indicated that both training in giving different responses and instructions to give original responses produced significantly more idiosyncratic responses on the new stimuli of the test list. In addition, although instructions had a more immediate effect during the training trials on increasing response idiosyncrasy, the effects of instructions and of training on the test list were independent—that is, the test for interaction was not significant. The authors suggest that the subjects may tend to generalize the instructions to be original from the training to the test list, and that the more training trials there are, the greater the probability that the subjects will generate these self-instructions to be original.

One final variable which has been demonstrated to be important in influencing response originality is that of the time interval between initial and test list. Maltzman and Simon (1959) noted that the number of uncommon responses was inversely related to the time between lists (the shorter the interval, the more uncommon the responses). Similarly, Maltzman et al. (1960) noted more uncommon responses after a 1-hour interval than after 48 hours had elapsed.

INTERPOLATION OF VERBAL MATERIAL

It is possible that the obtained originality effects are not a function of giving different responses to the repeated presentation of the stimulus list. Rather, it might be argued that the interpolation of any verbal material between the first and second WAT would result in more unusual responses (i. e., statistically less frequent) on the second test. Such a result would be consistent with the verbal context effects reported in Chapter 2.

Several studies of this type have been made, in which verbal material other than successive association tests has been interpolated between the initial and final WAT. For example, Maltzman *et al.* (1960) found that response originality was increased by simply presenting 125 words of high or of low Thorndike-Lorge frequency between initial and test list. On the other hand, when 125 pairs of unusual responses were presented for a forced-choice WAT, with instructions for the subject to pick the item which "goes best" with the stimulus, or when these same pairs were presented and the subject was instructed to underline the "most familiar" item, originality of test list responses was not increased (Maltzman *et al.*, 1960).

Gallup (1963) also investigated the effect of interpolated verbal tasks on subsequent associative responses. In this study, subjects were presented either with uncommon words as part of a vocabulary test or with arithmetic problems, or with intervening association trials in which the subject was required to give a response from a different grammatical class than that used on the initial trial. None of these conditions increased test list response originality, as compared to the standard control condition. However, the interpretation of the influence of these variables is somewhat equivocal, since their effect also did not differ from that of the repeated trials condition. That is, it is difficult to know whether associative originality was increased in all conditions, including control, or whether it was not demonstrated in any condition.

Response change as a function of interpolated activity has also been studied by Howard and Fiske (1961). In this study, a 15-minute interval between initial and subsequent WAT was filled with one of six tasks: paired-associate learning of low-strength associative responses to the WAT stimuli, paired-associate learning of designs as responses to the WAT stimuli, Arithmetic and Block Design problems from the Wechsler Adult Intelligence Scale requiring "high mental activity," crossing out letters and copying designs requiring "low mental activity," viewing neutral and then arousing pictures ("change in emotional state"), and viewing arousing pictures followed by neutral pictures ("emotional experience"). The results indicated that response changes (not necessarily more original) on the second test generally were most likely to occur where the initial response was weak (as determined by long reaction times). Furthermore, the learning of competing responses as an intervening task produced more response changes than the control paired-associate learning of designs.* Also, an intervening "change in emotional state" produced response changes, while neither "emotional experience" nor either type of "mental activity" produced much change.

*Cf. S. S. Shapiro (1965), who found intervening paired-associate learning of Primary responses and low-strength responses to produce response change (increase in number of Primary responses given on the WAT). However, this response change also occurred when no task was interpolated between the first and second WAT.

Two experiments by Maltzman *et al.* (1960) have studied the effect on originality of giving subjects the Unusual Uses test for varying numbers of trials, with the instructions to give a different response on each trial. However, training in giving different responses did not generalize from this task to increasing the response originality on a WAT test list.

The difficulty in transferring the tendency to give different responses between the WAT and other verbal tasks was also found in a study by Caron, Unger, and Parloff (1963). In this instance, prior to being tested on the RAT for ability to give original responses, subjects received either one presentation of the WAT (standard control), or five presentations with instructions to give either a different response or, alternatively, the same response, on each trial. Contrary to expectation, the three groups did not differ in their ability to make correct responses on the RAT, indicating either that training does not increase originality, or that this increase does not transfer to a different form of associative problem. What training did produce was an increasing number of *irrelevant* responses on the RAT; this effect, although true of both training groups, was more pronounced for those subjects trained to give different responses than for those repeatedly giving the same response.*

On the other hand, Freedman (1965) has been successful in increasing the number of "creative" responses by having subjects produce continuous associations to 10 stimuli prior to the RAT. Alternate groups of subjects who either defined the 10 stimuli, or who read aloud the responses produced by the first subjects (in a yoked-subject procedure), did not show a facilitative effect on the RAT. As the author points out, these findings suggest that it is the *production* of several (continuous) responses in a brief period (as opposed to a discrete response over successive trials, as in the Caron *et al.* study), rather than simply the *availability* of these responses (as was true for the yoked-subjects of this experiment) which is critical in facilitating RAT performance.

Studies of Satiation

Studies of verbal satiation also make use of repeated presentations of the stimulus word, under the assumption that repeated presentation will result in stimulus satiation—i.e., under the assumption that the stimulus temporarily will lose its meaning. The associative-response effects of this stimulus satiation (or, alternatively, of a word *related* to the stimulus)

---

*These findings are consistent with those of Maltzman *et al.* (1964) reported in Chapter 2. RAT performance was facilitated by practice in giving associative responses only when the stimulus words were *associatively* related to the correct RAT response; practice in giving responses to nonrelated stimuli merely increased (irrelevant) response productivity.

are compared to a control condition in which no satiation occurred, or in which the word satiated was unrelated to the WAT stimulus. Although both use repeated stimulus presentation, in satiation experiments one stimulus word is repeated consecutively and occurs with greater frequency than in the originality training studies.

The results of verbal satiation studies are not consistent. In some cases, self-satiation or associative satiation has been shown to increase the number of uncommon or irrelevant associative responses and to decrease the number and strength of relevant ones, as compared with conditions of no satiation or of unrelated satiation. For example, Smith and Raygor (1956) presented the stimulus word itself for approximately 30 seconds, during which time the subject alternately was to fixate, repeat subvocally, and write the word, following which he gave a discrete associative response to that stimulus word. This self-satiation procedure seemed clearly to increase the number of uncommon responses, as compared with the responses obtained from control subjects given the WAT only. Paul (1962), in a continued-association study, contrasted no satiation with four satiation conditions in which the subject repeated the satiator aloud for 30 seconds. The satiators were either the stimulus itself, a high- or a low-strength associate to the stimulus, or an unrelated word. The results indicated that both within satiation conditions, and as compared to the nonsatiated control subjects, all but the unrelated word condition decreased the number, m, of associative responses emitted, decreased the associative strength of the first response (Minnesota norms; Russell & Jenkins, 1954), and increased the latency for emission of the relatively strongest associative response (Minnesota norms; Russell & Jenkins, 1954). There was no difference between the effects of unrelated satiation and of no satiation.

These two studies provide the strongest support for the associative-satiation hypothesis. Two further studies offer weak support for this position. In one (Wolfensberger, 1963), the subject repeated the stimulus word aloud either 3 or 75 times, prior to a discrete-association test; control conditions included no prior repetition of the stimulus, or either 3 or 75 repetitions of an unrelated stimulus. The results of the association test indicated no significant differences among conditions for response latency or for number of uncommon responses, although the 75-trial self-satiation condition consistently resulted in slightly more uncommon responses in both the experiment proper and in pilot studies.

The second study which offers weak support for associative satiation (Kanungo & Lambert, 1963) suggested that memory for previous associative responses may be a determining factor in the effect of satiation on associative behavior. In this continued-association study, satiation was accomplished by repeating the stimulus word aloud for 20 seconds. Half of the satiated stimuli also had been given 24 hours previously as a standard WAT; the other half were "new" to the subjects. In addition, several nonsatiated stimuli were presented on both tests as a control for the effects of satiation and for the effects of prior testing with the same stimuli. The results indicated that the self-satiation of *new* stimuli decreased the number of relevant responses and increased the number of irrelevant responses, as compared either to the previous values for these stimuli or to the results for the other two types of stimuli—i.e., the "old" self-satiated stimuli and the "old" nonsatiated stimuli. However, the "old" self-satiated stimuli showed an *in*crease in the number of relevant responses and no change in the number of irrelevant responses; in both respects they were indistinguishable from the results obtained with the "old" nonsatiated stimuli. The authors suggested that the self-satiated stimuli which were repeated on the second association test failed to show satiation effects due to the subjects' *memory* of their previous responses. Nevertheless, the results obtained for *new* stimuli which were self-satiated did support the satiation hypothesis. A subsequent study of new stimuli which were not satiated (48-hour intertest interval) did not find the satiation results, indicating that these effects were not a function of stimulus newness, *per se.*

On the other hand, two studies have found conditions of no satiation or of unrelated satiation to be equally or more effective than associative or self-satiation in producing the satiation effects. Thus Fillenbaum (1963), in a discrete-association study, presented as satiators either the stimulus word itself, a synonym* of the stimulus word, or a word unrelated to the stimulus. In a series of experiments, satiation was attempted by having the subject write the satiator 30 times, or by having the subject say the word aloud either for 4 seconds, 1 minute, 3 minutes, or until he felt it to lose its meaning. Surprisingly, in no instance did self-satiation result in the greatest increase in uncommon responses; in fact, this type of satiation either produced more common responses or was indistinguishable in effect from the results of satiation via the unrelated control condition. (The only exception to this surprising result was found in that condition in which the subject continued satiation until *he* felt the stimulus to lose meaning; in this case, self-satiation produced more uncommon responses than unrelated satiation.)

Instead, satiation by repeated presentation of a *synonym* of the critical stimulus word resulted in the greatest increase in unusual associative responses (with the exception of the 4-second satiation interval, where synonym satiation and unrelated satiation were quite similar in that both produced more uncommon responses than did self-satiation). This finding of synonym

---

*All of which were, incidentally, associates of the stimulus word as well.

satiation being maximally effective in producing unusual responses was true even when the data were "corrected" to account for cases in which the synonym satiator was among the five most frequent normative associative responses (and thus was, by instruction, necessarily omitted from the subjects' response repertory).

A second study, by Gumenik and Spencer (1965), found unrelated stimuli to produce even greater satiation effects than either self-satiation or satiation using highly associated synonyms. In this discrete-association study, as in the preceding design, each subject was tested for all satiation conditions, with stimuli counterbalanced for satiation conditions across subjects. Satiation was accomplished by having the subject write the satiating word 30 times. The results of this experiment were consistent with those of Fillenbaum, insofar as self-satiation was found to be the least effective in increasing the number of uncommon responses; however, the highly associated synonym was almost equally ineffective. On the other hand, the unrelated control word was more effective than either the stimulus word or the highly associated synonym, but was less effective than weakly associated synonyms, in producing satiation effects. In addition, the percentage of responses in common to the test stimulus and the high associative synonym was greater following high associative satiation than following low, while the percentage of responses in common to the test stimulus and the low associative synonym was greater following low associative satiation.

The authors suggest that satiation by synonyms works to shift the meaning of the stimulus toward that of the synonym, and that the fewer associates in common between the synonym and the stimulus, the greater is this change in meaning, and hence the greater the diversity of associative responses found to synonyms of low associative strength. That is, they suggest that a change in set, rather than a generalization of verbal satiation from satiator to stimulus word, is responsible for the change in associative responses. However, the inconsistency in findings among the various studies in this area makes it difficult at this time to formulate any definitive interpretation of the processes involved.

Summary and Discussion

The technique of repeated stimulus presentation has been used both for originality training and for verbal satiation. The following results have been noted.

I. ORIGINALITY TRAINING

(1) Repeated presentation of the stimulus list has been found to influence the responses to subsequent tests.

(A) With instructions to give different responses on successive trials,
  (a) the number of idiosyncratic responses to the same test stimuli increases;
  (b) the number of idiosyncratic responses to *new* test stimuli increases,
    (i) with or without instructions to give original responses to the new stimuli.
    (ii) This effect is greater after 1 hour than after 48 hours; after one week, the trend reverses, such that a greater number of common responses is given.
    (iii) The effect increases with an increasing number of training trials.
(B) With instructions to give the same responses on successive trials, the number of idiosyncratic responses to new test stimuli is unchanged.
(C) It has also been found that the number of idiosyncratic responses increases on a second WAT, regardless of the presence or absence of repeated trials or of training.
(D) On the RAT:
  (a) *successive* trials with instructions to give the same or a different response did not increase the number of *correct* responses, but did increase the number of irrelevant responses;
  (b) producing *continuous* associations (versus producing definitions or *re*producing associative responses) increased the number of *correct* responses;
  (c) producing continued associations to an *associate*, B, of the correct response, A, with instructions to give a different response on each trial, increased the number of correct responses, A. (This effect was not found when a nonassociate, B', was substituted.)

(2) The effect of interpolation of other verbal material (i.e., not WAT stimuli) between the first and second WAT also has been studied.
  (A) The frequency of idiosyncratic responses on the second test is increased by the interpolation of 125 words of high or of low Thorndike-Lorge frequency.
  (B) The frequency of idiosyncratic responses on the second test is unchanged by the interpolation of a 125-item multiple-choice WAT for which the subject is to indicate the "best" or most familiar response, or by the interpolation of the Unusual Uses test, a vocabulary test, or an arithmetic test.
  (C) The learning of paired-associate responses to the test stimuli, as an interpolated task, is likely to produce associative-response

changes, especially where the initial associative response was weak. When these responses are associates of the stimulus, the Primary response frequency is increased.

II. Verbal Satiation

In the absence of consistent findings, this topic may best be summarized by indicating, first, those studies which found some evidence for associative satiation, and secondly, those which did not.

(1) Studies in which repetition of the stimulus word itself, or of an associate to the stimulus word, produced more satiation effects on association responses than did repetition of an unrelated word and/or no repetition preceding the WAT.

- (A) Smith and Raygor (1956): self-satiation > no satiation.
- (B) Paul (1962): self-satiation = strong associate satiation = weak associate satiation > unrelated satiation = no satiation.
- (C) Wolfensberger (1963): self-satiation ≥ unrelated satiation = no satiation.
- (D) Kanungo and Lambert (1963): "new" stimulus, self-satiation > "old" stimulus, self-satiation = "old" stimulus, no satiation. Also, "new" stimulus, self-satiation > "new" stimulus, no satiation.

(2) The following studies found repetition of the stimulus and/or of an associate to the stimulus to be no more effective than repetition of an unrelated word in producing satiation effects.

- (A) Fillenbaum (1963): synonym-associate satiation > self-satiation = unrelated satiation.
- (B) Gumenik and Spencer (1965): weak associate synonym satiation > unrelated satiation > strong associate synonym satiation ≥ self-satiation.

In the discussion, the satiation studies will be considered first. This will be followed by a return to the problem of originality training. The fact that the satiation studies vary in so many ways makes it very difficult to evaluate the reasons for the discrepant findings. As has been pointed out, each study used a different repetition technique to accomplish satiation. Furthermore, three studies evaluated the effect of satiation by using a written, discrete WAT (Fillenbaum, 1963; Gumenik & Spencer, 1965; Smith & Raygor, 1956), two by using a written, continued WAT (Kanungo & Lambert, 1963; Paul, 1962) and one by using an oral, discrete WAT (Wolfensberger, 1963).

To complicate the picture even further, the measures of response uncommonness differed. Two studies used as a response measure the *number*

SUMMARY AND DISCUSSION 109

of "uncommon" responses, as determined either from the response having a frequency of less than 35 on the 1954 Minnesota norms (Smith & Raygor, 1956) or by the response being assigned its rank value on the 1954 Minnesota norms (responses were scored one through five; any response other than the first five was assigned a rank of six) (Fillenbaum, 1963). Three other studies measured "uncommon" responses in terms of the associative strength of the *first* response given; associative strength was determined either from norms developed for that specific population (Gumenik & Spencer, 1965), or by use of norms based on other populations (Paul [1962] used the 1954 Minnesota norms, and Wolfensberger [1963] used Tresselt's 1958 norms). One study used the number of continued-association responses, m, as a response measure (Paul, 1962); one compared the number of relevant and irrelevant responses (Kanungo & Lambert, 1963); one noted the order of occurrence of the strongest response in a series of continued associations (Paul, 1962); and one measured reaction time (Wolfensberger, 1963).

Unfortunately, neither repetition technique, format of WAT, nor response measure used to evaluate satiation effects bear any consistent relationship to the success or failure of the study in demonstrating satiation.

A somewhat more promising approach to trying to disentangle these results comes from noting that in each of the two studies which failed to find self- or associative-satiation effects, the same WAT stimuli were used to test the different satiation conditions—i.e., the test list was held constant and the satiating stimuli were varied (Fillenbaum, 1963; Gumenik & Spencer, 1965). On the other hand, of the four studies which produced some self- or associative-satiation effects, three used different stimuli to test each satiation condition, thereby confounding the effects of types of satiation with those of the particular stimuli used. Only Smith and Raygor (1956), among the "successful" studies, used the same stimuli across conditions. However, it will be recalled that they compared only two groups—self-satiation with no satiation. We do not know what would have happened if, using the same test stimuli, unrelated satiation had been compared with no satiation.

Also unfortunately, Gumenik and Spencer did not include a no-satiation condition, and Fillenbaum included this control for only one of his five studies. In this one case, the same subjects were tested under standard conditions on the same 12 stimuli plus 38 new ones, two weeks following the satiation procedure. The results indicated no difference between the responses given in this control, no-satiation condition and those given following unrelated satiation. The results contrasting no satiation with self-satiation suggested (inconclusively) that self-satiation might produce more *common* associations, while synonym satiation resulted in fewer common associations than those obtained to no satiation. Fillenbaum relies on this finding to eliminate the necessity of a no-repetition control group in the four subsequent studies. However, the effects of memory for earlier associations, which was suggested by Kanungo and Lambert (1963) to be an important factor in satiation studies, were not considered in interpreting this control condition; nor was the potential influence of the 38 new stimuli taken into account (cf. Ch. 2, pp. 90–91). Either of these factors might have worked to increase the commonness of associations to the "control" condition. Thus it does not seem to the present author that Fillenbaum has convincingly demonstrated that self-satiation (as compared to no satiation) has no effect on response commonness, or might in some circumstances even increase it.

An adequate comparison of different satiation conditions with no satiation is crucial if we are to be able to decide if satiation is a specific associative effect, or if it is rather a general fatigue or inhibition effect. That is, we would like to know if the relationship of the satiator to the WAT stimulus is important, or if the repetition of any word just prior to the association test produces the same satiation effects. In order to answer this question fully, we have to know the effects of unrelated versus no satiation.

Fortunately, Paul (1962) and Wolfensberger (1963), although using different stimuli across different satiation conditions, used these same stimuli to test for the effects of no satiation. Their results indicated that the responses following self- or associative-satiation, as opposed to no satiation, showed satiation effects.* However, responses following unrelated satiation did not differ from those following no satiation. These findings, then, appear to rule out general fatigue or inhibition as an explanation of the satiation findings: they do not, however, allow us to make direct comparisons of the different satiation conditions, due to the confounding of stimuli and conditions. A further difficulty arises in Paul's study, in that the (nonsatiated) control group for the unrelated satiation condition showed greater satiation effects than any other (nonsatiated) control group. This result suggests that the stimuli which were used in the unrelated satiation condition were markedly different from those used in the self- or associative-satiation conditions, in terms of producing satiation effects. As a result, the shifting baseline of the control groups is confounded with the satiation conditions. In this case, the comparisons between unrelated satiation and self- or associative-satiation do not appear justified.

Just how specific stimuli might differentially affect satiation can only, at this point, be a topic for speculation. It is reasonable to assume, for example, that stimuli with strong Primary responses might elicit fewer

---

*It should be recalled that this was only a *trend* in Wolfensberger's study.

uncommon responses than stimuli with weak Primaries, regardless of satiation conditions. This assumption has, in fact, been demonstrated by Gumenik and Spencer (1965), who found that, using the same stimuli in each repetition condition, uncommon responses always were greatest for those stimuli with weak Primaries. Paul (1962) also noted that there were significant differences in the number and strength of responses evoked between the two stimuli used to test each satiation condition; as pointed out above, this difference among stimuli makes it impossible to compare the unrelated satiation condition with either self- or associative-satiation. Furthermore, the two stimuli used in this study to test the effects of high associative satiation both had very strong Primaries (76.2% and 60.5%), and it is noteworthy that this satiation condition was highly similar to its (no satiation) control group for the number-of-associations measure.

It would be convenient if we could, at this point, explain the successful satiation studies as being the result of accidental selection of stimuli such that those stimuli used to test the effects of unrelated and/or no satiation had stronger Primaries, thereby spuriously inflating the apparent decrease in number of common responses as a result of self- or associative-satiation. However, an examination of the stimuli used in the three studies which assigned different words to different conditions does not support this attempt at explanation. In Paul's (1962) study, the stimuli used in the unrelated satiation condition had *weaker* Primary responses than those stimuli used to test self-satiation or satiation using a high associate of the stimulus word. In Wolfensberger's (1963) study, the two stimuli were selected purposely to have Primaries of equal strength, and in Kanungo and Lambert's (1963) study, the stimuli of the different conditions were matched for m, which was probably more important than Primary strength, since a continued association task was used for the satiation measure. Nevertheless, it is conceivable that some other stimulus variable actually is responsible for the apparent satiation effects. Thus we would conclude that self- and associative-satiation result in greater satiation effects than no satiation,* but that we cannot, from the studies carried out this far, directly determine if these satiation conditions produce effects different from those produced by unrelated satiation.

Further Thoughts on Originality Training

Let us turn now to a consideration of the other area of study which has been discussed in this chapter. The studies of originality training have been based on the successive presentation of stimulus lists with instructions

---

*Except, perhaps, when stimuli with very strong Primaries are used.

to give a different response on each trial. Under such conditions, the number of idiosyncratic responses has been shown to increase.

If one considers the actual procedure involved—of presenting 25 stimuli and requiring the subject to give 125 different responses—it is clear that the technique of successive stimulus presentation and response elicitation in fact works to increase the complexity of the verbal context within which the (test) stimulus occurs. In Chapter 2, we saw that, unless contextual stimuli are chosen on the basis of knowledge of their producing a specific associative effect, the result of increasing contextual complexity is to decrease response commonality, and to increase response variability. Looked at in this way, it is not surprising that the originality training techniques increase both idiosyncrasy and variability of response.

That these associative-response effects may be due simply to the interpolation of additional verbal material prior to the association test (i.e., increasing the complexity of the verbal context), rather than to practice in giving "different" responses, receives some further support from Gallup's findings that the *second* association test always elicits more idiosyncratic responses than the first test, with or without training in giving different responses.* This idea is also supported by Maltzman's findings that response originality was increased by simply presenting lists of high- or low-frequency Thorndike-Lorge words prior to the critical test. Furthermore, practice in giving "different" responses on the Unusual Uses test did not increase response originality on a subsequent WAT.

However, it must be recalled that interpolation of successive WATs with instructions to give the *same* response did not increase response originality. This finding would seem to contradict the hypothesis suggested above—that it is the increased contextual complexity which accounts for the increasing response originality. However, it may well be that the instruction used—to give the "same" response—works to counteract the response idiosyncrasy effect. Support for this notion comes from the fact that response originality was not increased by the interpolation of 125 pairs of words together with instructions to pick the item which "goes best" with the stimulus, or to pick the one which is "most familiar." That is, both of these instructions focused on the "sameness" of the responses, and with neither of them was response idiosyncrasy increased.

In other words, it is being suggested that it may be the presentation of additional stimuli between training and test, without explicit training in giving a different response, which is sufficient to increase response original-

---

*Although Kanungo and Lambert (1963) found a decrease in number of idiosyncratic responses to the second association test, it is possible that this may be due to the length of the intervals—24 and 48 hours—between their first and second test. This point is discussed below.

ity, except in those situations where this intervening activity is accompanied by instructions to focus on sameness or commonality. In this case, a set to give common responses may be established inadvertently, with the result that any tendency toward increased response originality is obliterated.

There is also evidence to suggest that the response originality effects are transitory. It has been shown, for example, that more idiosyncratic responses are obtained after one hour than after 48 hours. Furthermore, several studies were reported in the Prologue which found that over periods varying from one week to several months, there was an overall *de*crease in the number of idiosyncratic responses made to subsequent WATs. In fact, a tendency for this reversal to occur (that is, to find an increase in the number of relevant responses and a decrease in the number of irrelevant responses) was noted after a period of 24 hours, using the same stimuli, and, in another investigation, after 48 hours using different stimuli (Kanungo & Lambert, 1963).

Another problem to be considered in connection with these studies is whether the associative-response changes which occur actually represent increased "originality." In part, of course, this is a definitional problem. However, fewer assumptions need to be made to speak of changes in response idiosyncrasy than are necessary to assume that there are changes in response originality, if the term "originality" is used to imply anything in addition to statistical infrequency. Furthermore, when an independent test (RAT) was used to measure originality, then training in giving several different associative responses did not increase the (RAT) originality score in the way that it did increase the association test originality score. Rather, facilitation of RAT performance depended on the stimuli of the training WAT being *associatively* related to the correct RAT response; practice in giving responses to nonrelated stimuli merely increased the number of irrelevant responses. These findings suggest, then, that the best interpretation of the word-association results of originality training studies (training in giving different associative responses) is that such training increases the number of idiosyncratic associative responses, which may or may not also be original responses.

There is a further point to be considered when trying to interpret the originality training effects, which derives from the similarity between these training methods and those of verbal satiation. Let us assume for a moment that, at least in some instances, the repeated presentation of a stimulus word does result in the satiation of that word's meaning (as seen in an increased number of idiosyncratic associative responses). If this is so, then it seems likely that at least part of the effect of originality training must also be due to satiation. That is, it seems reasonable to assume that the increased number of idiosyncratic (original) responses to a stimulus word following the repetition of that word during originality training is a result of the same process responsible for the increased number of idiosyncratic responses following the stimulus repetition of satiation procedures. Whether this repetition be called originality training or satiation, it is suggested that its effect is to inhibit temporarily the usually pre-potent associative responses of the repeated stimulus.

Furthermore, it can be argued that originality training and satiation are actually two names for the same process even when the stimuli in the originality training list are different from those in the test list. Thus, even though the stimulus itself has not been presented repeatedly, it is likely that some word on the originality training list will be associatively related to that stimulus, unless specific care has been taken to control for this factor. Since it appears from the studies cited that satiation via an associate is at least as effective as self-satiation, the repetition of an associate on the originality training list could produce satiation effects on the subsequent test.

These suggestions, of course, are speculative. However, in light of the knowledge that both contextual complexity and stimulus repetition are known to increase response idiosyncrasy, it would seem that some caution should be used in interpreting the effects of practice in giving different responses as indicating an increase in associative-response originality, if this term is meant to imply some phenomenon distinct from statistical infrequency.

Chapter 4

REINFORCEMENT

A series of studies have investigated the effect of reinforcement on WAT responses. A number of these investigations have been based on the principles and techniques of operant conditioning. Both positive and negative reinforcers have been used in an attempt to increase or decrease some predetermined class of responses. Following the emission of such a response, if the intent of the experimenter is to increase the probability of this type of response occurring on subsequent tests, positive reinforcement in the form of a verbal "good" from the experimenter, or, less often, some material reward (as a cigarette) will be given. If the intent is to decrease the probability of this type of response, it is followed by a negative reinforcer, such as a verbal "wrong" or an electric shock. Thus the response made by the subject determines whether or not reinforcement will be given, and the occurrence of this reinforcement, in turn, is expected to modify the subsequent frequency of occurrence of that response.

Positive Reinforcement

Maltzman, Seymore, and Licht (1962), using normal subjects, studied the effect of a verbal reinforcement ("good") which was given following each occurrence of a Primary, Secondary, or Tertiary response. The findings indicated that the frequency of such common responses to a new (non-reinforced) set of stimuli was increased. A material reinforcement (cigarette) resulted in the same type of increase for alcoholic subjects (but not for schizophrenics) (Sommer, Witney, & Osmond, 1962). However, in the former study this increase was found only if the subject was aware of the reinforcement contingency. Furthermore, while positive reinforcement could, in this case, increase the frequency of common responses, it was ineffective in increasing the frequency of uncommon ones. This result was also found in the originality training study of Maltzman *et al.* (1958), where reinforcement for giving a different response on repeated trials of an association test was no more effective in producing unusual responses than was such practice without reinforcement. Maltzman *et al.* (1962) have suggested that the inability of positive reinforcement to increase unusual responses may be due to two factors; first, such responses occur relatively less often and hence less reinforcement is possible, and second, a nonspecific class of responses is being reinforced (i.e., the class consisting of any response *other* than the most common responses), as opposed to reinforcing a more limited set of responses (i.e., the most common).

Negative Reinforcement

Negative reinforcement has also been shown to produce modifications in associative behavior. Bersh, Notterman, and Schoenfeld (1957), for example, demonstrated that preceding a stimulus with shock can decrease the popularity* of responses given to that stimulus, even when the shock is removed; however, response latency remained relatively unchanged in the presence of negative reinforcement. Similarly, Rotberg (1959), after initially rewarding the occurrence of antonym responses, found that continuous or aperiodic shock, or continuous negative verbal reinforcement ("wrong") would reduce the number of antonym responses given to new stimuli, both during the punishment period and subsequently, when punishment was discontinued. In this study, however, response latency was related to negative reinforcement, with the more severe punishment (shock) resulting in a longer reaction time than mild punishment ("wrong").

Hare (1965), in a similar study, varied both the schedule (100% versus 67%) and delay (0 seconds versus 5 seconds) of negative reinforcement (shock) following antonym responses; testing with new stimuli was continued until no antonym responses were made (or for a maximum of eight trials). The results indicated that both variables produced significant main effects in determining trials to criterion, with delay being relatively more important than schedule (the interaction was not significant). However, attaining criterion also was found to be dependent on the ability of the subject to verbalize the contingency of reinforcement. Neither of the acquisition variables produced differential effects on the rate of extinction of the avoidance response; extinction was accelerated by removal of the shock-producing electrodes, but even under these clear conditions of termination of negative reinforcement, the number of antonym responses emitted did not increase to the preexperimental operant level, indicating that the negative reinforcement was still affecting the response process.

Eriksen and Kuethe (1956) have shown that shock also can suppress

*As determined from associative-response frequency on the 1910 Kent-Rosanoff norms.

the occurrence of arbitrarily selected responses and have suggested that this occurs regardless of the subject's awareness of the reinforcement contingency. In this study, subjects initially were administered a 15-item successive WAT. Five of the discrete responses, arbitrarily chosen on the first trial, were followed by shock each time they occurred on subsequent trials. Testing was continued for 10 trials, or until no punished response occurred for two successive trials. Before the extinction trials, the subject was informed that the shock would be discontinued. Although the shocked and nonshocked stimuli now elicited the same total number of responses during a continuous-association task, the previously shocked stimuli elicited a significantly smaller number of responses which had occurred on the first trial, as compared to the nonshocked stimuli; that is, the previously punished responses did not occur to the stimuli which had initially elicited them. Thus, as the authors point out, the effect of negative reinforcement persisted despite the change to a different task and despite the subject's knowledge that shock would no longer occur.

Two lines of evidence suggested to the authors that response inhibition could occur without awareness on the part of the subject. First, the rate of avoidance learning and the continued suppression of the punished response even during extinction was the same for subjects who did, and who did not, report awareness of the reinforcement contingency. Secondly, the "aware" subjects showed an increase in reaction time to the critical stimuli over the first four trials, suggesting they were attempting to withhold punished responses and to substitute new ones. On the other hand, the "unaware" subjects showed a *decrease* in reaction time to the critical stimuli over the same four trials; in fact, these latencies were very similar to the reaction times obtained to the noncritical stimuli from both subject groups. Thus the learning and resistance to extinction of the aware and unaware subjects was the same, but their latency of response differed in a way consonant with the assumption that the aware subjects were consciously trying to modify their behavior so as to avoid negative reinforcement.

Although the authors believed they had demonstrated that negative reinforcement could suppress a response without the subject's awareness, the results of an experiment by R. B. Martin and Dean (1965) cast some doubt on this conclusion. In pilot studies, using a successive WAT procedure similar to that of Eriksen and Kuethe (1956), these authors had found that unless subjects had some partial knowledge of the reinforcement contingencies, they did not reach criterion (i.e., did not show suppression of punished responses) within 10 trials. Subsequently, they conducted an experiment in which the stimulus lists consisted of words of high, medium, and low Thorndike-Lorge frequency. Unlike Eriksen and Kuethe's procedure, one group of subjects was shocked for their Trial 1 responses to high-frequency stimuli, while a second group was shocked for their Trial 1 responses to low-frequency stimuli.* While shock again was found to be a significant determinant of the subsequent suppression of Trial 1 responses and of the variability of responses after Trial 1, stimulus *familiarity* was shown to interact with shock in determining reaction time. That is, high-frequency stimuli showed an increased reaction time to shock over trials, while low-frequency stimuli showed a *de*creased reaction time. Furthermore, when these curves were plotted for Trials 1 through 4, they corresponded quite closely to Eriksen and Kuethe's results for aware versus unaware subjects, respectively. Martin and Dean suggest that since the stimulus variable of familiarity was not controlled in the Eriksen-Kuethe study, the latter's finding—that reaction time was longer for subjects who were aware of the true reinforcement contingency—did not reflect a relationship between reaction time and awareness, but rather was due to the independent relationship to stimulus familiarity of both reaction time and of awareness.

In another study which appeared to demonstrate that conditioning could occur without the subject's awareness of which words were being reinforced, the effects of negative reinforcement were shown not only to suppress the occurrence of the punished response, but also to generalize to semantically related stimuli. Lacey and Smith (1954) presented subjects with an association test in which either the stimulus word *cow* or *paper* was followed by a shock. After several trials of such negative reinforcement, a change in the dependent variable (heart rate) followed on presentation of the conditioned stimulus word. Furthermore, if *cow* was the negatively reinforced stimulus word, the conditioned response was noted to generalize to other *rural* stimulus words in the list; this generalization to rural stimuli was not found if *paper* was the shocked stimulus. For this latter condition, there was some generalization of the conditioned response to nonrural stimulus words, but this occurrence was unreliable.

Chatterjee and Eriksen (1960) repeated these findings, but questioned whether Lacey and Smith's additional conclusion—that verbal conditioning occurs outside of the subject's awareness—was justified. By asking subjects some additional questions (e.g., if they had any hypotheses about when shock would *not* occur), and by analyzing the autonomic response data in terms of the difference between the stimulus which was actually shocked and stimuli which the subject expected to be shocked, the authors concluded that the conditioning of the autonomic response "was no more specific than

---

*In the Eriksen and Kuethe study, different subjects were shocked for different stimuli. Since the stimuli varied in familiarity, it is possible that the critical stimuli for some subjects were of greater familiarity.

the subjects' verbalizations" (p. 403). That is, the GSR was positively related to the subject's expectation of shock, rather than to an accurate unconscious recognition of the word which was actually shocked.

The effects of negative reinforcement also have been shown to generalize to temporally contiguous stimuli. L. Worell (1965) presented subjects with 48 highly meaningful CVCs as a WAT; two sets of four consecutive stimuli were preselected to be followed by shock. After a 5-day interval, there was no difference in the free recall of shocked versus nonshocked stimuli or responses; however, the overall recall level was very low (8.7% and 6.8%, respectively). When subjects were subsequently given a response reproduction test and a stimulus-response relearning task, the number of errors made to previously shocked stimuli significantly exceeded the number made to nonshocked stimuli. In general, the shocked stimuli showed an accumulation of aversive effects such that the stimuli in the middle of the set showed more errors than the first and last stimulus in the set of four. Furthermore, the stimuli immediately preceding and following the shocked sets also showed an increase of errors over other nonshocked stimuli, thereby demonstrating a generalization of aversive effects via temporal contiguity.

Positive and Negative Reinforcement

Finally, D'Alessio (1964) studied the joint effect of positive and negative reinforcement on associative responses. In this study, five arbitrarily chosen responses were followed by an aversive sound; this negative reinforcement could be avoided subsequently by giving any response other than the initial response word. In addition, one-third of the subjects received a positive verbal reinforcement for making such an avoidance response on all eight acquisition trials, one-third were positively reinforced on the second four trials only, and one-third received no positive reinforcement. During extinction (no negative reinforcement), one-half of the subjects were given positive verbal reinforcement for continuing to make the substitute response. The acquisition results indicated that there was no difference among groups for amount of repetition of the initial response to noncritical stimuli (i.e., no generalization of the tendency to avoid the initial response) and, in fact, no significant difference in avoidance responses to the *critical* stimuli. However, the maximally reinforced subjects (positive reinforcement on all eight trials) did show significantly greater avoidance of the punished response on the later acquisition trials than did those subjects receiving no positive reinforcement. Furthermore, this difference was maintained, such that during the later extinction trials subjects who had been maximally reinforced during acquisition were still making a greater number of avoidance responses. The presence of positive reinforcement during extinction did not produce a significant main effect, but did interact significantly with trials, such that subjects who received positive reinforcement during extinction continued to give avoidance responses for a greater number of trials. Thus there is some evidence that the introduction of positive verbal reinforcement during acquisition can hasten the acquisition of a verbal avoidance response and increase its resistance to extinction, and that this latter result can also be accomplished by the introduction of such reinforcement during extinction.

It is noteworthy, considering the preceding discussion of the relationships among awareness, reaction time, and stimulus familiarity (cf. p. 117) that the present study, which used stimulus words of high Thorndike-Lorge frequency, also found a lengthening of reaction time during the initial few acquisition trials, and noted that almost all the subjects were aware of the reinforcement contingency.

Summary and Discussion

I. POSITIVE REINFORCEMENT

    (1) This has been shown to have the following effects:
        (A) reinforcement of Primary, Secondary and Tertiary responses increased the frequency of these responses*, but
        (B) reinforcement of uncommon responses did not change the frequency of such responses.

II. NEGATIVE REINFORCEMENT

    (1) This has been shown to have the following effects:
        (A) when shock precedes the stimulus word,
            (a) the associative-response frequency is decreased, but
            (b) reaction time is unchanged.
        (B) When negative reinforcement follows antonym responses,
            (a) the number of antonym responses is decreased.* Furthermore, the rate of suppression, and resistance to extinction depend on
                (i) the *delay* of reinforcement, and
                (ii) the *schedule* of reinforcement.

(Delay is more important than schedule in determining the rate of suppression; they are of equal importance in determining the resistance to extinction of the avoidance response.)

*Starred items: this effect may require awareness of the reinforcement contingency.

(iii) Rate of suppression and resistance to extinction also depend on *severity* of reinforcement (shock versus "wrong"), which interacts with schedule in determining the decrease of antonym responses during both punishment and extinction. That is, for severe punishment, both continuous and aperiodic reinforcement produce the effect; for mild punishment, only continuous reinforcement produces the effect.
  (b) reaction time is increased*, and severe punishment results in a greater increase than mild punishment.
(C) When negative reinforcement follows arbitrarily selected responses
  (a) the frequency of such responses is decreased during punishment and extinction (even when the subject knows that shock is discontinued)*;
  (b) the response availability, m, to such stimuli during extinction is unchanged.
(D) Studies of semantic generalization indicate that an autonomic conditioned response will generalize to other stimuli from the same (restricted) semantic class of conditioned stimuli*.
(E) Studies of temporal generalization indicate that
  (a) response reproduction errors and stimulus-response relearning errors generalize to nonshocked, but temporally contiguous, stimuli.
  (b) in addition, response reproduction errors and stimulus-response relearning errors are maximal for shocked stimuli which are temporally surrounded by other shocked stimuli; that is, there is a spread and summation of effect.

III. NEGATIVE AND POSITIVE REINFORCEMENT EMPLOYED TOGETHER

(1) Following arbitrarily selected responses,
  (A) the rate of suppression of such responses is increased, and
  (B) the resistance to extinction of the substitute avoidance response is increased.

While it has been clearly demonstrated that reinforcement can modify associative responses, the locus of the reinforcement effect is not always clear. In certain cases, both positive and negative reinforcement have been shown to modify the frequency of occurrence of a class of *responses*, regardless of the stimuli. Thus popular responses have been increased, and antonym responses have been decreased. On the other hand, using virtually the same negative reinforcement procedure (i.e., shock following response production), the effects of reinforcement also have been manifest on the *stimulus* dimension. As an example, an autonomic conditioned response initially evoked by the rural stimulus *cow* was subsequently evoked by other stimuli belonging to the class "rural." In another example of stimulus generalization, stimuli which were temporally contiguous to the negatively reinforced stimuli began themselves to show the effect of reinforcement. In addition to this generalization along stimulus and along response dimensions, reinforcement has also been shown to have a highly specific effect on particular stimulus-response connections, while not affecting the availability of other responses to the same stimulus.

On the other hand, certain classes of responses and of stimuli (uncommon responses and nonrural stimuli) have not been affected by reinforcement. In both cases this can probably be best explained by the assumption that these classes are too broad and too vaguely defined, whereas the effects of reinforcement are limited to narrower, more restricted classes.

In fact, much of the evidence for reinforcement differentially affecting different classes of *stimuli* might as easily be interpreted as examples of response class conditioning. Thus one might focus on the fact that *responses* which are temporally contiguous to reinforced responses show a generalization of reinforcement effects; the method used to test for such effects (response reproduction and stimulus-response relearning) does not permit us to determine which of the two dimensions was being affected by reinforcement. Similarly, one might argue that the autonomic conditioned response did not generalize to other rural stimuli, but rather that the class of rural *responses*, implicitly evoked by these stimuli as well as by the critical rural stimulus, became inhibited and/or anxiety-arousing as a result of the negative reinforcement. Again, the method of testing does not make it possible to discriminate between stimulus and response effects.

Only in studies in which the stimuli are changed from the acquisition period to the test period is it possible to determine whether reinforcement has produced stimulus-specific effects, or whether the locus of the effect has been on the response dimension. The studies by Maltzman *et al.* (1962), Sommer *et al.* (1962), Rotberg (1959), and Hare (1965) all used new stimuli during the test stage, making it possible to determine that in fact it was the occurrence of certain types of responses, as distinct from the stimuli which produced them, which was being affected by reinforcement.

On the other hand, there have been no studies which could be said to demonstrate definitively that stimuli, as opposed to their responses, have been affected by reinforcement. To do this, following the same line of reasoning as given above to determine response effects, the same stimuli which had been previously reinforced would have to be represented with the subject being required to make new responses. The difficulty with this approach, however, is the possibility that the previous responses would occur implicitly, and would thereby activate the previous reinforcement effects.

The study which most closely approximates this procedure of presenting the same stimuli and requiring new responses is that of Eriksen and Kuethe, in which stimuli initially followed by a discrete response (Trial 1) were then presented for continued association (Trial 2). Interestingly enough, the shocked and nonshocked stimuli of Trial 1 did not differ in their response-eliciting capacity on Trial 2. Both types of stimuli elicited the same number, m, of responses. In addition to this demonstration that reinforcement did not affect the stimulus dimension, this study provides further evidence suggesting that reinforcement primarily affects the response dimension. This evidence comes from noting that although the stimuli produced an equal number of continued-associative responses, the previously shocked responses did not occur as often as their control counterparts. The combination of these two findings in the only study in which it is possible to test for stimulus, as distinct from response, effects, suggests that reinforcement acts on responses and generalizes along response dimensions.

Somewhat overlapping with the issue of the locus of the reinforcement effect is the question of the role of awareness in determining the occurrence of the effect. The large majority of these studies have found that awareness is necessary; those investigations which initially seemed to demonstrate conditioning effects without awareness have subsequently been found faulty in design or procedure. Yet, there are some findings which suggest that this issue is not yet closed. Thus, the fact that the avoidance of negatively reinforced responses continues even when the subject is told that no more punishment will occur, or when the sources of the punishment (i.e., the electrodes) are removed, would suggest that this effect is not completely under conscious volitional control. One of the difficulties in studying the role of awareness in determining the effects of reinforcement is the problem of establishing a definition and a reliable criterion for the presence of awareness. Another difficulty, which has been paid little heed, is that the awareness of the contingencies of reinforcement may vary over the course of the experiment. Thus a subject who is interviewed at the conclusion of the experiment may demonstrate considerable awareness; however, this does not necessarily imply that during the initial stages of the experiment, conditioning was not taking place without awareness of reinforcement contingencies. At this point, then, we must conclude that the role of awareness in verbal conditioning is not fully understood.

Chapter 5

STRESS

In this chapter, the effect of stress on the production of associative responses will be considered. These studies may be divided into two large groups, on the basis of the definition of stress: first, those in which stress is a subject variable (i.e., subjects are preselected on the basis of personality measures for degree of subjective stress experienced), and second, those in which stress is experimentally induced. Other studies of subject-variable effects will be included in Part II. However, *stress* as a subject variable is included here, since several investigations using experimental sources for producing stress have been concerned also with the interaction between this external stress and the preexperimental level of stress (anxiety) existing in the subject. In order to evaluate these latter interaction studies, it is helpful first to consider the separate effects of the subject variable.

Stress as a Subject Variable

A number of experiments have been conducted in which the effect of stress on associative responses has been studied by selecting subjects who score high on measures of anxiety; presumably, such subjects are in a continuous state of stress, a condition which is not true for low-scoring subjects. To select high-anxious, *HA*, and low-anxious, *LA*, subjects, the Taylor Manifest Anxiety Scale has been used most often; only in a few instances have other measures, such as the CPI Anxiety Scale (R. C. Johnson & Lim, 1964), the MMPI Psychaesthenia Scale (Kuethe, 1961), the Blacky Test (Smock & Thompson, 1954), or the Edwards Personal Preference Schedule (J. Worell & Worell, 1965), been used to infer the presence of intra-subject stress.

There has been general agreement in the finding that *HA* subjects produce more different responses, *D*, in a discrete-association task than do *LA* subjects (Buchwald [1959] using Kent-Rosanoff stimulus words; and Trapp and Kausler [1960] using CVCs). In addition, in Trapp and Kausler's study, the effects of anxiety were independent of the association value of the stimulus (based on the percentage of subjects for whom the CVC elicits at least one response). Apart from the findings of Mandler and Mandler (1962), to be discussed below, the only discrepant finding is that of Brody (1964), who found HA and LA subjects to be equivalent in the number of different responses, D, made to a WAT. However, when Brody's data were analyzed in terms of responses to stimuli of high and of low D values, the results indicated that HA subjects did give more different responses to high D stimuli, but gave fewer different responses to low D ones, resulting in an overall mean D score which did not differ from that of LA subjects.

Davids and Eriksen (1955) found that HA subjects produce more associative responses, m, in a continuous-association task, and R. C. Johnson and Lim (1964), while finding no relationship between anxiety and m, discovered that HA subjects produce proportionately more m responses to "good" than to "bad" stimuli, as compared with LA subjects.

If anxiety increases response heterogeneity, it might be expected that fewer Popular responses would be given by HA subjects. However, the findings on this question are inconclusive. Buchwald (1959) did find that HA subjects gave fewer Primary responses (defined by the responses of this sample to 40 Kent-Rosanoff stimuli, preselected to have a minimum Primary strength of 33% on the 1954 Minnesota norms). The differences between HA and LA subjects, however, were significant only for male subjects. Kanfer (1960), combining the results of male and female subjects, noted no difference between the number of Primaries (defined by the 1954 Minnesota norms) given by HA and LA subjects to 30 Kent-Rosanoff stimuli, preselected for high- (52%–83%) or low- (12%–26%) strength Primaries, while Kuethe (1961), with male subjects only, found (insignificantly) *more* Primaries (based on the responses of this sample) among HA subjects, for 50 Kent-Rosanoff stimuli (basis for selection not stated). Furthermore, Wolff (1965), using Kent-Rosanoff stimuli preselected for high- (61%–84%) or low- (24%–38%) strength Primaries, found no difference in the response commonality of HA and LA males, while moderately anxious (MA) males showed greater commonality, especially for stimuli with strong Primaries.* Sarason (1959) also found MA subjects to give more Primaries and to have higher response commonality than either HA or LA subjects, who did not differ. Finally, Nakamura and Wright (1965) found no difference in response commonality of HA and LA females to stimuli with strong Primaries.

* Response commonality was determined from the associative frequency of the response in the 1954 Minnesota norms. The *interaction* of anxiety level with type of stimulus will be discussed below (pp. 127–128).

The results of reaction time studies have been somewhat less equivocal, showing in general that anxiety is not related directly to response latency. Thus Mandler and Mandler (1962) found no relationship between anxiety and reaction time,* and this was true over a variety of stimuli (CVCs, adjectives, photographs, and a Rorschach card). Tecce and Glassco (1965) also found no difference in the reaction time of *HA* and *LA* subjects. However, they did note an (insignificant) trend toward an interaction between anxiety level and slope of the response gradient in determining reaction time. Thus stimuli for which there was no predominant Primary and several equi-probable responses (high response competition) resulted in a longer response latency in *HA* than in *LA* subjects, but the two subject groups did not differ on stimuli of low response competition. Nakamura and Wright (1965) also have found that *HA* and *LA* subjects do not differ in their reaction time to stimuli with strong Primaries.

Doris *et al.* (1963) similarly noted no differences among the reaction times of *HA*, *MA*, and *LA* subjects from the third grade. Again, however, an interaction with type of stimulus was noted. When the stimuli of this study were analyzed by affective category, the reaction time to emotional stimuli of *HA* subjects exceeded that of *MA* subjects, which in turn was greater than that of *LA* subjects; the reaction time to neutral stimuli did not show any effect of subject anxiety level. Smock and Thompson (1954) also noted this differential effect; the reaction to conflict stimuli was greater for *HA* than for *LA* subjects, while the reaction time to neutral stimuli was equivalent for the two groups. Only A. G. Goldstein (1961) found greater response latency in *HA* subjects, independent of the *D* value of emotionality of the stimulus.†

Finally, *HA* subjects have been found to give a greater number of disturbed responses (Smock & Thompson, 1954), responses with anxiety ideation (Davids & Eriksen, 1955), "body" responses on Secord's homonym WAT (Secord & Jourard, 1953), and negatively toned responses to CVCs (Trapp & Kausler, 1959). Furthermore, both L. Worell and Worell (1965) and Sarason (1959, 1961) have found *HA* subjects to make more response reproduction errors than *LA* subjects. However, this apparent relationship between intra-subject stress and associative-response disturbance was not supported in an investigation by M. J. Goldstein (1961), who found anxiety level to be unrelated to the occurrence either of rare responses or of reproduction errors.

---

*As well as finding anxiety unrelated to *m*, the number of idiosyncratic responses, and GSR.

†For a suggested explanation, see footnote p. 135.

Experimentally Induced Stress

ENVIRONMENTAL CONDITIONS

Another approach to the study of the effect of stress on associative responses has been to induce stress experimentally via manipulation of the external environment. This experimental manipulation may be designed to produce an objective, environmental, physical kind of stress; alternatively, experimental manipulation of instructions may be used to increase the degree of subjective stress experienced by the subject.

Studies of the first type—i.e., of experimentally induced, environmental stress—have included such dramatic procedures as food deprivation and parachute-jump training as the stressful condition, as well as less startling conditions, such as anticipation of examination results, increased muscle tension, time pressure, and distraction. For example, Kollar *et al.* (1964) tested subjects deprived of food for a period slightly less than a week and found some evidence for an increasing number of either "non-sequitur" or blocked responses. Furthermore, the reaction time of deprived subjects to "food" stimuli increased with increasing deprivation, while that of control subjects did not. Brozek *et al.* (1951), testing subjects over a 24-week period of semistarvation, found (insignificant) evidence for fewer popular responses and more "personalized" responses (the latter significant if only "food" stimuli were considered), and a greater probability of recall of the stimulus word *hungry* among the food-deprived subjects, as compared to controls.

Wispé (1954) deprived subjects of food and water for 0, 10, and 24 hours, and presented both need-relevant (food and water) and neutral stimuli for continued association. The number of food and water responses increased up to the tenth hour of deprivation, but decreased thereafter. Furthermore, for the longest period of deprivation (24 hours), there was an increase in the number of responses referring to acts which would be instrumental in obtaining food or water, while the number of responses simply naming objects which would satisfy the need decreased. Thus, as the author points out, after the tenth hour of deprivation there is a shift in the number and kind of associative responses, possibly due to the fact that the previous responses have not provided gratification to the subjects.

Two other studies also have found evidence for an interaction effect between the condition producing the stress and the type of stimulus used on the association test. In an investigation by Epstein and Fenz (1962), the subjects were parachute-jump trainees and matched college controls. The stimuli were chosen to represent varying degrees of relevance to parachuting, as well as including anxiety and neutral words. For both "parachute" and "anxiety" stimuli, the GSR was greatest for parachutists tested on the jump day, next greatest for parachutists tested on a nonjump day, and least for the control subjects. Furthermore, the greater the relevance of the stimuli to parachuting, the greater the GSR for the experimental subjects. However, on neutral stimuli, the GSR of control subjects exceeded that of experimental subjects. Similar findings were obtained for a measure of reaction time and for the number of "parachute" responses produced.

In the second study (W. R. Johnson, 1951), college athletes were given a WAT within the hour just prior to competition. The stimulus list included words which were relevant either to athletics or to psychosexual problems, and also included neutral stimuli, thus providing a baseline control for each subject. In addition, nonathlete college subjects were tested as a control group. While the athletes showed a greater GSR to psychosexual stimuli than to athletic stimuli (with neutral stimuli eliciting the least response), their GSR to the athletic stimuli exceeded that of the control group to the psychosexual stimuli. On the other hand, neutral stimuli resulted in a smaller GSR for the stressed athletes than for nonstressed control subjects. Unfortunately, the control subjects were not tested on the athletic stimuli and the athletic list always followed the psychosexual list, so that two important variables were left uncontrolled. However, it is possible to conclude that, under stress conditions of imminent athletic competition, the GSR of such stressed subjects was increased to emotional (psychosexual) stimuli and decreased to neutral stimuli, relative to the control group. Whether stress caused the athletes' GSR to athletic stimuli to exceed that of nonstressed subjects to psychosexual stimuli, as the authors suggest, cannot be determined, due to the confounding of number and order of lists with type of stimulus.

In a less dramatic study of experimentally induced, environmental stress, Saltz (1961) administered a WAT to subjects while they were waiting for an examination to be graded. The stimuli of this test were preselected from the Kent-Rosanoff list to have Primaries of high (61% and above), medium (41–60%), and low (20–40%) associative strength. The responses to this stressed test were compared with those of the same subjects tested either a week before the exam or a week after they had received their grades. The stress condition was found to significantly decrease the number of Primary responses, although the number of idiosyncratic responses remained unchanged. Neither the order of stress and nonstress conditions, nor any of the interactions among stress, association strength, and order of conditions was significant.

Mandler and Parnes (1957), in an attempt to induce a failure-stress situation, interrupted subjects in the middle of a continued association task and admonished them for doing "poorly." This procedure was noted to increase the output of *m* responses. Kuethe (1961) demonstrated that increasing the muscle tension of a *HA* subject (by requiring him to lift a weight on a pulley) reduced the frequency of occurrence of Popular responses, as compared to *LA* subjects. Siipola, *et al.* (1955) found that time pressure (instruction to make a rapid associative response) increased the number of contrast responses (which were also necessarily of the same form class), and Flavell *et al.* (1958) found time pressure to increase the number of "perseveration" and "distant" responses. In the latter study, when a reward was offered for making a "fast" response, an additional increase in clang responses, and a decrease in subordinate responses was noted. However, the additional requirement to make a (distracting) motor response did not further modify responses, as compared to those obtained under time-pressure conditions alone.

Both Flavell *et al.* and Siipola *et al.* interpret their findings as indicating that time pressure results in a response which is "closer" to the stimulus. In this regard, Flavell is referring to the associative process stopping at an earlier point on the (structural) associative pathway between the stimulus and response. Siipola, although similarly referring to the subject's tendency to become stimulus-bound (i.e., by responding within the same form class or dimension as that of the stimulus), focuses on this phenomenon of sticking to the stimulus as a technique used by the subject to avoid making a personal response, despite the increased pressure, or stress, of the situation. It does not appear, however, that these two interpretations are incompatible; both authors are describing the same phenomenon, one from a structural, and one from an adaptive, point of view.

In later sections (cf. Chapters 7, 8, and 10) it will be suggested that contrast responses of the type to which Siipola *et al.* are referring are actually short-circuited responses.* That is, these responses are not mediated but rather depend on the development of direct connections between the stimulus and response. We would suggest that it is this factor which allows them to be given so rapidly. If these responses are not, or cannot be, given, then in order to meet the time-pressure requirements, the subject must halt the associative process sooner, and hence responses which are "closer" to the stimulus occur.

INSTRUCTIONAL STRESS

Still other studies have been concerned with the effects of instructions which are designed to evoke a subjective sense of stress in the subject. It has been found that when subjects were instructed that the Kent-Rosanoff

---

*The use of contrast responses to avoid unacceptable responses has already been discussed in Chapter 1.

WAT was actually a measure of personality (Sarason, 1959) or of intelligence (Sarason, 1961), these stress-inducing instructions decreased both the number of Primary responses and response commonality (based on the number of responses which exceeded an associative response frequency of 10% on the 1954 Minnesota norms) and increased the number of reproduction errors. Furthermore, it has been demonstrated that the effect of instructions on inducing subjective stress interacts with the preexperimental anxiety level of the subject in determining associative responses. In the Sarason studies (1959, 1961); there was a significant interaction between the effect of instructions and the preexperimental anxiety level, such that *HA* subjects were most responsible for producing the decrease in number of Primary responses and in response commonality. In addition, there was a tendency ($.10 < p < .05$) for the number of reproduction errors to reflect this interaction between instructions and preexperimental anxiety level, with *HA* subjects being more affected by instructions than any other group.

However, when Wolff (1965) used stimulus lists made up either of 10 stimuli with very strong (61%–84%) or 10 stimuli with weak (24%–38%) Primaries, he found neither stress instructions (telling the subjects the WAT was actually a personality test) nor an interaction between instructions and preexperimental anxiety level to be significant in determining response commonality (based on the frequency of occurrence of that response in the 1954 Minnesota norms). Rather, strength of Primary response showed a tendency to interact with anxiety level in determining response commonality. Thus stimuli preselected for low-strength Primary responses showed only an insignificant tendency to produce higher response commonality for *LA* and *MA* subjects than for *HA* subjects.* However, on stimuli preselected for high-strength Primary responses, while *HA* and *LA* subjects did not differ, *MA* subjects showed significantly greater response commonality than the average of the *HA* and *LA* groups.

That the relationships among inner stress (anxiety), experimentally induced stress, and word association are not yet understood is further demonstrated in a study by J. Worell and Worell (1965), in which stress-inducing instructions had the same effect on some aspects of the associative response process, but the reverse effect for other aspects, as compared to those found by Sarason (1959). High- and low-conflicted subjects were selected by means of response to the Edwards Personal Preference Schedule, answered once in respect to preferred behavior and once for actual behavior. Conflict was measured by the amount of discrepancy between the

―――――――
*Cf. also Tecce and Glassco (1965), cited on p. 126, for further tentative evidence of this interaction between response competition and anxiety level.

two tests. The experimenters then administered the 25 Kent-Rosanoff stimuli of strongest, and the 25 of weakest, Primary response strength; subjects were to give three responses to each stimulus, and then were tested for response recall.

The results indicated that high-conflict subjects showed lower response commonality and more reproduction errors. As level of subject conflict increased, response commonality decreased (as measured either by the number of responses which exceeded an associative-response frequency of 10%, or the number of responses among the top 25 versus the bottom 25 responses, on the 1954 Minnesota norms). A (negative) relationship also was found between conflict and recall of the first and third response,* and between conflict and recall of all responses combined. Furthermore, the interaction of subject anxiety level and Primary response strength was found to be a significant determiner of response commonality (as measured by the number of responses with a frequency of 100 or greater on the 1954 Minnesota norms). Stimuli with high-strength Primaries produced significantly greater response commonality for low-conflict subjects than for high-conflict subjects; stimuli with low-strength Primaries did not differentiate between the two subject groups.†

The final result of this study (J. Worell & Worell, 1965) indicated that stress-inducing instructions had no effect on the commonality of responses, but did significantly *decrease* the number of reproduction errors (in contrast to Sarason's findings of increased response reproduction errors). The interaction between instructions and level of subject anxiety was not significant for either measure.

Summary and Discussion

I. INTERNAL STRESS, OR *SUBJECT ANXIETY*

This has been noted to have the following (inconsistent) effects:
  (A) The associative frequency of the Primary response is
      (a) decreased (Buchwald, 1959),
      (b) unaffected (Kanfer, 1960), or
      (c) increased (Kuethe, 1961).
  (B) Response commonality is
      (a) unchanged for *LA* versus *HA* subjects (Nakamura & Wright, 1965; Sarason, 1959; Wolff, 1965)
      (b) increased for *MA* subjects (Sarason, 1959; Wolff, 1965), or

---

* Recall of second response was not tested.
†These findings are inconsistent with those of Wolff (1965), who did not find any difference in the response commonality of *HA* or *LA* subjects to either type of stimulus.

(c) decreased for high-conflict subjects (J. Worell & Worell, 1965)
(C) Response heterogeneity, D, is increased or unaffected,*
(D) Response availability, m, is increased or unaffected*.
(E) With the exception of one study†, reaction time has not been found to be directly related to subject anxiety level*.
(F) Response reproduction errors are
(a) increased (Sarason, 1959, 1961; J. Worell & Worell 1965), or
(b) unaffected (M. J. Goldstein, 1961).
(G) The number of disturbed, anxiety, or negatively toned responses is increased.

II. STUDIES OF THE CONSEQUENCES OF *EXTERNAL STRESS*

These are divided into two groups: the effects of experimental manipulation of environmental conditions, and the effects of experimental instructions.

(A) Environmentally induced stress
(a) decreases the frequency of the Primary response, and
(b) increases response availability;‡
(c) it also increases the number of response disturbances, unusual responses, and of
(d) stimulus-bound, or close, responses,
(e) the frequency of contrast responses also has been noted to increase as a result of time pressure.
(B) Stress induced via instructions
(a) decreases the frequency of Primary responses.
(b) Measures of response commonality have been
(i) unaffected (Wolff, 1965; J. Worell & Worell, 1965), or
(ii) decreased (Sarason, 1959, 1961).
(c) Response reproduction errors have been
(i) increased (Sarason, 1959, 1961), and
(ii) decreased (J. Worell & Worell, 1965).

III. LEVEL OF SUBJECT ANXIETY AND INTERACTION WITH STIMULUS VARIABLES IN DETERMINING ASSOCIATIVE RESPONSES

The interaction of subject anxiety with the
(A) Preexperimental Primary response strength of the stimulus

---

*Starred items: In these studies there were significant interaction effects between subject anxiety and type of stimulus in determining the response measure.
†M. J. Goldstein (1961; cf. footnote, p. 135).
‡But cf. interpretation, p. 137.

(a) did not affect the obtained frequency of the Primary response (Kanfer, 1960);
(b) had inconsistent effects on response commonality:
    (i) Wolff (1965) found that for Primary response frequencies of 24–38%, $HA = MA = LA$ subjects; for Primaries of 61–84%, $MA > HA = LA$ subjects.
    (ii) Nakamura (1965), with stimuli having Primaries of 13–33%, found inconsistent results; with Primaries of 35–83%, $HA = LA$ subjects.
    (iii) L. Worell (1965), using Kent-Rosanoff stimuli with the 25 weakest Primaries, found $HA = LA$ subjects; for stimuli with the 125 strongest Primaries, he found $LA > HA$ subjects.
(c) For reaction time, Nakamura found stimuli with Primaries of 13–44% to have inconsistent results, and for Primaries of 35–83%, $HA = LA$ subjects.
(B) Preexperimental D value of the stimulus
    (a) affected response heterogeneity, D: $HA > LA$ subjects for high D stimuli; for low D stimuli, $LA > HA$ subjects,
    (b) did not significantly affect reaction time, although there was a tendency for high D stimuli to produce longer reaction times in HA than in LA subjects,
(C) Preexperimental association value of the stimulus did not affect response heterogeneity, D,
(D) Emotionality of the stimulus
    (a) affected response availability, m. The "good" to "bad" stimulus m ratio was greater for HA than for LA subjects;
    (b) it also affected reaction time. For emotional stimuli, reaction time was longer for HA than for LA subjects. For neutral stimuli, HA and LA subjects did not differ.

III. Level of Subject Anxiety and Interaction with Experimental Stress-Inducing Procedures in Determining Associative Responses

(1) The decrease in frequency of the Primary response found with stress-inducing conditions or instructions is primarily due to HA subjects.

(2) The relationship of this interaction to response commonality has not been consistent:
    (a) Wolff (1965) and L. Worell (1965) found no significant interaction effect;
    (b) Sarason (1959, 1961) found that the decrease in response commonality following stress-inducing instructions was primarily due to HA subjects.

(3) Nor has it been consistent for response reproduction errors:
   (a) L.Worell (1965) found no significant interaction effect, but
   (b) Sarason (1959, 1961) found a tendency for instructions to affect *HA* subjects more than *LA* subjects.

IV. EFFECT OF THE RELATIONSHIP BETWEEN EXPERIMENTAL STRESS-INDUCING PROCEDURES AND STIMULUS VARIABLES

The effect of this on the production of associative responses also has been studied. The interaction of experimental procedures with the pre-experimental Primary strength of the stimulus was not significant in its effect on the obtained frequency of Primary response.

V. TRIPLE INTERACTION BETWEEN TYPE OF STIMULUS, EXPERIMENTAL PROCEDURE, AND SUBJECT ANXIETY LEVEL

(1) Both reaction time and GSR
   (A) are increased to emotional stimuli under stress conditions for *HA* more than for *LA* subjects, but
   (B) are increased to neutral stimuli under stress conditions for *LA* more than for *HA* subjects.
(2) Both reaction time and number of unusual responses
   (A) are increased to "food" stimuli under food-deprivation conditions for *HA* (food-deprived) subjects more than for *LA* (nondeprived) subjects,
   (B) are equal to other stimuli under food-deprivation conditions for *HA* and *LA* subjects.

One of the most striking contradictions in the findings of these studies is that of the relationship of subject anxiety to the relative frequency of Primary responses. In Buchwald's study, increasing anxiety decreased the number of Primaries; in Kanfer's study, *HA* and *LA* subjects gave an equal number of Primaries, and in Kuethe's study, increasing anxiety increased the number of Primaries. Since all three studies used Kent-Rosanoff stimuli, it is unlikely that the findings are a function of the nature of the stimulus words. However, the bases for selection of anxious subjects did differ; in Buchwald's study, the criteria for *HA* and *LA* subjects were scores of 23 and 10, respectively, on the Manifest Anxiety Scale, and in Kanfer's study, the criteria were 21 and 8. On the other hand, Kuethe's subjects were assigned to *HA* and *LA* groups subsequent to their initial assignment to experimental groups, by splitting each experimental group at the median value obtained for that group on the MMPI Psychaesthenia Scale ($r = .92$ between *Pt* and *MAS*). This technique of a *post hoc* median split suggests that Kuethe's top group may actually have consisted of a large percentage of *MA* subjects.

Since both Wolff and Sarason have shown that *MA* subjects give a greater number of strong associative responses than *LA* subjects, it seems likely that Kuethe's increased number of Primaries with increasing anxiety was due to a *post hoc* classification which resulted in a *LA* group being contrasted with a *MA* group.

An analysis of the subject differences may also explain the discrepancy between the findings of Buchwald and Kanfer. It will be recalled that Buchwald found a significant difference due to anxiety only for males; Kanfer combined the results of males and females and found no differences due to anxiety level. (Possibly, if Kanfer had made a separate comparison for *HA* and *LA* males, he would have found a difference.) In both studies, the same criteria were applied for selection of male and female subjects. However, M. J. Goldstein (1961) found that the distribution of anxiety scores differs for men and women. Thus, to select *HA* subjects, he set a cutoff score of 20 for males, and 24 for females; to select *LA* subjects, the scores were 10 for males, and 7 for females.* Goldstein's analysis suggests that Buchwald's *HA* criterion score of 23 resulted in the males of his group being more anxious than the females, while the males of his *LA* group (criterion = 8) were probably slightly less anxious than the females. The *HA* and *LA* males thus were more differentiated than were the *HA* and *LA* females, so that a comparison of *HA* and *LA* groups would more likely reveal a difference for the males (as was found), if in fact some relationship between anxiety level and Primary response strength does exist.

Support for this explanation comes from Wolff's study, in which the criterion for selecting *HA* males was 19 and *LA* males 12. Using these less stringent criteria, *HA* and *LA* males did not differ in response commonality. Similarly, Nakamura and Wright found no difference in the response commonality of females, where the criteria for *HA* and *LA* were 18 and 12, respectively. Thus far, a comparison of the response commonality of female subjects who are as extremely differentiated as the males in Buchwald's study has not been made.

In summary then, the discrepant results are most likely due to different criteria for subject selection: first, the fact that Kuethe used a *post hoc* 50-50 split, and second, the fact that Buchwald and Kanfer, while selecting *HA* and *LA* subjects from the extremes of the distribution of anxiety scores, applied the same cutoff score to both males and females, while other evidence suggests that the scores of the two groups are different in distribution. In general, this points up the potential difficulty in using adjectives such as *high* or *low* to describe the standing of subjects on some variable,

---

*This may explain why Goldstein's study was the only one to obtain significantly longer reaction times in *HA* subjects, regardless of stimulus variable values.

when the empirical referent may actually be "more than" and "less than," and when one "high" may not equal another "high."

In addition to this problem in subject selection, these studies indicate that it is very difficult to talk about the effects of anxiety per se. Often the effects are contradictory, or there is *no* apparent effect (cf., e.g., the findings on response heterogeneity, D, response availability, m, and reaction time). Rather, it is necessary to consider the effects of anxiety in different stimulus situations, or under different environmental conditions. The interaction of subject anxiety with these two variables is discussed below.

When the relationship between anxiety and response heterogeneity, response availability, or response latency is considered, it becomes apparent that it is necessary to speak of the effects of anxiety in specific stimulus situations. For example, contrary to other findings, Brody found subject anxiety unrelated to response heterogeneity. However, closer examination of the data revealed that HA subjects increased response heterogeneity to high D stimuli and decreased response heterogeneity to low D stimuli. Similarly, Johnson and Lim found no difference in response availability, m, for LA and HA subjects when compared over all stimuli. However, when the stimuli were divided according to affective value, the m ratio for "good" to "bad" stimuli indicated that the *relative* response availability to "good" stimuli was significantly greater for the HA subjects (i.e., the relative availability of responses to "bad" stimuli was less). Similarly, subject anxiety level appears unrelated to the response measure of reaction time, until the data is further divided to answer the question: response to what kinds of stimuli? Looked at this way, we see that anxiety increases reaction time to emotional stimuli but does not affect neutral stimuli, that there is an insignificant tendency for anxiety to increase reaction time to high D stimuli, but that, as is true for low D stimuli, anxiety is unrelated to reaction time for stimuli with strong Primaries.

The effect of subject anxiety on associative responses has also been found to vary under different environmental conditions. Thus on measures of frequency of Primary response, Sarason found no difference between HA and LA subjects, and Kuethe found slightly more Primaries for HA subjects; yet under stress conditions, both found fewer Primary responses among the HA subjects than among the LA subjects.

The preceding studies also give us an opportunity to consider to what extent environmentally induced stress produces results similar to those produced by internal stress—i.e., subject anxiety. Looking at the results, we can see that at least for some response measures the two sources of anxiety produce the same effects. Both sources of stress have been shown to increase the occurrence of unusual or disturbed responses, as well as to increase the number of responses emitted in a continued-association task.* In terms of measures of response commonality, experimental stress and subject stress generally have had no effect, although in both cases one study has found decreased commonality. However both instructions and environmental conditions designed to induce anxiety have been found to decrease the number of Primaries, but the effects of subject anxiety on this measure have not been consistent.†

In addition to the effects of environmental versus internal stress, it is also possible to compare the extent to which the interaction of environmental stress with stimulus variables produces the same associative effects as the interaction of internal stress with stimulus variables. For example, neither experimental anxiety nor subject anxiety interact with the Primary response strength of the stimulus in determining the number of Primary responses actually obtained. However, subject anxiety (but not experimental anxiety) does interact with the Primary response strength of the stimulus to determine response commonality. The results obtained by the two studies demonstrating this interaction, however, differed in direction. That is, although Wolff (1965) found stimuli with low-strength Primaries to produce no differences in commonality for *HA*, *MA*, and *LA* subjects, and J. Worrell and Worrell (1965) found such stimuli to produce equal response commonality for high-conflict and low-conflict subjects, the results for stimuli with high-strength Primaries differed. Wolff found stimuli with high-strength Primaries to produce greater response commonality for *MA* than for *HA* or *LA* subjects (the latter two groups being equal),‡ while Worrell and Worrell found these stimuli to produce greater commonality for *LA* (low-conflict) than for *HA* (high-conflict) subjects. These findings can be reconciled only if we assume that Wolff's *MA* subjects are equivalent to Worell's low-conflict subjects.

*Whether the experimentally induced increase in m was due to *stress*, or, more simply, was the result of the experimenter's admonishment to "do better" (of which the most reasonable interpretation, given the situation, would be to "produce more responses") is questionable.

†It is possible to think of the difference between giving an oral response and a written response to a WAT as a difference in the amount of stress placed on the subject. However, the characteristic finding of *increased* response commonality in the oral response condition suggests that this stress is of a different type, and might be referred to more appropriately as social pressure.

‡As was also found by Nakamura and Wright (1965).

As another example, both experimental and subject anxiety have been found to interact with stimulus emotionality in determining reaction time. For both types of anxiety, reaction time to emotional, but not to neutral stimuli is increased more for *HA* than for *LA* subjects. However, whereas reaction time to neutral stimuli is decreased by experimentally induced anxiety, it is unrelated to level of subject anxiety.

These findings may also be considered to demonstrate the cumulative effects of anxiety with those of the affective quality of the stimulus. That is, both subject anxiety (insignificantly) and stimulus emotionality (significantly) function independently to increase reaction time, and when combined in the same situation their effects are additive, with the result that reaction time is increased even further. However, the effects of subject anxiety and stimulus emotionality do not always cumulate in the manner which might be expected—i.e., emotionality and high anxiety do not always line up against neutrality and low anxiety. For example, in R. C. Johnson and Lim's study (1964), the ratio of response availability *m*, for "good" as opposed to "bad" stimuli was greater for *HA* than for *LA* subjects. As independent variables there is some evidence that *HA* subjects give more *m* responses than *LA* subjects; on the other hand, "good" and/or neutral stimuli elicit more *m* responses than "bad" and/or emotional stimuli. Since in the Johnson-Lim study the total *m* was unrelated to anxiety level, the interaction effect means that anxiety further increased responses, *m*, to "good" stimuli and decreased responses to "bad". Thus, rather than anxiety adding to the effect of its congruent stimulus value (emotionality)* to increase the number of responses, *m*, to emotional stimuli, anxiety combined instead with the noncongruent value, by increasing the number of responses to neutral stimuli.

In conclusion, these studies indicate that the effects of anxiety—whether naturally occurring or experimentally induced—depend both on the stimulus situation and on which aspect of the response is being considered. In some cases, the two sources of anxiety will produce the same effect, and in some cases, the results are quite different. It was also suggested that it may be possible to resolve apparent contradictions by realigning the points of equivalent anxiety on the measurement scales used. Nevertheless, it seems unlikely that externally provoked, experimental anxiety, could be expected to produce effects identical to those produced by subject anxiety which has continued over a long period of time. While in some respects the effects may overlap, chronic subject anxiety in all probability requires the individual to develop some more extensive methods for coping. It is reasonable to expect that these methods might involve the modification

---

* As was true in the case of reaction time considered above.

and/or reorganization of previous habits or patterns of thought, which in turn would be reflected in word-association behavior.

As an illustration of how subject anxiety may alter associative processes to produce response effects which are counter to what might be reasonably predicted, let us reconsider the relationship between subject anxiety, stimulus emotionality, and response availability, m. In at least one study, it has been demonstrated that subject anxiety increases m, while several studies have indicated that stimulus emotionality decreases m. It would be expected, then, that the relative number of responses to emotional stimuli could be increased by using anxious subjects. In fact, the opposite effect was found; subject anxiety decreased the number of responses to emotional stimuli. This is an unexpected finding, unless we consider certain implications of being a chronically anxious individual.

First of all, it has been suggested in Chapter 1 that the decreased response availability to emotional stimuli can be understood as a result of the occurrence of implicit avoidance responses, which in turn requires the adoption of a new strategy to find an acceptable response. From this point of view, it is possible to understand why anxiety further restricts the number of responses available to emotional stimuli. That is, it is reasonable to assume that the highly anxious individual has developed an even greater number of avoidance responses to potentially disturbing stimuli, in an attempt to control his anxiety. Over a period of time, he has learned to manage his anxiety by avoiding those situations which would be likely to increase his discomfort.

It is further suggested that there are different methods learned to avoid the arousal of anxiety-producing ideas. On the one hand, associative connections may be restricted to a few neutral ideas, functionally eliminating other associative pathways. This kind of avoidance is seen in the defense mechanisms of repression and, in a more extreme form, denial. On the other hand, the avoidance of anxiety-producing ideas by attempting to find alternative, less anxiety-provoking, acceptable, responses is seen in the defense mechanisms of rationalization and intellectualization. This distinction leads to different predictions about the associative behavior of (anxious) individuals who utilize one or the other of the defensive maneuvers.*

In the former case, we would expect to find increased reaction time, blocking, and inability to give any response. In the latter case (using defenses of rationalization and intellectualization), we might or might not find a decreased number of responses available, depending on the

---

*Typically, it is the individual with a hysterical character who utilizes associative constriction as a defense, and it is the obsessive-compulsive character who substitutes neutral (i.e., nonemotional) ideas for affective associations.

success with which the individual had been able to find substitute associations, which in turn probably depends on the length of time over which this defense had been utilized. However, we would expect to find an increased reaction time, as long as we can assume that the implicit responses to be avoided are still being aroused by the stimulus.

There is, however, one type of defense mechanism based on associative constriction which should not produce associative blocking, at least for certain stimuli. Reaction formation is a defense mechanism which depends on the individual's ability to respond in the opposite way to which he feels. Hence, for those subjects who utilize this defense, if the emotional stimulus word has a contrast response available, they should give as rapid responses as those obtained from "normal" subjects. However, measures of response availability would be expected to reveal associative constriction after this first contrast response is emitted.

The approach outlined above suggests, then, that subject anxiety should not be expected to produce any single effect, or set of effects, on associative responses. Rather, it is suggested that the continuing existence of this type of internal stress will result in the development of different methods for coping, and that each of these will have different effects on associative behavior. Experimentally produced stress, on the other hand, would not be expected to *produce* such coping mechanisms. However, if they already exist, stress which is experimentally caused may call them into play. Again, no single effect on associative behavior could then be expected. If we consider, in addition, the capacity postulated for certain stimuli to elicit implicit avoidance responses, thereby requiring some change in response strategy, it becomes apparent that the relationships among subject anxiety, experimental stress, and stimulus variables will be quite complex—as the studies reviewed in this chapter have demonstrated.

PART II

SUBJECT VARIABLES

Chapter 6

DEMOGRAPHIC VARIABLES

Age

In this section, the associative-response effects of age, sex, educational level, and socioeconomic status will be considered. Age has been the most widely investigated demographic variable, with studies focusing on the strength, variability, and nature of associative responses of subjects varying from nursery school level to old age.

Studies of the associative strength of Primary responses have been carried out with subjects spanning a wide age range. Palermo (1964, 1965) studied the (oral) responses of 50 girls and 50 boys in each of Grades 1 through 4; 100 stimuli, drawn partly from the Kent-Rosanoff list and partly to represent other grammatical classes, were used. The data indicated an increase in Primary response strength over this age range. Palermo (1963) has also made a large-scale study of the (written) responses of 250 girls and 250 boys from Grades 4 through 8, Grade 10, and Grade 12, and of 500 female and 500 male college students; the stimuli were the 100 Kent-Rosanoff words plus 100 additional familiar (Thorndike-Lorge *A* and *AA*) words, chosen to represent other grammatical categories. Again, he found the frequency of the Primary response to increase with age. S. S. Shapiro (1964b) investigated the (written) responses of 100 girls and 100 boys from Grades 4, 6, and 8; the stimuli were 65 CVC trigrams (52 of which were real words). In this study, however, the three age groups were approximately equal in strength of Primary responses. Dörken (1956) studied the (oral) responses of subjects from nine age groups (ranging in age from 10 to 79 years) to 10 neutral stimuli which had high-strength Primary responses; the stimuli were chosen from the Verdun Association Test. The data indicated a progressive increase in Primary response strength until age 39; after this point, Primary response frequency began to decline. The author suggests that this reflects an increasing conservatism and involvement in the affairs of society, until the end of the thirties. This process is seen as being followed by a gradual withdrawal from certain activities, which is accompanied by a decline in the commonness of associative response. While this may partially explain the observed inverted U function, most likely there are other important subject variables which differed across the several age groups. The responses of older subjects also have been studied by Tresselt and Mayzner (1964a) who noted a significant decrease in Primary response strength across age groups 18–33, 34–39, and 50–87—a finding which roughly parallels that of Dörken, although again the possible effects of other subject variables are left uncontrolled.

Contradictory findings were obtained by Riegel and Birren (1965), who contrasted an 18–33-year-old group with a 60–80-year-old group. In this study of oral responses to Kent-Rosanoff stimuli, there was no difference in the overall mean Primary response strength between the two groups. However, for the older group only, Primary response strength decreased with the serial position of the stimulus. The explanation of the discrepancy in these findings is not clear, but it may be partially due to the fact that these subjects were matched for scores on the WAIS Vocabulary subtest, and were roughly equivalent in educational level mean of 14.0 years for the younger and 13.2 years for the older subjects).

In another study of the effects of age on associative responses, DiVesta (1964a) administered a controlled association test to 100 children from each of Grades 2 through 6. The subjects were restricted to responses which would modify the noun provided in a sentence frame (e.g., The car is _____; The _____ car). The data indicated that the frequency of the most common response (i.e., the Primary) increased over the five grades. Interestingly enough, however, the number of different lower associative-strength responses also increased with age, suggesting that a child's verbal associations become both more stereotyped and more diversified with increasing age.* Other evidence for this finding that an increase in Primary response strength is not paralleled by an increase in consistency of responses lower in the hierarchy comes from the studies of Palermo (1963, 1964, 1965). As mentioned above, the frequency of the Primary response increased from Grade 1 through college; the Secondary response frequency also showed this increase. However, with the exception of the third and fourth ranking responses in Grades 1 through 4, responses lower in the hierarchy did not show an increase in strength with age.

Studies of the relationship of age and response heterogeneity, D, have

---

*Although not discussed by the author, there is a difficulty in drawing the conclusion that the number of different responses of low association strength increases as a function of age, since the older subjects in DiVesta's study (1964b) were given a written association test while the younger subjects had an oral test, and Palermo (1964) has found a written test to increase the number of infrequent responses obtained.

also found this increasing diversity of associative responses. In the DiVesta study (1964a) noted above, D increased from Grade 2 through 6. Albright and Albright (1951) studied the 30-second continuous associations of nursery-school and kindergarten children to pictorial stimuli, and found that the proportion of heterogeneous responses (number of different responses, m, as well as the number of idiosyncratic and unique responses) was greater for kindergarten than for nursery-school subjects. Tresselt and Mayzner (1964a), comparing younger adults (18–21 years) with older adults (55–87 years), found a greater number of heterogeneous responses among the older subjects. Riegel and Birren (1965) also found greater response heterogeneity among the older subjects (60–80 as against 18–33 years), and this was noted to increase even more as a function of the serial position of the stimulus. However, Palermo's findings (1963) that D decreases for each stimulus word for subjects representing Grades 4 through 8, Grade 10, Grade 12, and college level suggests that there is not steady increase in response heterogeneity with age. Rather, it appears that response heterogeneity increases until fourth or fifth grade,* and then begins to decrease—a decrease which continues into college, increasing again in later years. The findings of Davidson and Longo (1960) for the number of idiosyncratic responses over three successive trials to lexical and pictorial stimuli were consistent with this hypothesis. Ten-year-olds gave more idiosyncratic responses than did junior-high-school subjects; however, by college age, the number of idiosyncratic responses had begun to increase again.†

There is also some evidence to suggest that response availability follows a similar developmental trend. In a test of oral, 30-second continued associations to pictorial stimuli, there were no differences in the number of responses, m, given by nursery-school and kindergarten children, although there was greater variability (larger standard deviation) in the number of responses obtained from the older group (Albright & Albright, 1951). However, by the time the child reaches elementary-school age, differences in response availability do appear. Thus S. S. Shapiro (1964b), in a study of 100 boys and 100 girls at each of three grade levels, noted that the number of responses, m, to CVC words significantly increased from Grades 4 to 6 to 8.

Two additional studies suggest that there may be a reversal in this trend of increasing response availability with age, as was found with strength of Primary response and response heterogeneity. Birren, Riegel, and Robbin (1961) compared a group of young adults (18–33 years) with a group of older adults (60–80 years) for the number of continuous-association

---

*Although DiVesta (1964a) found D to increase through Grade 6, it must be recalled. that his sixth-grade (and half of his fifth-grade) subjects took a *written* WAT.
†Cf. also Becher (1960, p. 154) for change during college years.

responses elicited in a 2-minute interval.* The results indicated that the younger subjects gave significantly more m responses. Further analysis of the data, in terms of time required to produce each response, indicated that the differences could not be attributed to speaking time per se; that is, it took the older subjects an average of 2.33 seconds per word to produce 30 associative responses,† while other studies have shown that the normal speaking rate for this age group is about 0.4 seconds per word. The slowness and paucity of continuous responses given by the older subjects, then, seemed to be due to a lessening of available associative responses, rather than to differences in rate of emitted speech. One other source of indirect evidence for the hypothesis that response availability decreases after young adulthood comes from Rocklyn, Hessert and Braun (1957), who obtained 60-second continued associations to 24 of Noble's stimuli. When product-moment correlations were computed between Noble's m values (Noble, 1952) and those of the Rocklyn et al. study, there was a slight decline with age; for younger adults (20–29 years), $r = .96$; for middle-aged subjects (30–49 years), $r = .94$; for older adults (50–66 years), $r = .92$. Although the correlation continued to be quite high, the decrease in the value of the coefficient with age was due to a decrease in the average m value in the older groups.

As suggested above, it appears that there are age trends in the development of different aspects of the associative-response process. Several studies have considered associative-response change as a developmental process, and have attempted to determine whether a continuous or step-wise function would better describe this process. Thus Palermo (1963), in comparing subjects from Grades 4 through 8, 10, 12, and college, noted considerable overlap in the rank order of identical associative responses from one grade to the next. However, despite this between-grade continuity, the responses of the fourth-graders were considerably different from those of the college students. S. S. Shapiro (1964b) also noted this similarity in response across Grades 4, 6, and 8. About half of the subjects of each group gave the same Primary response; where the Primaries differed, the Primary response of one subject group often occurred as the Secondary or Tertiary response of the other group. Tresselt and Mayzner (1964a) have also pointed out that, despite the decrease in frequency of Primary response in their older-subject group (55–87 years), 72% of the Primary responses for the older and younger (18–21 years) subjects were "essentially the same" (p. 65).

---

*These are the same subjects as those used in the Riegel and Birren study (1965) reported above.
†The younger subjects took an average of 1.67 seconds per word.

An extensive attempt to describe the nature of the process involved in the development of associative responses has been carried out by DiVesta (1964b). One hundred children from each of Grades 2 through 6 were given a controlled-association test in which their responses were restricted to modifiers of nouns presented in sentence frames; response distributions were constructed as for the usual WAT. From these data, it was possible to determine the frequency of occurrence of each modifier, the number different nouns to which modifier was applied, and a partial entropy value, H, based on the first two measures. In addition to these values describing the use of modifier, similar information was obtained for each noun: the frequency of each modifier response to each noun, the number of different responses to each noun, and a partial entropy value, H. Then, using the 100 modifiers which had the highest H values for sixth-grade subjects as a standard, the H values for each of these modifiers in each of Grades 2 to 6 was correlated with that modifier's value in each other grade. Under the assumption that changes over time in H values indicate changes in the meaning of the stimuli, the matrix of intercorrelations obtained in the above fashion then reflects the degree of change from year to year. The results indicated that for nouns (concepts), the changes over time are moderate from year to year. However, over longer periods of time, the changes in H are greater for nouns than they are for adjectives, which have higher correlations between the H values of disjunctive age levels. This finding is interpreted as indicating that for subjects of this age group, changes in the meaning of concepts (nouns) is greater than changes in the modes of modifying. The author suggests that if frequency of experience with a word is important in determining its meaning, then for nouns this experience occurs during school years, while for adjectives this change in meaning is based largely on experiences of preschool years. Furthermore, the finding that the matrix best ordering the intercorrelations conformed to a simplex model suggested to the author that the learning of these associative-response habits "is a continuous and incremental process rather then a process occurring in discrete, independent stages." (p. 508).

Studies of associative reaction time like those of response heterogeneity, also suggest a U-shaped developmental trend. Davidson and Longo (1960) found that 10-year-old subjects had a longer reaction time than junior-high-school subjects, who in turn took longer than college subjects. On the other hand, a comparison of 60-to-80-year-old adults with 18-to-33-year-old adults showed a reversal in this trend (Riegel & Birren, 1965). In this study, the older subjects had longer associative reaction times than the younger adults, and this difference was shown not to depend on slower speech in the older subjects (see p. 144). Finally, as has been pointed out in the section on emotional stimuli (Ch. 1, pp. 49–50), Powell's data (1955), which used reaction time difference scores as a measure of conflict, can be interpreted as presenting meaningful developmental trends in the rise and fall of different areas of psychosocial concern.

In addition to these studies specifying the quantitative characteristics of associative-response distributions at different stages of development, studies adopting an alternative approach have focused on the occurrence of associative responses from different grammatical form classes, semantic categories, degrees of familiarity, and levels of evaluative meaning.

The largest number of studies representing this approach to the study of the development of associative responses has been concerned with the grammatical form class of the associative response in relation to the form class of the stimulus. For example, Albright and Albright (1951) noted that the grammatically most frequent associative responses to pictorial stimuli among nursery-school and kindergarten children were nouns and noun plurals. The younger subjects gave slightly more noun responses, while the kindergarten subjects gave significantly more verbal nouns and compound plural responses. R. W. Brown and Berko (1960), studying associative responses to stimuli from six grammatical classes, noted that the tendency to respond with words from the same grammatical class as that of the stimulus (paradigmatic response) increased over first, second, and third grades, with adults making the largest number of paradigmatic responses; at the same time, the number of responses from different form classes decreased. The authors explain this increase in grammatically homogeneous responses as a function of the subject's increased experience with words occupying a particular part-of-speech position in sentences. Ervin (1961) also noted this increase in paradigmatic responses over Grades 1, 2, 3, and 6. In addition, she noted that this increase occurred earlier for words which frequently appear in the final position of a sentence, as opposed to those which often occupy a medial position. She suggests that the gradual decline of syntagmatic associations is due to the fact that initially, in young children, there is not much variation in the words which customarily follow one another; hence, fairly strong sequential associations are established. However, with increasing age, the length and variety of sentences which follow any particular word is greatly increased, with the result that the associative strength of any particular sequence is markedly decreased.

Entwisle, Forsyth, and Muuss (1964) also found syntagmatic responses to decrease over the period from 5 to 11 years, while paradigmatic responses increased. Furthermore, the decrease in syntagmatic responses was noted to occur first for nouns, then for adjectives, and then for verbs. On the other hand, the increase in paradigmatic responses is largest and most rapid for adjectives; the apparently smaller increase in paradigmatic responses to nouns is due to the fact that "primitive noun responses"* drop out with increasing age. Palermo (1963, 1965) also noted an increase with age in the percentage of paradigmatic responses among the first five associative responses. The earlier increase in paradigmatic responses to adjectives was also evident in this study, in that stimuli from all grammatical classes except adjectives elicited more paradigmatic responses from Grade 12 than from Grade 4 subjects; for adjectives, the younger subjects gave as many paradigmatic responses as did the older group. A downward extension of this study to include children in Grades 1 through 4 (Palermo, 1965) indicated the same increase in paradigmatic responses with age, except that paradigmatic responses to adjective stimuli reached a peak by Grade 2.

On the basis of their data (predominantly from individual-oral tests), Entwisle *et al.* (1964) have described the developmental course of associative responses as follows: in addition to the occurrence of "primitive noun responses,"* they noted that children aged 4 to 5 also give many multiword and many clang responses.† During the next year, the percentage of noun responses begins to decline, and paradigmatic responses to adjectives, and possibly to verbs, begin to increase. From 6 to 8 years, the percentage of noun responses sharply decreased. At the same time, the number of paradigmatic responses increased markedly such that by 8 years the number of paradigmatic responses to adjectives appeared to have reached an asymptote; syntagmatic responses, at a maximum during the first part of this age period, drop sharply during the latter part.‡

From 8 to 10 years, verbs show a marked increase in paradigmatic responses, while syntagmatic responses have declined to adult levels. The authors further suggest that there is some evidence that the pattern of associative responses may be more stereotyped at age 10 than it is for adults.

Regarding this issue of the developmental change in the ratio of paradigmatic and syntagmatic responses, Deese (1962a) has noted that since adults show the greatest number of paradigmatic responses to nouns

---

*"Primitive noun responses" refers to the fact that kindergarten subjects give many noun responses, regardless of the form class of the stimulus, presumably reflecting the fact that nouns are the first words learned, have a concrete referent, etc.

†Ervin (1961) also noted the occurrence of clang responses in kindergarten subjects, and found these to decrease over Grades 1, 3, and 6.

‡Kagan *et al.* (1964) also have found a continuous increase in the number of "coordinate" (paradigmatic) responses to noun, verb, and adjective stimuli over Grades 1 through 4, and have additionally noted that the largest increase in paradigmatic responses occurs between Grades 1 and 2 (ages 6 to 7).

and high-frequency adjectives, while data from young children shows a predominance of syntagmatic responses to these stimuli, this suggests that the lexical structure of nouns and familiar adjectives (as opposed to their sequential structure) must be acquired slowly and is dependent on experience with the language.*

Several studies have been concerned with the developmental trend in the occurrence of contrast and supraordinate responses. The number of contrast responses has been found to increase over Grades 1 through 4 (Kagan *et al.*, 1964; Palermo, 1964, 1965) and over Grades 4 through college (Palermo, 1963). Supraordinate responses also were noted to increase from Grade 1 through 4, although they occured less frequently than contrast responses at all age levels (Palermo, 1964). This increase in supraordinate responses was found to continue until Grade 6, after which the frequency of this type of response decreased. However, children in Grade 4 have been noted to give more supraordinate responses than college students (Palermo & Jenkins, 1962).† Some variability in the peak of supraordinate responding was noted, depending on the familiarity of the stimulus; thus stimuli of low Thorndike-Lorge frequency reached a peak later (Grade 7 or 8) than did those of higher familiarity. On the other hand, Peters (1952) found that when stimuli are selected on the basis of ease in eliciting supra- or subordinate responses, and when adult subjects are instructed to respond with either a supra- or subordinate response, then there is a tendency for the number of supraordinate responses to increase with age; subjects under 28 years gave fewer such responses than did subjects 28 to 38 years old, who in turn gave fewer than subjects over 38 years.

The developmental trends of several other associative-response variables have been investigated in isolated studies. Albright and Albright (1951), combining their nursery-school and kindergarten subjects, found that 67% of the continuous-associative responses obtained were among the 500 most common Thorndike-Lorge words, 24% were among the second 500, and the remaining 9% were among the second 1,000 most common words. In this same study, it was found that nursery-school subjects made more naming responses (repeating the names of the stimuli in the pictures) than did kindergarten subjects; for the younger group, the two most frequent responses to each of the 10 stimuli were naming responses, while for the older subjects only 6 of the 20 most common responses were picture naming. Pollio (1964a) determined the extent of the relationship between the S. D. rating of a stimulus and its Primary response for children

---

*Cf. also DiVesta (1964b), reported on p. 145.

†Flavell *et al.* (1958) found 35-year-old males to give more supraordinate responses than 20-year-old male and female college students, but the two groups differed on two critical variables: educational background and sex (see p. 155).

(based on Woodrow and Lowell's 1916 data for children aged 9 to 12 years) and for college students (based on Russell and Jenkins' 1954 normative data). For children, the correlations between stimuli and Primary responses were .64, .69, and .44, for the Evaluative, Potency, and Activity scales, respectively;* for adults, the corresponding correlations were .52, .26, and .36. The differences between children and college subjects on the Evaluative and the Potency stimulus-response correlations were significant; the author points out that the lower correlations for the older subjects is due to the large number of *contrast* Primary responses in this group. He concludes that the mediating link between a stimulus and its associative response is based, in part, on similarities in connotative meaning, and that this type of mediation is more important in determining word associates for children than for adults.

Milgram and Goodglass (1961) have studied the effect of instructions on children in Grades 2 through 8. Using two forms of a multiple-choice WAT with an abstract and a concrete response alternative, one group of children was instructed to respond as "young children" would, and then to respond as "adults" would. A second group gave spontaneous, uninstructed—i.e., "self—responses. For Grades 2 and 3, neither "young children" nor "adult" instructions modified the number of abstract responses obtained; however, from Grade 4 and up, "adult" instructions resulted in significantly more abstract response choices than "child" instructions, with the spontaneous responses of uninstructed subjects falling in between. This effect was shown to be independent of word familiarity, since the same pattern was obtained for the most and least familiar stimuli.

However, the nature of this relationship may also change with age. Herr (1957), in a study of 800 male and 800 female adults instructed to give the response that "most people" would give, noted response commonality to be negatively correlated with age ($p < .01$);†

Summary

The following is a summary of the associative response effects of age. There will be a discussion of this, as well as other demographic variables, at the end of the chapter.

(1) Primary responses
    (A) increase in frequency from age 5 to the mid-30s, and then decrease;

---

*These results might be questioned in light of the marked changes in children's responses since 1916.

†The measure of response commonality was based on standard scores developed for each response distribution. This relationship held only for normal, but not for schizophrenic, subjects.

(B) a possible exception to this occurs for highly familiar, simple words (CVCs), which do not discriminate among grade-school children of different ages.

(2) Response heterogeneity, D, increases from nursery-school age to age 10, then decreases until college, then increases.

(3) Response availability, m, begins to increase at kindergarten level, increases to Grade 8 and perhaps beyond, then decreases from college to older adulthood.

(4) Reaction time decreases from age 10 to college, then increases to older adulthood.

(5) Examination of the words which constitute the associative response hierarchy shows
   (A) considerable response overlap from year to year, and
   (B) that changes are continuous and incremental rather than occurring in discrete, independent stages;
   (C) during school years, changes are greater for nouns than for adjectives; the meaning of adjectives appears to be fixed earlier.

(6) Studies of the grammatical form class of associative responses indicate that
   (A) primitive noun responses decrease from nursery school age on,
   (B) syntagmatic responses decrease from age 5 to college, and
   (C) paradigmatic responses increase from age 5 to college.
      (a) This increase occurs earliest (5–6 years) for adjectives, reaching an asymptote by age 8;
      (b) an increase for verbs occurs most markedly between 8 and 10 years;
      (c) a relatively small increase for nouns is due to the fact that noun responses are already very frequent at age 5.

(7) Supraordinate responses
   (A) increase for Grades 1 through 6, and then decrease;
   (B) for stimuli of low Thorndike-Lorge frequency, the increase continues to Grades 7 or 8.
   (C) are given more often in Grade 4 than by adults.

(8) Contrast responses increase from Grade 1 through college.

(9) Studies of the conceptual "distance" between the stimulus and its response (the extent to which the response is stimulus-bound) have found that
   (A) naming responses (to visual stimuli) are greater in nursery-school-age than in kindergarten children;
   (B) clang responses decrease from kindergarten on;
   (C) the similarity between the stimulus and response in S. D.

ratings is greater for children (1916)* than for adults (1954), on both the Semantic Differential Evaluative and Potency dimensions; children depend more on connotation, less on word-word habits.
(10) The effect of instructions
    (A) to give "adult" and "child" responses is nil until Grade 4;
    (B) to give the responses "most people" would give, is negatively related to age, in an adult sample;
    (C) to give supra- or subordinate responses results in an increase in supraordinate responses with age, in an adult sample.

Sex

A second demographic variable to be considered in this section is that of sex. Other measures of verbal behavior characteristically find differences between male and female subjects, and to the extent that the WAT shares in the general realm of verbal abilities, it is not unreasonable to expect sex differences to affect associative responses. As in the preceding section, we will consider the effects of this variable on the strength, variability, and nature of associative responses.

The extensive word-association studies by Palermo and Jenkins have indicated that, at all age levels from Grade 1 through college, females give a greater number of Primary responses than do males (Palermo, 1963, 1964; Palermo & Jenkins, 1965a). They also found that college females gave different words as Primary responses to 16% of the stimuli (100 Kent-Rosanoff, plus 100 additional words). It should be noted that the greater number of Primary responses among females was not due to the effects of particular stimulus words; when the frequencies of Primary responses for males and females were compared over all stimuli, the significant correlation obtained ($r = .97$) indicated that the relative strength of Primary responses to different stimuli was the same for the two groups, despite the overall greater frequency for females. In addition, it was found that college males give as many paradigmatic Primary responses as do college females.

S. S. Shapiro (1964b) found that, for boys and girls from Grades 4, 6, and 8, about 50% of the Primary responses were the same across sex groups. Tresselt, Leeds, and Mayzner (1955) also studied differences between young-adult males and females in responding to the Kent-Rosanoff stimuli and found that only 5% of the Primary responses differed for the two groups, and that, overall, the number of Primary responses among females was

*See footnote, p. 149.

greater than among males. These authors also noted their impression that the choice of response words lower in the associative hierarchy showed greater male-female differences than those found in the choice of Primary responses.

Other studies of response commonality lend some support to the hypothesis that the findings for males versus females on responses lower in the associative hierarchy may not parallel those for Primary responses. Thus Palermo (1963) and Palermo and Jenkins (1965a) found that a significantly greater percentage of females give the first three responses in the associative hierarchy, and that this trend continues until the fifth response; for responses lower in the hierarchy, females do not differ from males in response frequency. Possibly this finding helps explain the results of the Grooms and Osipow (1963) study,* which used compound stimuli consisting of a Kent-Rosanoff stimulus and its Primary response as word-association stimuli. They found that the associative responses of males and females to these compounds did not differ in commonality, nor in the extent to which their response hierarchies paralleled those given to the individual stimuli (Russell & Jenkins, 1954); this finding, however, may be due to the fact that the responses elicited were generally of low strength.

Interestingly enough, although stimulus-response strength, as measured by frequency of Primary response, has been found to differentiate between males and females, reaction time—which presumably also measures stimulus-response strength—has not been found to differentiate between the two groups. For example, Wallenhorst (1965) compared the responses of male and female college subjects to 100 (predominantly neutral) stimuli and found no difference in reaction time. Powell (1955), studying subjects aged 10 to 30, and Doris *et al.* (1963), studying third-grade subjects, obtained the same results with neutral stimuli. However, in the latter study, the difference between the sexes in reaction time to emotional stimuli approached significance at the .05 level (direction of difference not given), and in the Powell study, a longer reaction time to emotional stimuli was obtained at an earlier age for female than for male subjects.

Studies of the number of different responses given by males and females have found greater response heterogeneity, D, among males, at all ages from first grade through college (Palermo, 1963; Palermo & Jenkins, 1965a). However, there is some evidence that the availability of responses to females may be greater than that to males. Archer (1960), asking subjects if CVCs did, or did not, elicit an association, found that females were more inclined to report an association than were males. Matthews

---

*See Part I, Chapter 2, pp. 87–88.

(1965), using a written continued-association task, found college-aged females to give consistently more *m* responses than males. This difference was less after 2 minutes than after 1, suggesting to the author that differential writing speed should be considered in interpreting the results. On the other hand, S. S. Shapiro (1964b), studying children (Grades 4, 6, and 8), used a modified continued-association task, and found no sex differences in the number of responses, *m*, obtained. It is possible that this lack of difference was due to the method of restricting the subjects to five responses. However, the author has indicated that most of the subjects made no more than three responses—that is, did not reach the possible limit.

Several studies of the nature, or type of responses given by male and female subjects have been conducted. For example, males have been found to give more supraordinate responses than females, both for Grades 1 through 12 (Palermo & Jenkins, 1963) and in college (Palermo & Jenkins, 1965a). This stylistic difference was also noted by Peters (1952) with adult subjects given instructions to respond with a supra- or sub-ordinate response. On the other hand, females have been found to give more contrast, or opposite, responses than males over the entire age range from Grade 1 through college (Palermo, 1963). If we consider the giving of supraordinate responses by adults to be less well-adjusted* or less mature,† and a contrast response to be developmentally more mature, then the findings of males giving more supraordinate and fewer contrast responses at each age level is consistent with other findings regarding the relative verbal abilities of male and female subjects—that is, that females tend to be more advanced than males. However, when Flavell *et al.* (1958) classified the associations of subjects into 16 categories, presumably representing mature and immature responses, no differences between male and female subjects were obtained. Finally, Freedman (1965) has found that males and females are equally successful in giving the correct associative response to the RAT, either with or without prior associative facilitation.

Summary

The following is a summary of the associative-response effects of sex. There will be a discussion of this, as well as of other demographic variables, at the end of the chapter.

(1) Primary response strength is greater in females than in males.
(2) Response commonality is greater in females than in males.

*As suggested by Peters (1952).
†As found by Palermo (1964).

(3) The frequency of responses of rank 5 and lower in the associative hierarchy is not different for females and males.
(4) The reaction time of females and males
  (A) does not differ for neutral words;
  (B) for emotional words, females may have longer latencies than males.
(5) Response heterogeneity, D, is greater for males than for females.
(6) Response availability, m
  (A) is greater for female than for male adults;
  (B) is the same for female and male children.
(7) Paradigmatic Primary responses are given as often by male as by female college students.
(8) Supraordinate responses are given more often by males than by females.
(9) Contrast responses are given more often by females than by males.
(10) RAT problems are solved as often by females as by males.

Educational Level and Socioeconomic Status

Only a very few studies have been concerned with the influence of these variables on associative responses. Becher (1960), for example, found greater response commonality among female college freshman than among college seniors, or than among the same freshman girls tested 4 years later. However, with instructions to give the response "most people" would give, Herr (1957), testing 1600 adults, found a low, but significant ($p < .01$) positive correlation with educational level. Entwisle and Forsyth (1963) noted that method of test administration affected the degree of response commonality obtained for children from higher socioeconomic-status homes, but not for lower-status children. For the former subjects, the individual-oral method, as opposed to group-written, increased response commonality.

In Becher's (1960) study, it also was noted that female college seniors have more idiosyncratic responses than freshman girls or than themselves tested four years earlier. Deering (1963), on the other hand, contrasted females who had completed high-school with those who had some college, and found no differences in the number of idiosyncratic responses to both affective and neutral stimuli. However, Deering's samples differed in that the high-school subjects were older than the college subjects (27.2 versus 25.2 years), whereas Becher's seniors were 4 years older than the freshman. Also, Deering's college females appear to have been brighter than the high-school subjects, as suggested by the fact that the latter made more response reproduction errors and more errors on a test of stimulus recognition.

In another study of response disturbances, Flavell *et al.* (1958) found that college students, as opposed to hospital aides with a tenth-grade average educational level, made more completion and perseverative (relevant and irrelevant) responses, while the aides showed more blocking and made more supraordinate responses. On the other hand, Peters (1958), using the multiple-choice format of his supraordinate test, found Ph. D. psychologists ($N = 7$) to give more supraordinate responses than advanced college students, who in turn gave more than college sophomores. It is possible, however, that this reversal from Flavell's findings is a result of the test format, since the maladjustment findings of the previous investigation (Peters, 1952) were also reversed in this study. Also, in both Flavell's and Peters' studies, educational level was confounded with age; in both cases, the subject groups giving the largest number of supraordinate responses were also considerably older.

Finally, a comparison of the Air Force sample tested by Noble (1952) and the college sample tested by Noble and Parker (1960) suggests that response availability, m, is positively related to educational level.

Summary

The following is a summary of the associative response effects of educational level and socioeconomic status. A discussion of this, as well as of the other demographic variables, follows.

(1) Response commonality
  (A) is greater for college freshman than for college seniors;*
  (B) is greater for high-socioeconomic-status children than for low-status children, when tested using the individual-oral method;
  (C) is positively correlated with educational level, under instructions to give the response "most people" would.

(2) Idiosyncratic responses have been found to occur with equal frequency in subjects of a college- and of a high-school-level* population.

(3) The findings regarding supraordinate responses are confounded with age differences.

(4) The findings regarding response disturbances are also confounded with age differences.

*Starred items: These findings are likely due to the greater age of the latter group.

Discussion

In discussing the effects of age on associative responses, it is being assumed that the subject groups representing different age levels are comparable in other respects, and that the differences in associative responses reflect changes related to changes in age. This is, of course, a questionable assumption. Obviously, the 60-year-old subjects studied, in addition to being a number of years older than the college-aged subjects, also grew up in a considerably different cultural milieu, where mass communication media—believed to account for the increase in response stereotypy today*—did not exist as they do for today's students. If one wishes to study the effects of age—or more exactly, aging—on associative responses, then the appropriate contrast group for today's 60-year-olds might better be those college subjects tested in the 1920s—e.g., the data presented in Schellenberg's 1927 norms.

To a lesser extent, this consideration also applies to comparing 5-year-olds with 20-year-olds. Nevertheless, we will assume that there are a variety of influences on associative responses which are most parsimoniously grouped under the general classification of aging, and that consistent trends in the development of associative responses are functions of increasing age rather than of particular experiences unique to one age group.

With this in mind, let us consider first the growth and development of the associative-response hierarchy. From age 4 on,† the strength of the Primary response increases as does both the availability and heterogeneity of responses. At about age 10, response heterogeneity begins to decrease, while Primary strength and response availability continue to increase. These trends, as well as decreasing reaction time, appear to continue from age 10 until college. During college, response heterogeneity and reaction time again begin to increase—a trend which continues into late adulthood. At the same time, response availability is decreasing. Only Primary response strength continues to increase, and this trend persists until the mid-thirties, when the decline which persists until old age begins.

It also appears that the associative meaning of adjectives becomes stereotyped at an earlier age (possibly at the preschool level) than does that of nouns. In addition to the age-related changes in response entropy on which this statement is based (DiVesta, 1964b), it is also supported by the findings of studies on the *type* of responses given at different age levels. In general, syntagmatic responses decrease from age 5 to college, while paradigmatic responses increase. However, for adjectives, this increase has reached a maximum (equal to adult level) by age 8. For verbs,

---
*See pp. 218–19 for discussion of this issue.
†The youngest age yet studied.

the marked increase does not occur until a few years later; for nouns, the eventual increase in paradigmatic responses is difficult to detect due to the initially high level of noun responses in very young children; it can only be inferred by the drop-out of these primitive noun responses (noun responses given indiscriminantly to all stimuli).*

It has also been noted that there is a gradual change in the type of semantic relationship which exists between the stimulus and the response. Among very young children, associative responses are frequently stimulus-bound; that is, these children repeat or echo parts of the stimulus. At about age 6, responses begin to show more evidence of being cognitively mediated, with an increasing number of supraordinate and contrast responses occurring. In early adolescence, supraordinate responses begin to decline, while contrast responses continue to increase to college age. Since the correspondence between the S. D. ratings for stimulus-response pairs has been noted to be greater for children than for adults, it has been suggested (Pollio, 1964a) that children's associations depend more on the connotation of the stimulus word, while adults' associations reflect highly overlearned word-word habits.† If this is so, the chronological development of associative responses might be described as a movement away from responding to the physical properties of the stimulus toward a cognitively mediated associative process, and finally to responding in a reflex-like, "unthinking" fashion, where the cognitive link is short-circuited.

The relationship between sex and associative responses appears relatively clear-cut. At every age, responses from female subjects may be characterized as being more stereotyped than those of male subjects. It has been suggested that the occurrence of stronger Primaries, greater response commonality, greater number of contrast and fewer supraordinate responses in females is indicative of their greater verbal ability. However, the fact that the two groups do not differ in the number of paradigmatic responses, in reaction time, and in correct responses on the RAT, raises some question as to the interpretation of the relative "maturity" of their associative behavior. To the extent that responses from male subjects represent more diversified paradigmatic responses and are more likely to include supraordinate responses, it would appear that these associations are being conceptually mediated and that the greater response heterogeneity

---

*The basis for the development of paradigmatic responses has been discussed in Chapter 1 (pp. 69–70).

†This interpretation of the data depends on being able to assume that the associations of children in 1916 are comparable to those of children today. Material to be presented subsequently (pp. 218–20) makes this assumption questionable. The general idea, however, may nevertheless be valid.

is a function of this mediation. In this case, it is difficult to consider the greater stereotypy and reflexive quality of female responses as being verbally more "mature."

Finally, we should point out that, with the information presently available, it is difficult to determine the effect of educational background on word-association responses. The studies relating the effects of education to response commonality and type of associative response are consistent with those found for increasing age, and are difficult to interpret due to the confounding of the two variables.* From those studies in which confounding was not a problem, it is possible to conclude that the response commonality of subjects from a higher educational level (and/or from a higher socioeconomic background) is more affected by certain situational and instructional variables than is that of lower-status subjects.

*This criticism could equally well be made of studies that compare different age groups, which also differ in amount of education.

Chapter 7

ORGANISMIC VARIABLES

In addition to the demographic variables discussed above, another class of more global factors—here termed organismic variables—has been investigated for its effects on associative responses. These variables—such as intelligence, values, and personality characteristics—are both more subjective and more complex than those previously discussed. At the same time, they are probably more central to the conception that the human organism is a determining factor in the production of associations, and for this reason they have been grouped together under the general heading of organismic variables.

Intelligence and Verbal Ability

A few studies have specifically selected subjects who are of low-grade intelligence in order to study their associative processes. Horan (1956) obtained oral responses to the Kent-Rosanoff WAT from 732 children, aged 9 to 14 years with a median IQ of 69 (range 40–75). Horan found that the associative-response frequency—i.e., response commonality—of these subjects increased with age, while failure to respond and number of idiosyncratic responses decreased. It was also noted that the familiarity of the stimulus (Thorndike-Lorge frequency) was unrelated to associative-response measures for this group of subjects. Interestingly enough, the responses obtained from these subjects were more similar to those obtained from Kent and Rosanoff's adults (1910) than to those from Woodrow and Lowell's children (1916), although the latter were presumably of lower mental age.

Wolfensberger (1963) also studied the associative responses of high-grade retardates and noted no significant difference between the response commonality of this group and a group of normal subjects to two Kent-Rosanoff stimuli (average Primary response strength = 75.5%); nor did the retardates and normals differ in the effects of several satiation conditions (see Chapter 3, p. 104). However, the retardates did show a consistently longer reaction time than did the normals.

Silverstein and McLain (1961) studied the responses of an older group (mean age = 36.5 years) of slightly duller retardates (mean IQ = 51.4) to the Kent-Rosanoff and Menninger WATs. As might be expected, response commonality (associative-response frequency) and the rated "goodness" of the associative response increased with increasing IQ; however, at least for the Menninger word list, commonality and "goodness" of response decreased with increasing age. Neither of these findings were dependent on sex or on length of hospitalization. The explanation of why responses should become less common with increasing age in this study (as opposed to Horan's findings) may be due to the absolutely older age of the Silverstein sample and/or the presence of emotional words on the Menninger word list.

In a second investigation, Silverstein and McLain (1964) studied the associative responses of 100 retardates (mean age = 34.9 years, mean IQ = 55.1) to the Kent-Rosanoff and Menninger WAT. The responses were scored for 67 categories, which represented three different areas: disturbances in anticipation of the response (e.g., repeating the stimulus), goodness of concept formation (e.g., number of common responses), and disturbances in memory (e.g., number of response reproduction errors). The results indicated that disturbances in response anticipation correlated negatively with IQ and positively with age and length of hospitalization; goodness of concept formation correlated positively with IQ and negatively with hospitalization and age; disturbances in memory correlated negatively with IQ and positively with age. None of the diagnostic types of retardation was significantly related to any of the 67 response categories. Sex, which was unrelated to performance in the previous study, was important in the present study; females showed more failures to respond on the Kent-Rosanoff test and more blocking on the Menninger test—findings which the authors suggest was probably due to using a male experimenter.

The authors also noted that the more severely retarded subjects showed more "close" response disturbances,* while less severely retarded subjects showed more "distant" disturbances. This suggests to the authors that for the severe retardates there is a halting of the associative process in the analytic phase, while for the less severely retarded subjects the disturbance occurs in the synthetic phase.† The authors also suggest that since

---

*As defined by Rapaport et al. (1946) and Flavell et al. (1958).

†The term "analytic phase" refers to the first part of the associative process which occurs between the stimulus and response, while "synthetic phase" refers to the latter part of that process. For a fuller description, see Schafer (1953).

neither age nor hospitalization were found to be directly related to intelligence, and yet all three were related to deterioration in functioning on the WAT, this test must then be tapping an area of cognitive functioning not tapped by conventional intelligence tests.

Further information about the responsivity of retardates to emotional stimuli comes from an investigation by Doust and Schneider (1955). In this study, stress was measured by changes in the percentage of oxygen saturation in the blood. Using reactivity to neutral stimuli as a baseline, the relative anoxaemia to emotional stimuli for high-grade retardates and senile dements was found to be slightly less than for neurotics and normals, but was greater than for depressive and schizophrenic patients.

A most interesting study on the paths of associative arousal as a function of degree of retardation has been conducted by Luria and Vinogradova (1959). The basic paradigm for this investigation consisted of pairing a conditioned stimulus (word) with a conditioned response (e.g., button press); in normal subjects, this conditioned response was also noted to be accompanied by an orienting response (as measured by a finger plethysmograph). Further investigations of normal subjects revealed that a stimulus word which was similar in meaning to the conditioned stimulus, while not eliciting the conditioned response, would elicit the orienting response; however, a stimulus word which was similar to the conditioned stimulus only in *sound* would not elicit the orienting response. When these same procedures were used with retardates, a consistent pattern was found. For high-grade retardates, the conditioned stimulus elicited the conditioned response and orienting response; a word similar in *meaning* elicited the orienting response (as was true for the normal subjects); however, a stimulus word similar in *sound* also elicited the orienting response, and with shorter response latency than the meaningfully similar stimulus— a finding which the authors interpret as indicating that a sound-mediated response is a more direct process than a meaning-mediated response.

For slightly more retarded subjects, some changes occured in the pathways of association. The conditioned stimulus still elicited the conditioned response and the orienting response; however, words similar in meaning did not elicit an orienting response (unless they were nearly identical— e.g., kitten-cat), while words similar in sound did elicit the orienting response. Finally, for the most severely retarded subjects, the conditioned stimulus elicited the conditioned response and orienting response, stimulus words similar in meaning elicited no response, but words similar in sound elicited *both* the conditioned response and the orienting response. Furthermore, the range of words which qualified as being sound-similar was considerably enlarged for this group of severe retardates.

In addition to these studies of retardation, several studies have findings which provide some information about the relationship between level of normal intelligence and nature of associative response. Investigations of the relationship between commonality of response and intelligence have been conducted both with children and with college subjects. Entwisle and Forsyth (1963) divided fifth-grade children into high IQ (123+), medium IQ (95–105), and low IQ (85 and below) groups, and noted an increase in response commonality (frequency of the three most common responses) with increasing IQ. However, this positive relationship was much less strong for fifth-grade than for first- or third-grade subjects. This change with age may account for Herr's (1957) finding that response commonality (based on standard scores developed for each separate response distribution) was unrelated to intelligence test scores for high-school seniors or college freshman. This result led him to conclude, "Apparently intelligence apart from education is a negligible fact in communality of thought" (p. 262).

A similar trend was noted by Tobiessen (1964) when he compared composite scores on tests of language skills with associative-response measures. For boys, language-skills scores were significantly correlated with number of adult Primary responses, number of contrast responses, and number of paradigmatic responses, for Grades 4 and 6 (although the correlations were lower for Grade 6). By Grade 8, none of the correlations was significant, but all three again increased to significance by Grade 10. For girls, only the number of paradigmatic responses at Grade 4 was related to language skills scores.

Also relevant to this problem is a study by Kjeldergaard and Carroll (1963) of high-school students, which found that scores on verbal ability tests related differently to two different kinds of Primary responses. While verbal ability was unrelated to the number of "opposite" Primaries given (consistent with Herr's findings), there was a small but significant positive relationship between verbal ability and the number of nonopposite Primaries. This suggests that intelligence may play a role in determining responses based on conceptual, mediational processes, but not in the manifestation of responses based on word-word habits. However, Peters (1958), using the multiple-choice version of the supraordinate WAT with college subjects, found the relative number of supraordinate response choices to be unrelated to intelligence scores based on the Raven matrices test.

Two other associative-response measures, however, have been found to be related to intelligence. Clarke (1955), in a study of normal and neurotic soldiers, found a greater incidence of reaction time-motor disturbances (see p. 201) among the less intelligent subjects; intelligence was also correlated (positively) with the number of stimulus words recalled, and in fact was more important than the neurotic-normal dichotomy in determing recall.

Summary

The following is a summary of the findings regarding the relationship of intelligence and verbal ability factors to associative responses. A discussion of these occurs at the end of the chapter.

(1) Studies of mentally retarded subjects have found that
    (A) response commonality (associative-response frequency)
        (a) increases with increasing IQ level
            (i) this has also been found true for normal subjects of grammar-school age, but not for adults, and
            (ii) when the stimuli had very strong Primaries, high-grade retardates did not differ from normals;
        (b) increases with age, for children,*
        (c) decreases with age, when the subjects are older, more retarded, and tested with emotional stimuli.
    (B) reaction time increases as IQ level decreases*.
    (C) Response measures are unrelated to Thorndike-Lorge frequency of the stimulus.
    (D) Failure to respond, and the number of idiosyncratic responses decrease with age.
    (E) Response disturbances
        (a) in the areas of response anticipation and response reproduction, increase with decreasing IQ.
        (b) which indicate the subject is stimulus-bound ("close" responses), increase with decreasing IQ.
        (c) of the "distant" type are more likely to occur with less retarded subjects.

(2) Studies of the relationship between associative responses and verbal ability have found
    (A) for boys, the number of adult Primaries, contrast responses, and paradigmatic responses increases with increasing verbal ability, in Grades, 4, 6, and 10 (but is unrelated in Grade 8).
    (B) for girls, the number of paradigmatic responses increases with increasing verbal ability in Grade 4 only.
    (C) for high-school students,
        (a) number of opposite-Primaries was unrelated to verbal ability.
        (b) number of nonopposite Primaries was positively related to verbal ability.

*Starred items: This finding also holds true within the normal range of intelligence.

Values and Interests

Some attention has been given to the relationship between the values or interests of an individual and the type of associative responses he gives. In the only study specifically concerned with the influence of values on popularity of associative responses, J. J. Jenkins (1960) determined the response commonality scores (based on the number of Primary responses to 200 selected stimuli) of subjects for whom scores on the Allport-Vernon Study of Values and Strong Vocational Interest Blank also were available. The only relationship obtained with Allport-Vernon scores was for the Aesthetic scale; male subjects with high aesthetic scores gave fewer Primary responses. Although unrelated to any particular area of interest, it was noted that subjects with interest profiles which showed a large change over a 6- to 12-month period were also low on response commonality.

An attempt also has been made to determine the relationship between response availability, m, to stimuli representing different values and the relative strength of those values within the individual. Bousfield and Samborski (1955) selected 60 noun stimulus words, 10 to represent each of the Allport-Vernon values, and presented each of these to college undergraduates for a 60-second continued-association task. The distribution of responses to each stimulus was used to establish standard scores, and then each subject's response to each stimulus was scored. Subsequently, these scores were used to determine the subject's association score for each Allport-Vernon value. Rank order correlations between these response availability scores and scores on the Allport-Vernon test were generally low, with only the relationship for the Religious and Theoretical areas being significant.

This approach to the study of the relationship between response availability and value was also used by Van Krevelen (1956). In this study, undergraduate college students ranked statements describing the six types of value orientation represented in the Allport-Vernon scale; they also gave 60-second continued associations to five stimuli representing each of the six values. Standard scores based on each response distribution were used to determine the availability of responses for each value, for each subject. Rank order correlations between these availability scores and the subject's ranking of value statements were low and significant only for the Political area. However, when only the statements given the most extreme rankings were compared for response availability, m, significantly more responses were given to those stimuli representing the area of the "most liked" (rank 1) statements, and the area of the "next most liked" (rank 2) statements, while fewer responses were given to those stimuli representing the area of the "least liked" (rank 6) statements. Although other such comparisons were not significant, it was generally found that response availability increased as the subjective ranking of the value increased. There is also some evidence for this phenomenon existing with nonsense material. Anderson (1965) found response availability to be positively correlated with preference for individual letters (although this correlation was weaker than that between m and the familiarity of the letter).

The relationship between values and reaction time to stimuli representing those values has been studied by McGinnies (1950) and by Dunn, Bliss, and Siipola (1958). In the latter study, females who scored among the top 15 out of 264 subjects on one of the six Allport-Vernon value scales were selected as subjects. Subsequently, these values were grouped into an "extraceptive" class (Economic, Theoretical, and Political), and an "intraceptive" class (Aesthetic, Religious, and Social). On a WAT administered without time pressure, the overall reaction time of "extraceptive" subjects was found to be less than that of "intraceptive" subjects. Furthermore, the median reaction time (in seconds) for the six separate subject groups (chosen on the basis of value scores) was rather distinct, with a rank order of Economic (3.4), Political (4.1), Theoretical (4.3), Social (6.5), Religious (7.1), and Aesthetic (8.7).

In McGinnies' investigation (1950), the interaction between the values of the individual and the type of stimulus in determining reaction time was studied. The results indicated a significant correlation between Allport-Vernon scale scores and the mean reaction time of the six stimuli which represented each of the six values. Although the general trend was for reaction time to decrease as the importance of the value to the subject increased, for two of the 25 stimuli this trend was reversed.

The study by Dunn et al. (1958), mentioned above, also investigated the relationship between the subjective values of the individual and the *type* of associative response given. They found, for example, the "extraceptive" subjects gave more contrast responses than did "intraceptive" subjects, while the latter group was more likely to respond to adjective stimuli with syntagmatic (noun) responses and to be aware of the processes intervening between the stimulus and response.

Crown (1950), using a multiple-choice WAT consisting of a "normal" and "abnormal" response alternative, found some suggestive evidence that the number of "abnormal" responses was related to "war-mindedness," "anti-semitism," and tendency to give "empathic" answers on an inventory of social attitudes. However, the scales on which the latter scores were based were very short, and both the reliability and validity of the scales seems questionable.

Several studies have investigated the extent to which subjects give associative responses with *content* which represents their dominant values— i.e., response words which represent that value domain. For example,

Kimbrough and Cofer (1958) used Thurstone's scale to measure the attitude of subjects toward law, and then determined the number of associative responses with law content to stimuli which varied in their relevance to law. The results indicated that for stimuli of high or low relevance, the attitude of the subject was not important; however, for stimuli of moderate relevance, subjects with more favorable attitudes to law gave more law-relevant responses. In another study, Havron, Nordlie, and Cofer (1957) constructed a multiple-choice WAT in which the two response alternatives either represented a Religious versus a Political-Economic alternative, or, on a second test, represented Radical versus Conservative or Authoritarian versus Equalitarian attitudes. Subjects also were tested on the Allport-Vernon test, the F scale, and a Conservative-Radical questionnaire. The results indicated that the choice of Religious or Political-Economic responses correlated .68 to .81 with scores for these traits on the Allport-Vernon test. Choice of Radical versus Conservative responses and Authoritarian versus Equalitarian responses correlated with the questionnaire scores ($r = .42$) and, to a lesser degree, with F scale scores ($r = .18$).

In another investigation of the interaction between subjective values of the individual and type of stimulus in determining content of associative response, McGinnies (1950) noted that when subjects respond to stimuli representing their high values they give more responses from that value domain and more evaluative responses (responses which make an appraisal of the stimulus). On the other hand, when subjects respond to stimuli from an area of low value to them, they give more responses which are opposite in meaning or connotation of the stimulus, and more which are attitudinally neutral. In other words it appears that subjects make responses which are congruent with their value orientation.

Deese's factor analytic approach to determining underlying associative structure (see Prologue, p. 34) has been used by Feldman (reported in Deese, 1965) to compare the responses to religious stimuli of subjects who scored high and low on the Allport-Vernon Religious scale. The associative-response overlap coefficients among the 15 stimuli were determined separately for each subject group (highs versus lows), and two separate factor analyses were then performed. While the first two factors in each analysis indicated that the two subject groups had essentially the same associative structure, certain critical differences, corresponding with value orientation, were noted. Most strikingly, the overlap coefficients and factor loadings for the religious stimuli were higher for high Religious value subjects than for the low-value subjects. Furthermore, although the first two factors of the two groups were highly similar, subjects high in Religious value had the stimulus words *divine* and *spirit* loaded on the first factor, while the low scorers did not. On the other hand, *sermon* and *clergyman* did load on this first factor for low-, but not for high-scoring subjects.

Finally, the role of individual values in determining the particular meaning of the stimulus to which the individual will respond, has been studied by Brook and Heim (1960). In this pilot study, the stimulus words were homophones with meanings which referred to more than one area of interest. The homophones represented the areas of Sport, Religion, Science, Politics, Practicality, Outdoors, Aesthetics, and Academic interests. An associative-response-score measure of interest was determined by weighting responses according to infrequency of occurrence. Thus a subject who responded to an infrequently used meaning of the stimulus would receive a high score for that response. When this weighted associative-response-score measure of interest was compared with the experimenter's interview-based ratings of the subjects' interests, the correlations were uniformly positive and, with the exception of the Academic areas, significant.

Summary

The following is a summary of the findings of the relationship between the values and interests of the individual and his associative responses. A discussion of these findings occurs at the end of the chapter.

(1) Number of Primary responses
    (A) is negatively related to score on the Allport-Vernon Aesthetic scale, for male subjects;
    (B) is unrelated to scores on the Strong Vocational Interest Blank; but
    (C) is negatively related to test-retest interest profile change.

(2) Response availability, m, to stimuli which represent different values
    (A) in general, is positively related to the strength of those values in the individual, but
    (B) there is some disagreement as to whether this is equally true for all value areas.

(3) Reaction time
    (A) is relatively shorter for subjects with strong Economic, Political, and Theoretical values and relatively longer for subjects with strong Social, Religious, and Aesthetic values;
    (B) to stimuli representing particular values is negatively related to the strength of that value for the individual.

(4) Associative-response overlap to stimuli representing a particular value is greater for subjects for whom that value is especially important.

(5) Contrast responses are more likely to be given by subjects high on Economic, Political, or Theoretical values and less likely by subjects high on Social, Religious, or Aesthetic values.

(6) Syntagmatic (noun) responses to adjective stimuli are more likely to be given by subjects high on Social, Religious, and Aesthetic values and less likely by subjects high on Economic, Political, and Theoretical values.

(7) The *content* of associative responses has also been found to be related to the personal values of the individual, the content of the stimulus, and the interaction between the two.

- (A) The choice of response alternatives on a multiple-choice association test depends on the consonance of the alternative with the values of the individual.
- (B) For stimuli of moderate relevance to law, the frequency of occurrence of responses with law content is directly related to the positiveness of the subject's attitude toward law.
- (C) The meaning of a homophone stimulus which is responded to is consonant with the subject's values.
- (D) When stimuli represent areas of high value to the subject, there is a greater frequency both of responses from that value domain and of evaluative responses.
- (E) When stimuli represent areas of low value to the subject, there is a greater frequency both of contrast responses and of evaluatively neutral responses.

Personality

A series of experiments have tried to relate personality factors to different measures of associative response. Generally, "personality" has been determined from scores on objective personality questionnaires, and these scores have been used either to establish criterion groups or to correlate with associative-response measures. Fewer studies have been based on rating or behavioral measures of personality.

There have been several investigations of the relationship between personality factors and the tendency to give Primary responses. For example, J. J. Jenkins (1959) had the classroom instructor rate the "social sensitivity" of students who also took a WAT. He noted that the ability of subjects to increase their number of Primary responses, under instructions to give the response "most people" would, appeared to be positively related to their degree of social sensitivity. Following up this hypothesis, Horton, Marlowe, and Crowne (1963) gave subjects a "social desirability" test to determine need for social approval, and also administered the Kent-Rosanoff WAT under either relaxed or speed conditions; following this test, a second test under "most people" instructions was administered. A significant interaction between need for social approval and the effect of conditions was found; subjects with low need for approval gave more Primary responses under speed than under relaxed conditions. However, contrary to Jenkins' finding, need for social approval was not related to the ability to increase the number of Primary responses under "most people" instructions.*

Other studies have attempted to relate the occurrence of Primary responses to a wider variety of personality factors. Block (1960), for example, administered the CPI to subjects who scored high and low on response commonality. An item analysis of the CPI questions failed to reveal any significant relationships between personality and giving many or few Primary responses, for either male or female subjects. J. J. Jenkins (1960) found number of Primary responses to be negatively related to an overall measure of maladjustment, as determined from the MMPI, and to correlate negatively with the amount of personality profile (MMPI) change over a 6- to 12-month period. Kjeldergaard and Carroll (1963) attempted to relate scores on the scales of the Guilford-Zimmerman Temperament Survey and the Minnesota Counselling Inventory to the occurrence of two types of Primary responses—opposites and nonopposites. They found a low positive correlation between certain of the personality test scores and the occurrence of Primary responses, but of the 72 correlations obtained, only six were significant at the .05 level, and all of these were based on female subjects.

On the other hand, Cobb (1952), using a behavioral criterion to select 50 female campus leaders, did find differences in the responses of these subjects, as compared with a sample matched for sex, age, class, and rural-urban background. Using Goodenough's WAT (1942), the results indicated that the high-leadership subjects had responses of significantly higher asssociative frequency than did low-leadership subjects.

The effect of styles of ego-control on response commonality has been studied by Nakamura and Wright (1965). Female subjects who scored relatively high on neurotic over-control or, alternatively, on neurotic under-control, were administered a WAT in both a sitting and a lying position. The over-controlling subjects were found to give significantly more uncommon

*While it is likely that there is a difference between social sensitivity and need for social approval, to the extent that both imply an orientation toward the social group and an awareness of the customs of that group, it might be expected that both variables would be positively related to the ability to give responses characteristic of the group, when requested to do so.

responses while lying than sitting, while the under-controlling subjects were not affected by position. Furthermore, the two groups were differentially affected by the social conditions of testing. The over-controlling subjects gave more common responses when the experimenter was present in the same room than when the experimenter was observing from a second room (for the lying position only), while the under-controlling subjects gave fewer common responses when the experimenter was present (for both sitting and lying positions).

In the other study of response commonality, Smith and Raygor (1956) selected subjects who scored high and low on a "permeability" scale; high scorers were flexible, imaginative, and extraverted, while low scorers were less sensitive to stimuli, rigid, withdrawn, and introverted. These subjects were then administered a WAT under standard and under satiation conditions (see Chapter 3, p. 104). For the Impermeable subjects, the number of uncommon responses after satiation exceeded the number given before; for Permeable subjects, the number of uncommon responses was approximately the same on both tests. The authors suggest that the increase in uncommon responses following satiation is due to temporary inhibition of responses higher in the hierarchy, and that the refractory period for this inhibition may be longer for Impermeable than for Permeable subjects.

Two studies have investigated the relationship between personality and response availability. Davids (1956) presented male subjects rated high and low on alienation with 100 noun stimuli, for 20-second written continuous association. For all classes of stimuli (alienated and neutral, high and low Thorndike-Lorge frequency), alienated subjects have more responses, m, than did nonalienated subjects. R. C. Johnson and Lim (1964), however, did not find scores on the CPI scales to correlate with response availability, as determined from 60-second continued association to "good" and "bad" stimuli. However, when the response availability ratio of "good" to "bad" stimuli was calculated, the authors found that subjects who were high scorers on Inhibition and Anxiety and who were low scorers on Ego Strength, gave many more responses to "good" than to "bad" stimuli; subjects who made better-adjusted scores on these personality variables gave a more equal number of responses to "good" and "bad" stimuli.

The effect of personality on associative reaction time has been studied in five experiments. Machover and Schwartz (1952) found a significant correlation ($r = .45$, $p < .01$) between scores on the MMPI Depression scale and reaction time; subjects who were more depressed took longer to make a response.* Dunn et al. (1958) used the Guilford STDCR to select subjects scoring in the top and bottom 15% (total $N = 222$ males) on scales of

---

*But cf. Bodin and Geer (1965, Ch. 8, p. 202).

Inhibition-Impulsivity and Introversion-Extraversion. Twenty-five neutral Kent-Rosanoff stimuli were presented without time pressure. The results indicated that the reaction time of Inhibited subjects was significantly longer than that of Impulsive subjects; the results of the comparison of Introverted versus Extraverted subjects was in the same direction, but not significant. In the Nakamura and Wright study (1965) cited above, longer reaction times were obtained in the lying, as opposed to the sitting, position for subjects who were neurotic over-controllers; position was unrelated to reaction time for neurotic under-controlled subjects.

In another study of reaction time (Eriksen, 1952), personality types were established by choosing subjects on the basis of their reaction to an interrupted-task experiment. Subjects who had a high memory for tasks which had been "failed" were considered to be Intellectualizers or Rationalizers, while subjects who had a high memory for "successes" were considered to be Repressers. When the two groups were compared for reaction time to neutral and emotional stimuli, they did not differ. However, the reaction time of the Represser subjects was related inversely to the recognition threshold of the stimulus, while the reaction time of the Intellectualizer subjects was either not related, or related directly to the stimulus recognition threshold.

A rather extensive study of stimulus recall was conducted by Carlson (1954). Following the associative-response reproduction trial, subjects were tested for recall of the (emotional and neutral) stimulus words. Two measures were calculated from these data. The first, reproduction failures recall, was determined from the percentage of *forgotten* stimulus words on which the subject had made response reproduction errors, minus the percentage of *remembered* stimuli on which such errors were made. The second measure, reaction time recall, was based on the percentage of *forgotten* stimuli for which the initial reaction time was above the subject's median reaction time, minus the percentage of *remembered* stimuli with reaction times above the subject's median. These measures were then related to scores on selected MMPI scales. When the effect of scores on the Neuroticism scales were partialed out, Hysteria and Cyclothymia were positively related to the reproduction failure recall measure, while Psychaesthenia was negatively related to this measure. The relationship between the personality variables and reaction time recall was not significant.

There also has been some attempt to relate personality with the type of associative response obtained. For example, in the study by Cobb (1952) cited above, female campus leaders were not different from nonleaders in giving masculine versus feminine responses on Goodenough's WAT, but they did give significantly more leadership responses (as determined from

Goodenough's key). Also, the leaders used shorter words as responses, had a high ratio of verbs to nouns, had fewer emotional responses, especially of a negative character, and they took less time to complete the test.

In the Dunn *et al.* study (1958) cited above, Impulsive subjects gave more contrast responses than Inhibited subjects (significant), and Extraverted subjects gave more contrast responses than Introverted subjects (insignificant). The same pattern existed for awareness of the processes intervening between the stimulus and response. However, Machover and Schwartz (1952), using a WAT consisting of positively and negatively toned adjectives, found that subjects scoring high on the MMPI Depression scale gave significantly more contrast-adjective responses to positive adjective stimuli and significantly more concrete-noun responses to negative adjective stimuli. These results were interpreted as indicating that the subject's response serves as a homeostatic device to maintain his mood. Thus, if he is depressed, he will give opposite responses to positive stimuli, but confirmatory (noun) responses to negative stimuli.

Finally, a series of studies have investigated the relationship between personality and the occurrence of "body" responses. Secord (1953) developed a WAT consisting of 75 homonym stimuli with body and nonbody meanings (e.g., colon). The number of body responses elicited by these stimuli was found to be positively related to the number of Rorschach responses which indicated bodily concern and to be negatively related to subjects' scores on a "body acceptance" scale. In a subsequent study, Secord and Jourard (1953) again found the number of body responses to be related to degree of bodily dissatisfaction, but this was significant only for female subjects. The occurrence of body responses was not found to be related to general self-satisfaction, but there was a significant positive relationship with anxiety scores for both male and female subjects.

However, when Weinberg (1960) repeated this latter study, the number of body responses was not found to be related either to anxiety or to bodily dissatisfaction. Rather, he found a relationship between giving body responses and insecurity (as measured by Maslow's test (1942).

Summary

The following is a summary of the main findings of the relationship between certain personality traits and word-association test responses. A discussion of these findings occurs at the end of the chapter.

(1) Number of Primary responses
    (A) under instructions to give the response "most people" would

(a) is positively related to ratings of "social sensitivity," and
(b) is unrelated to questionnaire scores of "need for social approval";
- (B) increases in subjects who are low in "need for social approval," under speed, as compared to relaxed, conditions;
- (C) is unrelated to performance on the CPI, Guilford-Zimmerman, and Minnesota Counselling Inventory personality questionnaires;
- (D) is negatively related to MMPI measures of maladjustment and degree of response profile change over time.

(2) Response commonality
- (A) is positively related to leadership behavior in college females;
- (B) in over-controlled (female) subjects
    (a) is decreased in a supine, as opposed to a sitting, position, and
    (b) is increased by the presence of the experimenter, when in a supine position;
- (C) in under-controlled (female) subjects
    (a) is unrelated to body position (supine versus sitting), and
    (b) is decreased by the presence of the experimenter;
- (D) is decreased in rigid, introverted subjects after satiation, but
- (E) is unaffected by satiation in flexible, extraverted subjects.

(3) Response availability, m
- (A) is positively related to alienation (male subjects);
- (B) is unrelated to CPI scale scores;
- (C) however, the m ratio for "good" stimuli/"bad" stimuli was positively related to scores on CPI Inhibition and Anxiety scales, and negatively related to Ego-strength scores.

(4) Reaction time
- (A) is positively related to Depression, Inhibition, and Introversion, and
- (B) is negatively related to Impulsivity and Extraversion;
- (C) in over-controlled (female) subjects is increased in a supine position, and
- (D) in under-controlled (female) subjects, is unrelated to position.

(5) Contrast responses occur more often for
- (A) Impulsive than Inhibited subjects
- (B) Extroverted than Introverted subjects
- (C) Depressive than nondepressive subjects, to positively toned adjectives
- (D) Nondepressive than Depressive subjects, to negatively toned adjectives.

(6) There is some evidence that the occurrence of "body" responses is related to bodily concern.

Response Sets and Cognitive Styles

In addition to the preceding organismic variables, it has been noted that subjects often have a characteristic style of responding on association tests. Thus some subjects typically may give very common responses, while others may give highly unusual ones. This intra-subject consistency has been referred to as a response set, or, more, generally, as a cognitive style. This style is as characteristic of the individual as are his values, and intellectual and personality traits. A number of studies have investigated these styles of response and the factors which are presumed to underlie their occurrence.

A few studies have focused on one of the several possible response styles and have tried to relate other variables to that style. For example, Carroll *et al.*, (1962) studied high-school students who gave many contrast responses to opposite-evoking stimuli. They found that subjects with high opposite scores also gave contrast-like responses to stimulus words which are not ordinarily perseived as having an opposite; subjects who gave few contrast responses to OES did not show this tendency.

In a similar way, J. J. Jenkins (1960) contrasted subjects who gave many Primary responses with those who gave few. The high commonality subjects were found to give more Paradigmatic responses, while low commonality subjects gave more Syntagmatic responses. In a test of response consistency over time, high-commonality subjects tended to give the same responses as previously and to remain in the high-commonality group, while the responses of low-commonlity subjects changed from one test to the next (although they remain equally unusual).

The issue of commonality versus idiosyncrasy as a response style has also been studied by Dokecki, Polidoro, and Cromwell (1965). The associations of three groups of schizophrenic and normal subjects were scored for number of idiosyncratic responses to Kent-Rosanoff stimuli. The groups were divided at the median to determine high- and low-commonality subjects. After a 48-hour interval, all subjects were retested. For all groups, the high-commonality subjects showed greater response consistency on the retest, leading the authors to conclude, "Regardless of the presence or absence of psychopathology the idiosyncratic responder does differ reliably from his cultural counterparts with respect to stability over time" (p. 315).

Prior studies of commonality (e.g., Peterson & Jenkins, 1957) had suggested that this response style might be related to the personality trait of conformity. However, this hypothesis was not supported by later studies (e.g., Block, 1960; J. J. Jenkins, 1960).

Mandler and Parnes (1957) also noted a consistency, across stimulus classes, for subjects to give idiosyncratic responses. In tests of 30-second continued association to four types of stimuli (nonsense syllables, adjectives, line drawings, and a Rorschach card), subjects were consistent in giving, or not giving, statistically infrequent responses. Subsequently, the authors categorized the associative responses into a variety of categories, and these associative scores were then factor-analyzed. Two main factors emerged from this analysis: one reflected the output frequency (the number of associative responses, m) and accounted for the largest source of variance. The other factor reflected the popularity of the responses which were emitted. These two factors appeared to account adequately for the associative-response behavior of the subjects.

Other studies, however, suggest that associative-response styles may reflect, or be determined by, more than two factors. For example, Wallenhorst (1965) felt it was possible to identify five response sets: giving antonym responses to adjectives, giving contrast verb responses (e.g., climb-fall), giving object responses to verbs, giving object responses to adjectives (e.g., red-house), and giving synonym responses. However, these five styles were interrelated; the product-moment correlation between giving adjective-contrasts and verb-contrasts was $+.70$ ($p < .01$); between giving object responses to verbs and to adjectives, it was $+.28$ ($p < .01$), and between antonym and synonym responses it was $+.24$ ($p < .05$). Additionally, it was noted that subjects who chose a relatively large proportion of responses from one response set had a significantly faster reaction time.

M. J. Goldstein and Jones (1964) also determined the intercorrelations among several response measures in their study of schizophrenic response disturbance. Inspection of the matrix of intercorrelations revealed three clusters, or types, of associative disturbance: cognitive and memory disruption (as seen in "distant," autistic, and clang responses and in response reproduction errors); reaction time disturbances (as seen in the difference between both the means and variances of reaction time to emotional and to neutral stimuli, and in the overall reaction time variance); and defensive maneuvers (as seen in perseverative responses). The authors noted that subjects who show one type of associative disturbance to emotional stimuli will be likely to show that same type of disturbance (but less often) to neutral stimuli. They thus suggest that emotional stimuli do not result in a qualitatively different type of response, but rather they increase the *number* of response disturbances. They also suggest, since cognitive and memory disruption was not found to overlap with reaction time disturbance, that disturbance in content of associative responses is independent of disturbance in the temporal patterning of responses.

Still another approach to the study of response sets and the underlying basis for associative responses is that taken by Nunnaly *et al.*, (1963). Starting with the assumption that there are three different response sets—Evaluative (positive and negative), Denotative, and Categorization—they constructed either binary-choice, or multiple-choice, association tests, with responses to represent two (or more) of these response styles. When the binary- and multiple-choice forms of the test were compared for the subjects' frequency of choosing responses representing the three styles, correlations of approximately + .50 were obtained. In a second study (Nunnally & Hodges, 1965), additional response styles were added to the binary-choice test, and the response choices were factor-analyzed. The results indicated the existence of the original three factors, plus additional antonym, synonym and spatial relation factors. The authors suggest that the initial three factors may be similar to Osgood's definition of semantic meaning, while the latter three are more similar to an associative definition of meaning.

A factor analytic approach has also been employed by Moran *et al.* (1964). In this large study, different 25-item WATs were administered on 4 days in succession; the results were scored for 15 response categories and were then factor-analyzed. From this analysis, four factors emerged—three reflecting response sets and one representing general ability to cope with the task. The first factor, termed "functional," reflects the subject adopting an object-referent set and interpreting the task as one of naming a common object which is associated with the stimulus. The authors hypothesize that such subjects have a concrete, denotative attitude toward words. The second factor, "synonym-superordinate," reflects the subject adopting a conceptual-referent set and interpreting the task as one of specifying a word which is logically related to the stimulus. The authors hypothesized that these subjects have an abstract, conceptual attitude toward words. The third factor—contrast-coordinate," reflects the subject adopting a speed set and interpreting the task as literally being to respond as quickly as possible.

Over the 4 days, subjects consistently demonstrated the same set to different stimuli, leading the authors to postulate the existences of idiodynamic response sets. Also, it was noted that a subject's commonality score depended on the number of stimuli in the list which were compatible with his set. That is, for each stimulus the Primary response may be characterized as representing one particular response set; an individual's commonality score is determined by the interaction between the type of stimulus and his response style. Response disturbances were greatest when type of stimulus was incompatible with the subject's response style.

When this same investigation was repeated with schizophrenic subjects, the results were rather different. After the first day, on which the response sets emerging from the factor analysis were the same as for normals,* sharp differences appeared. Rather than factors based on structural response

---

*Leading the authors to conclude that normal and schizophrenic subjects have common associative structures.

categories, the factors of the second through fourth days were dominated by response fault variables (e.g., no response, multiword response, or response reproduction errors). Although the structural response sets of the first day were still operative, the loadings on these structural variables were low and were scattered among the new response fault factors. It was also noted that there was a tendency for specific types of response faults to be associated with different structural response sets,* and that over the period of 4 days the frequency of specific faults increased, while the frequency of other faults decreased.

Cook *et al.*, (1965) applied Moran's concept of idiodynamic response sets to a further study, in which the stimuli were numeral homonyms (e.g., eight-ate). They found that subjects with a "contrast-coordinate" response set were most likely to give numeral (coordinate) responses to the numeral homonym stimuli. On the basis of these and other results in the study (see Ch. 2), the authors concluded that associative responses are determined both by stimulus conditions and by subject response styles, and that the latter have more enduring and reliable consequences.

Finally, three studies have been concerned with nonlexical aspects of response style. Hsü (1951) factor-analyzed PGR records of college subjects who were given 24 verb stimuli and asked to imagine a past personal experience associated with the stimulus. The author suggests there are five types of PGR profiles which emerge from this analysis, but the low factor loadings and few stimuli used do not solidly support his interpretation.

Baker (1951) has offered an hypothesis regarding WAT extra-lingual responses (e.g., uhms, coughs, and yawns) which is based on psychoanalytic theory. According to this point of view, subjects who make such responses before the response proper are indicating some passive resistance to the experimenter and the WAT, while subjects who make such responses afterward are indicating active resistance. In either case, the subject who gives such extra-lingual responses is seen as attempting to silence the examiner and thereby remove an external source of tension. Finally, Veness (1962) has noted that parapraxic response faults are characteristic of some subjects, and that such slips of the tongue are determined more by subject response style than by the nature of the stimuli.

Summary

The following is a summary of the findings regarding response sets and cognitive styles. A discussion of these occurs at the end of the chapter.

(1) High commonality versus low commonality:

(A) High commonality subjects can also be characterized as giving

*The clearest example of this was the relationship between reaction time faults and the "conceptual-referent" set.

more paradigmatic responses and identical responses on a retest, while
- (B) low commonality subjects can be characterized as giving more syntagmatic responses and more different responses on a retest;
- (C) no personality correlates of these two styles have yet been discovered.

(2) Several different classifications of response style have been suggested. An attempt to relate these different approaches will be made in the Discussion.

(3) It has been found that response set is related to reaction time, response commonality, and response disturbance.
- (A) Reaction time was decreased by choosing many responses from one set.
- (B) Response commonality was directly related to the number of stimuli in the list which had as Primaries responses which were compatible with the subject's response set.
- (C) Response disturbances were increased when the type of Primary evoked by the stimulus was incompatible with the subject's response style.

Selected Subject Groups

As a final section in this discussion of organismic variables, we will consider a limited number of studies which have been made of selected subject groups. These studies range from subjects selected on the basis of creativity to those selected on the basis of physical pathology.

Several studies of the associative behavior of creative individuals have been conducted. Three of these have been concerned with S. A. Mednick's contention (1962) that the associative-response hierarchies of creative individuals have a different structure from those of less creative ones. Creative individuals are postulated to have more associative responses of equal habit strength available (flat gradient) while less creative individuals are postulated to have a steep response gradient. To test this hypothesis, S. A. Mednick (1962) first demonstrated that scores on the RAT (see Prologue, p. 15) correlate significantly with professors' ratings of creativity—in this case, of architecture and graduate psychology students. He then found that RAT scores (and hence presumably creativity) were significantly related to response availability, m, as determined from a 60-second continued-association test. In a subsequent study (M. T. Mednick *et al.*, 1964a), stimuli of various types were selected (nouns and adjectives, high and low Thorndike-Lorge frequency, producing flat and steep response gradients); subjects gave continued associations for 2 minutes. Again, response availability, m, was positively related to creativity, with high RAT scorers giving more responses than medium RAT scorers, who gave more responses than low scorers. However, somewhat different results were obtained when Maltzman *et al.* (1964) selected from a sample of 45 male subjects those making the highest ($N = 15$) and lowest ($N = 15$) scores on the RAT. These subjects were then given a WAT in which each stimulus was presented six times in immediate succession, with instructions to give a different response on each presentation. When the two groups were compared for the shape of their associative-response hierarchies on each trial (based on response frequencies), high and low creativity subjects were found to be quite similar on each of the six trials, although high RAT subjects showed a tendency to give more original (low-frequency) responses on the first trial. However, when the entire range of RAT scores ($N = 46$) was used, there was no significant relationship between creativity and number of original responses occurring over the six trials.

In a rather different type of study, Wild (1965) gave 30 art students a brief character description first of an original individual, and then of a conventional person; the subjects were instructed to respond to the WAT as they thought each of these fictional characters would. The subjects ability to shift from giving more original responses on the first WAT to giving fewer original responses on the second test was related to ratings of creativity made of these students by their teachers. The ten most creative students were significantly more capable of making this associative-response shift than were the ten least creative ones.*

In addition to these studies designed specifically to investigate the associative responses of creative individuals, several other subject groups have been studied. A large number ($N = 667$) of employed professional engineers, representing six different aspects of engineering, who had been rated for degree of success of the job, were studied by Hills (1958). Each subject was presented with eight "common words" and was asked to write as many synonyms as possible in a 12-minute period. Both number of responses and response commonality were found to be related to job success, while number of uncommon responses was unrelated to success. However, the relationships obtained were not very great, and attempts to cross-validate the findings were not successful.

P. E. Johnson (1964) tested female high-school students who had completed studying, who were currently studying, who were planning to study, or who were not planning to study physics; the stimuli represented 18 concepts from physics. When the associations were scored for number

---

*There was no significant relationship between shift and IQ.

of stimuli also given as responses, the following (significant) ordering of subject groups was obtained: "currently studying" gave more such responses than "completed," who gave more than "planning to study," who gave more than "not planning to study." This same rank order was obtained when the groups were measured for inter-item associative strength (based on all 18 stimuli). The author concludes that the obtained number of inter-related associations among physical concepts depends on the degree of involvement of the individual in physics. It would seem to the present author that the findings may also reflect an interaction between involvement and effectiveness of priming (see Chapter 2).

Another study (Kundu, 1958) compared the accident records of industrial employees over a 2-year period. Words related to accidents were used as association-test stimuli, and both reaction time and frequency of Primary response were determined. For some stimuli, there did appear to be some differences between accident-prone subjects and others, but no statistical tests were done and a number of subjects were dropped from the study for failure to comprehend the language; at best, the findings can only be considered suggestive.

Finally, the responses of male castrates and control subjects, matched for sex, age, and IQ, were studied by Yamamoto and Seeman (1960). Twelve nonsexual and eight sexual stimuli were administered for discrete oral associations; the results indicated no difference in the reaction time of the two groups. Boyd and Valentine (1953) tested dysmenorrheac and control subjects on a word-association test which consisted of a variety of emotional stimuli interspersed with neutral words. They noted an insignificant tendency for reaction time and pneumographic measures of respiration to be greater in the dysmenorrheac group, as well as a significantly larger GSR and a greater number of unusual responses for that group. Furthermore, while the control subjects had slightly (insignificant) larger abnormal scores to the stimulus words with oral connotations and to the initial buffer stimuli, the dysmenorrheac subjects had higher abnormal scores to stimuli with sexual, health, family, and sadomasochistic overtones. In addition, they had higher scores for neutral words—a finding which was interpreted as being due to the carryover of anxiety from the preceding emotional stimulus.

Summary

(1) Creativity
   (A) has been shown to be positively related to response availability, m;
   (B) was unrelated to the number of idiosyncratic responses given to each of six stimulus presentations, although there was a slight

tendency for creative subjects to give more idiosyncratic responses on the first trial;
(C) increases the ability to shift from an original to a conventional response set.

(2) Isolated studies of engineers, physics students, accident-prone subjects, and individuals with physical disabilities have also been reported. It is difficult to determine the generality of these findings.

Discussion

This discussion of the relationship between certain organismic variables and the nature of responses given to a word-association test tries to point out some of the main trends which can be discerned from the investigations in this area. Not surprisingly, studies of variables for which a variety of different measures have been used to establish criterion groups have had few definitive, consistent findings. Thus, for example, it is difficult to determine the reliable effects of personality on associative behavior, when the measures of personality have differed across studies. Perhaps partly for this reason, there are as yet few reliable principles which relate personality traits with associative response behavior. Somewhat more successful have been the studies of value (where the Allport-Vernon test of values has been the predominant measuring instrument) and studies relating intelligence (as measured by a standard intelligence test) to associative behavior. In the following discussion, the role of intellectual level in determining associative responses will be considered first. This will be followed by a discussion of the effects of values, personality traits, and cognitive style.

The effects of intellectual level have been examined in both the normal and subnormal range. Comparisons made across these two ranges indicate that within each group there is a certain parallel of the relationships between increasing intelligence and associative-response behavior. That is, brighter mental retardates have faster reaction times, just as do brighter normal subjects. Also, brighter retardates show greater response commonality (higher associative-response frequency), just as is found with brighter grade-school-aged children in the normal range of intelligence. Similarly, the response commonality of both retardates and normals increases with age until adolescence, and then decreases as middle and old age are approached.

However, there is a critical difference between the two groups. While intellectual level is positively related to associative-response commonality in retardates, it is unrelated to response commonality in normal adults. Another aspect of this absence of relationship is seen in the finding that level of verbal ability in high-school students is unrelated to number of antonym Primary responses (although it *is* positively related to number of nonantonym Primaries). To understand this lack of correspondence between the two groups, as well as the absence of relationship between intelligence and response commonality in the normal adults, it is necessary to consider more closely the types of responses made by each group. At the lowest level of retardation, the associative responses obtained are very "close" to the stimulus, often being based on sound similarities. These stimulus-bound and clang responses, which also occur in very young children of normal intelligence, probably indicate that associative pathways leading away from the stimulus have not yet developed. For the normal child, these will develop with time; for the severe retardate, they may never develop. In this sense, the older nosological term of "mental defective" may have been more appropriate than the current "mental retardate." It is not just that these individuals are retarded. They also are defective in the sense that they are missing the associative pathways based on—as will be discussed below—the conceptual connections that ordinarily develop in normal adults.

At a somewhat higher level of retardation, there is evidence that some associative pathways have developed. However, these may be along rather peculiar lines, as seen from the occurrence of "distant" associations* in this group. Nevertheless, in addition to the sound-based responses (which continue to appear), conceptually based responses also occur. This development occurs around age 6 in normal children. In both groups, it is accompanied by an increase in response commonality. It is in this sense of an increasing number of conceptually mediated responses that intellectual level is related positively to response commonality within the retardate range.

However, it would appear that individuals in the retardate range never get beyond this point in the development of associative pathways. On the other hand, in the normal range of intelligence, after the childhood development of conceptually based associative pathways, in subsequent years some of these pathways are "short-circuited." That is, a direct connection between the associative response and the stimulus is established, rather than the response being conceptually mediated via an associative pathway.

It is suggested that the development of these direct, nonmediated responses depends on the repeated exposure of the individual to certain stimulus words. In other words, it is suggested that the occurrence of these responses is a function of the frequency of occurrence of the word in the

---

*i.e., associations which are conceptually too far removed from the stimulus.

language—i.e., of stimulus familiarity.* In persons of normal intelligence such associations have become so highly overlearned by adolescence that their occurrence does not discriminate between brighter and duller individuals. On the other hand, there is some evidence that conceptually mediated associations continue to be related to level of intelligence.†

This distinction between direct nonmediated responses and conceptually mediated responses is helpful, then, in explaining the somewhat unusual finding that response commonality is unrelated to intelligence in normal individuals but *is* related in mental retardates. First of all, we must remember that intelligence is related to *conceptual* mediation. Secondly, while most adult Primaries do not depend on conceptual mediation, some do, and even more important, Secondary and Tertiary responses do. However, in normal adults, the occurrence of highly overlearned Primary responses, which is dependent in part on stimulus familiarity, overshadows the occurrence of conceptually mediated Secondary, Tertiary, and Primary responses.

For retardates, the situation is somewhat different. In this group, the characteristic absence, or low degree of conceptual mediation, means that the groundwork was never laid for the subsequent development of short-circuited responses—i.e., of responses which bypass the mediating link. It is hypothesized, then, that retardates do not have available these direct, short-circuited Primary responses, but that higher level retardates, who have some capacity for conceptually mediated responses, do give more of the mediated Primary responses and do give conceptually mediated Secondary and Tertiary responses, and it is the occurrence of these which accounts for the relationship between response commonality and intellectual level in retardates.‡ This is a hypothesis to be tested; nevertheless, it has some indirect support in the finding that retardates' responses are not affected by stimulus familiarity, while among normal individuals the nonmediated Primaries are more likely to be given to more familiar (adjective) stimuli than to less familiar (adjective) stimuli. Thus, in normal individuals, the occurrence of nonmediated Primaries is responsible for familiar stimuli

---

*Support for this suggestion is seen in the fact that more nonmediated, contrast responses are given to adjective stimuli of high Thorndike-Lorge familiarity than to adjectives of low familiarity.

†Cf., e.g., the positive relationship between verbal ability and frequency of nonantonym Primaries.

‡The question might be raised as to why, if they develop conceptually based responses, these retardates do not go on to develop short-circuited responses. One possibility is that, due to their disability, these individuals have less interaction with the normal verbal society in which we live, and thus have less opportunity to experience the kind of response overlearning being postulated.

having a higher response commonality. However, if this type of Primary response is not available to the individual (as is the case being postulated for the retardate), then stimulus familiarity will not be a determining factor of associative-response commonality.

It might be argued that rather than assuming a discontinuity between the two intellectual categories, by postulating that a different type of associative response occurs in persons who are within the normal range of intelligence, it would be more parsimonious to assume a continuity between the groups and to explain the lack of relationship in the brighter group as the result of a ceiling effect. That is, it might be argued that up to some level (say IQ of 70) there is a relationship between intelligence and response commonality, but that at that point commonality reaches a maximum, so that any additional increases in intelligence cannot be reflected in the response measure.

There are two reasons that this does not appear to be a satisfactory alternate explanation. First, it implies that all adults of normal IQ have reached a point of maximum response commonality—an implication which is clearly not supported by empirical findings. Furthermore, as will be discussed below, there are consistent differences among people as to degree of response commonality, related to both cognitive and personality variables. Secondly, it overlooks the findings which indicate that, when an associative response must be conceptually mediated, there *is* a relationship between intelligence and response commonality. For these reasons, then, it is suggested that the two subject group differ as to type of associative responses available to them, and that this difference accounts for the relationship between intellectual level and response commonality in the retardate, but not in the normal group.

Investigations of the relationship between values and associative responses have generally taken one of two approaches. One approach tries to determine if the responses of individuals who are high on one value can be differentiated, in some general way, from those of individuals who are equally high on some other value. The other approach investigates the relationship between the strength of a value for a particular individual and the nature of the associative responses he gives to stimuli which represent that value.

On the whole, the first approach—the attempt to relate having specific values to different measures of associative response—has not been very successful. The few significant findings which have been obtained are probably best understood as a result of the degree of contact which the individual has had with his verbal society. This idea will be elaborated in the subsequent discussion of the relationship between personality factors and associative responses. Suffice it to say here, then, that individuals with strong Economic or Political values probably interact more with society, and these are the groups which give stronger (more rapid) and more common associative responses. On the other hand, individuals with strong Aesthetic or Religious values, who might be expected to be more introspective and less involved with everyday social interactions, have weaker and less common associations.

Studies relating the strength of subjective values to the associative responses given to stimuli which represent those values have been somewhat more successful. Availability of responses to such value-consonant stimuli has been found to be a positive funcion of the strengh of the value, as has the rapidity with which the response is made. Several studies have indicated that the content of the specific associative responses emitted will depend on the values which are dominant for that individual. That is, subjects choose responses from those domains which represent their strongest values. Furthermore, there is some evidence that the underlying associative structure of high- and low-value subjects may be relatively similar, but that the two groups may differ in the shape of the response hierarchy which represents the value and in the relative ordering of responses within that hierarchy.

It is suggested, then, that the interaction effects observed between value-related stimuli and the subjective values of the individual represent a summation of response potential. That is, as a result of experience with the language, there is a certain culturally determined response potential for any response word, when considered in connection with any stimulus. That response may, in addition, have another source of excitatory potential deriving from the value system of the individual. What is being suggested, then, is that there is more than one source of input which determines the effective response potential—i.e., that internal, as well as external, stimuli may have cumulative effects in determining the occurrence of associative responses. This idea will be discussed more fully in Chapter 10.

As is true for studies of value, attempts to relate personality variables directly with associative-response measures have not been very successful. More often, the effect of personality on associative behavior has been seen in the interaction of personality with an additional variable. For example, scores on given personality tests are often found to be unrelated to measures of response commonality or response availability. However, measures of personality have been found to interact differentially with certain other experimental variables—satiation versus no satiation, body position during testing, presence or absence of an examiner—in determining associative responses.

In general, the personality factors which differentially affect associative-response reactions to different situational variables can be sorted into two clusters. The first cluster, or personality type, may be characterized as being inhibited, introverted, rigid, and depressive, while the second type tends to be impulsive, extraverted, flexible, and expressive. The associative responses of these two groups under varying experimental conditions are characteristically different. As will be suggested below, one explanation of these differences may be made on the basis of the differing degrees of interaction which the two types of individuals have with (verbal) society.

It appears that the associative responses of the first personality type (Inhibited, Introverted) are determined to a relatively smaller degree by the verbal milieu in which that individual lives. The existence, in this type of person, of weaker, less culturally determined associations is inferred from noting the lower response commonality in such individuals, from the fact that the common associations which do exist are extinguished more readily by satiation procedures, and from the fact that they occur less often when the environmental supports (such as an upright body position) are removed. That these culturally determined responses do, nevertheless, exist in the associative hierarchy of these individuals is seen in the fact that the presence of an examiner can increase the frequency with which they are given.

The additional findings—that fewer contrast responses are obtained from these individuals—suggests a possible explanation of the weaker S-R associations found in this group, which is consistent with their personality description. If we assume that it is the repeated exposure to certain stimuli in the culture which determines the occurrence of the nonmediated, short-circuited responses mentioned in the earlier discussion of association and intelligence, then it is not surprising that a group of subjects who are characterized as being inhibited and introverted—i.e., those whose predominant orientation is *away* from interaction with society—should give relatively fewer of those responses.

On the other hand, the associative responses of the second personality type (Impulsive, Extraverted) are to a much greater extent determined by the verbal culture, as indicated by the increased response commonality which characterizes this group. There is also evidence that their responses are highly overlearned, as seen in the fact that satiation procedures or changes in body position do not affect measures of response commonality. Both of these facts can be interpreted as meaning that these extraverted subjects have more direct, short-circuited responses available, which in turn is consistent with the hypothesis put forward above—that it is the repeated exposure to stimuli which is a determining factor in the establishment of such direct nonmediated responses. That is, it is suggested that it is the subjects who are extraverted, outgoing, and actively involved in society who will be exposed most often to the words of the language and who will, in turn, show the greatest commonality of response. In addition, to the extent that these individuals are also impulsive, their predilection will be to give responses which are "unthinking" and which discharge the task obligation as quickly as possible. Nonmediated responses fulfill both of these requirements quite well.*

It has also been found that these subjects show a *de*crease in response commonality when the examiner is present, as compared to when he is absent. If we assume that the presence of the examiner creates a certain amount of social pressure on the subject, then we want to understand why the presence of this kind of pressure results in responses which are less reflective of social norms. This somewhat unexpected result can be explained if we assume that the social pressure these individuals experience takes the form of a perceived expectation that they treat the task with serious consideration. The subject then momentarily abandons his impulsive style in order to "stop and think," and as a result he gives more conceptually mediated responses. The occurrence of such responses, in turn accounts for the decrease in response commonality.

To summarize: the effect of personality on associative responses—at least the restricted aspects of personality considered in the studies reported here—can be understood in terms of the way in which personality factors determine the amount of interaction the individual has with (verbal) society. Those individuals who are oriented toward society will come in contact with certain verbal stimuli more frequently than will those who are oriented away from society. It is hypothesized that it is the repeated exposure to these stimuli which is related to the development of short-circuited, direct associative responses. In turn, the occurrence of these nonmediated responses is a strong determinant of response commonality scores. Hence, the associative behavior of extraverted individuals will be characterized by high-response commonality which, when they respond to social pressure by trying to "stop and think," may in fact decrease. On the other hand, introverted individuals have a personal response set which depends less on cultural language patterns. However, the presence of an examiner may exert enough social pressure to force these subjects to adopt, temporarily, a more socially oriented set, and this in turn accounts for the increase in response commonality.

A variable which somehow cuts across this introverted-inhibited versus extraverted-impulsive dimension of personality is that of creativity. It appears than the creative individual can be characterized as having more responses available and having a tendency to give more idiosyncratic

---

*The assumption being made here is that nonmediated responses can be given more rapidly. In this connection, we recall the finding that, at least for some subjects, time pressure increases the number of contrast responses obtained (cf. Flavell *et al.*, 1958, and Siipola *et al.*, 1955, discussed in Chapter 5). (Contrast responses are assumed to be direct and nonmediated.)

responses. The former characteristic—of increased response availability—has also been found to be true of successful engineers. However, successful engineers are characterized, in addition, as having high-response commonality, in contrast to the subjects of the "creative" groups studied. This finding raises a question of whether the associative basis of creativity (cf. S. A. Mednick, 1962) is the same in all fields of endeavor—e.g., whether one should expect the associative behavior of individuals who are creative in the arts to be the same as that of individuals who are creative applied scientists. The patterns of association which contribute to creativity in one area may not be facilitating in another field.

It has been noted in the above discussion that, under certain experimental conditions, the individual may adopt a different response set—e.g., his associative behavior may become either more socially oriented or it may become more cautious and reflective. Other studies have shown that subjects can change their response sets as a result of certain instructional variables (see Chapter 2). In addition to this ability to change response sets, the present chapter has reported a series of studies which demonstrate that, under normal circumstances, subjects will adopt one characteristic set. This typical response set, or cognitive style, represents one of a small number of such sets which it is possible to adopt, and it appears to be a characteristic of the individual which is stable over time. It is also a characteristic which is closely related to response latency, for the choice of many associative responses on the basis of a single response set results in a shortened reaction time. It also has been demonstrated that a subject's commonality score depends on the number of stimuli in the WAT which ordinarily elicit, as Primary responses, words which are compatible with that individual's response set.

The set to give common responses is one such cognitive style, but there are others. These structural response sets have been variously identified, and, depending on the level of analysis, may range in number from three to six or more. It seems possible, however, to combine the findings of the several studies, so as to identify three, or perhaps only two, basic styles of associative response. Thus the "object-referent, functional" set of Moran et al. (1964) may include two of the response sets identified by Wallenhorst (1965)—that of object responses, both to verbs and to adjectives. Similarly, Moran's "conceptual-referent, synonym-superordinate" set may subsume Nunnally et al.'s denotative categorization set (1963) and, to a lesser extent, their synonym response set. Finally, Moran's "speed, contrast-coordinate" response set includes Nunnally's contrast and spatial relation sets. In additon, since giving contrast responses is correlated with giving synonym responses, there must be a point of overlap between the "conceptual-referent" set and the "speed" set.

If one additional type of response tendency—that of giving evaluative responses—is added to the "functional" set, then the "functional" and "conceptual" sets together include all the types of responses which Nunnally suggests are based on semantic meaning.* On the other hand, the "speed" set includes those responses Nunnally suggests are due to associative meaning.

To summarize: semantic meaning is related both to "functional" response sets, including object responses and evaluative responses, as well as to "conceptual" response sets, including synonym, superordinate, categorization, and denotative responses. Associative meaning is related to the "speed" set, which includes contrast responses and certain synonym and coordinate responses which are based on spatial contiguity.

It seems possible to relate this interpretation of the response set findings to the earlier discussion of the associative behavior of two personality types. If the preceding analysis of associative behavior is valid, then we would predict that under normal circumstances the introverted, inhibited individual uses a response set based on the semantic meaning of the stimulus, while the extraverted, impulsive individual uses a set which depends on the associative meaning. However, under conditions of social pressure, the introverted individual tends to adopt a response set based on associative meaning, while the extraverted individual now adopts a set based on semantic meaning.

This analysis of response sets supports the general distinction between conceptually mediated responses and nonmediated, short-circuited responses being postulated in this chapter. Semantic meaning sets are based on conceptually mediated responses, while the associative meaning set is based on nonmediated responses. This distinction between the two types of responses can be found, in addition, in the results of studies of response disturbance. Here, also, there appear to be relatively stable patterns, or sets. One of these response disturbance sets—that of cognitive and/or memory disruption—appears to be related to conceptually mediated responses. Another—that of reaction time disturbance—may have more to do with the associative short-circuiting of nonmediated responses. The third response disturbance factor—that of general defensiveness—probably cuts across both types of response.

In summary then, we are suggesting that postulating two different types of associative responses may be helpful in understanding the relationship between several organismic variables and associative-response behavior. The relationship between level of intelligence and response commonality

---

*Alternatively, evaluative responses might be seen as representing the affective meaning of the stimulus.

within the mentally retarded range is hypothesized to be the result of an increasing number of conceptually mediated responses. The lack of such a relationship in the normal range of intelligence is understood to reflect the large number of nonmediated responses given by this group, which is at least partly a function of stimulus familiarity.* The higher response commonality of extraverted, impulsive, and socially oriented individuals is also understood as reflecting an increased frequency of nonmediated responses as a result of the greater interaction of these individuals with their (verbal) society. The lower response commonality of introverted, inhibited, and introspective individuals, on the other hand, is hypothesized to be due to their giving a larger number of conceptually mediated responses, reflecting, in turn, less interaction with (verbal) society. Finally, apart from dividing subjects according to personality type, it has been demonstrated that unselected subjects characteristically adopt one or another associative response style or set, and that the distinction between conceptually mediated versus short-circuited responses can be seen as a feature which distinguishes these sets.

*This assumption implies, incidentally, that there should be a stronger relationship between intelligence and response commonality in this group if less familiar stimuli were used.

Chapter 8

PATHOLOGICAL CONDITIONS

In the first part of this chapter, the effects of functional pathology on associative responses will be considered. Subsequently, the effects of experimentally induced altered states of consciousness will be discussed. Following this, the effects of organic pathology on associative behavior will be presented. Finally, the relationship between certain types of therapeutic treatment and change in associative responses will be discussed.

Functional Pathology

A number of studies of the effects of functional pathology on associative responses have been carried out. The large majority of these have investigated the responses of psychotic (schizophrenic) patients, with less attention given to the effects of neurosis or character disorder. These studies may be grouped conveniently in terms of the types of subject groups which have been compared: some investigations have contrasted schizophrenics with "normal" (nonpsychiatric) individuals, others have compared different subtypes of schizophrenia, and still others have compared schizophrenics with nonpsychotic psychiatric categories. In addition, a few studies of the influence of treatment on schizophrenic associative responses have been conducted.

SCHIZOPHRENIC VERSUS "NORMAL"

Let us consider first those studies contrasting the responses of schizophrenics with those of normal individuals. With one exception, these investigations have found measures of S-R associative strength to be consistently weaker for schizophrenic subjects. Thus R. C. Johnson *et al.* (1964), Lehmann and Dörken (1953), Sommer, Dewar, and Osmond (1960) and Wynne (1964) found schizophrenics to give significantly fewer Primary responses, and Moran *et al.* (1964), as well as Shakow and Jellinek (1965), found less response commonality among schizophrenic subjects. In the latter study, response commonality was determined from a composite index based on number of Primary responses, number of idiosyncratic responses, and number of unusual responses given to the Kent-Rosanoff stimuli. Retesting of schizophrenic subjects at 3- to 4-month intervals over a 16-month period indicated virtually no change in commonality, while normal subjects retested after only 2 weeks showed a significant increase (Shakow, 1963). On the other hand, Moran *et al.* (1964), using associative frequency as a measure of response commonality, found that for certain types of schizophrenic subjects (those adopting an "object-referent" set or a "concept-referent" set—see Chapter 8), response commonality increased over a 4-day period, as the response sets became less preemptive. On the other hand, the commonality scores of normal subjects remained consistent, at their initially high level, over this period of time. In another study of the consistency of associative responses over time, Sommer *et al.* (1960) found schizophrenic subjects to give significantly fewer identical responses than did normals, when retested on the Kent-Rosanoff WAT after a 1-week interval. Storms and Broen (1964) also have noted that schizophrenics show greater response instability on repeated association tasks than do normals.

Lehmann and Dörken (1953), after first establishing the normal range of reaction times for each individual stimulus word, found the reaction time of schizophrenic patients to be above the normative limit significantly more often (48.1%) than that of normal subjects (11.5%). Faibish (1961) also found reaction time in schizophrenics to be longer than for normals. Furthermore, he noted a significant interaction between pathology and type of stimulus word in determining reaction time, with schizophrenics showing a relatively longer reaction time to multiple-meaning stimuli (as opposed to single-meaning stimuli).

Other response measures also suggest a less stable, less well organized associative network in schizophrenics. Deering (1963) found schizophrenic subjects to give more idiosyncratic responses (although this was true only for emotional, but not for neutral, stimuli), and Cramer's (1965b) study suggested that schizophrenics give more heterogeneous responses (higher D) to both emotional and neutral stimuli than do normal subjects. Also, R. C. Johnson *et al.* (1964) found schizophrenics to have fewer responses available, m, to both emotional and neutral stimuli than normals. Furthermore, both Deering (1963) and Moran *et al.* (1964) found schizophrenics to make more response reproduction errors. Deering also found that the schizophrenics made more errors than normal subjects in a subsequent test of stimulus recognition, for both emotional and neutral stimuli.

The findings on response disturbance and occurrence of deviant responses in schizophrenics, as opposed to normals, are consistent with the above results of greater response instability. Thus Faibish (1961) found schizophrenics to give more deviant associative responses, although this was true only for multi-meaning stimuli (normal subjects gave more deviant responses to single-meaning stimuli). Milgram (1961) found schizophrenics to give more "repetition" and "irrelevant-perseveration" responses (but fewer "meaningful-perseveration" and "multiword" responses), and Flavell *et al.* (1958) found schizophrenics to give more perseverative, clang, and "distant" responses. Similarly, Moran *et al.* (1964) noted that schizophrenics show more response disturbances (no response, distant response, reaction time disturbance). Furthermore, the schizophrenic subjects were quite variable on these measures over the 4-day period of testing, while normal subjects' scores were quite consistent.*

In terms of semantic category of response, Milgram (1961) noted schizophrenics to give more supraordinate responses; however, this result is confounded by the fact that the patient group consisted of all male subjects, a variable which has been shown to increase the number of supraordinate responses (see Chapter 7). Furthermore, when this test was presented in a multiple-choice format (with one supraordinate, one subordinate, and two unrelated response alternatives), the patient group gave *fewer* supraordinate responses than did normals. On the other hand, Flavell *et al.* (1958) found schizophrenics to give fewer *sub*ordinate responses, and fewer synonym responses than normals. Finally, Moran *et al.* (1964) found schizophrenics to be lower on all "structural" response variables—i.e., on all measures of synonyms, antonyms, supraordinate, coordinate, and subordinate responses. Thus, while different investigators, using different stimuli and different response measures regularly have found some semantic categories of response to differentiate between schizophrenic and normal subjects, it does not yet seem possible to make any definitive statement about categories which would consistently discriminate between the two subject groups.

Four studies have investigated the effect of instructions, or set, on schizophrenic associative responses.† Both Herr (1957) and Wynne (1964) administered selected stimuli from the Kent-Rosanoff WAT to schizophrenic and normal subjects, with the instructions to respond as "most

---

*An additional finding by Wild (1965)—that schizophrenics did not differ from schoolteachers in number of unusual responses—is difficult to interpret due to the unsatisfactory criteria for "unusual" responses—i.e., an unusual response was one which did not appear on the 1910 Kent-Rosanoff norms or, for the alternate WAT, did not appear on the 1946 Menninger norms, which included only responses with a frequency of 7% or greater. Thus any response which had entered the cultural domain since 1910 or, alternatively, any response with a frequency of greater than 0% but less than 7% was scored as "unusual."

†For the effects of instruction on the responses of normal subjects, see Chapter 2.

people" would. In Herr's study, the schizophrenic and normal subjects were matched for age, education, and regional background; response commonality was based on standard scores worked out separately for each response distribution. The results indicated that normals obtained higher commonality scores than schizophrenics—i.e., were better able to respond as "most people" would; however, this discriminating difference depended on the responses to only one-third of the 80 word-association items used. The results of Wynne's study were consistent with these findings. Compared to free-association responses, "most people" instructions increased the number of Primary responses for normal subjects but had little effect for either acute or chronic schizophrenics.*

In the study by Wild (1965), schizophrenic and normal subjects were read a character description of an original and then a conventional individual, and were asked after each description to respond as they thought such a person would. The associative responses obtained in this way were compared with responses previously given under standard instructions. The ability to "shift" the type of response given was greatest for art students, less for schoolteachers, and least for the schizophrenics. However, although this rank order indicated the number of unusual responses obtained after "original" instructions, it also was the rank order for number of unusual responses obtained after "conventional" instructions. That is, compared to the subjects' initial level of unusual responses (obtained from the standard free-association test), instructions to give more conventional responses resulted in art students and teachers becoming slightly *less* conventional, while schizophrenic subjects did not change. This finding would seem to suggest that the instructions were ineffective, in terms of producing an appropriate change in the responses of any of the subjects.† What does emerge, however, is that schizophrenics exhibit less change as a result of instructions than do normals.‡

Finally, Milgram (1960), in a study reported more fully in the following section on organic pathology (see p. 206), gave schizophrenic and normal subjects a multiple-choice WAT consisting either of masculine and feminine, or of adult and child, response alternatives. Subjects (all male) were matched for age and IQ; educational level of the schizophrenics was

---

*It should be noted that this was not Wynne's conclusion, but is that of the present author made on the basis of the reported results.

†a point not discussed by the author.

‡It is possible that this finding might be related to the fact that the schizophrenic subjects had significantly less education than the normals. However, Herr (1957), while finding the ability of normal subjects to give common responses under "most people" instructions to be positively related to educational level, did not find this relationship to hold for schizophrenic subjects.

lower (see third footnote, p. 194). The results indicated that in this multiple-choice format, schizophrenics were as capable as normals to choose "adult," "child," and "feminine" responses, but were less successful when instructed to choose "masculine" responses.

SUBTYPES OF SCHIZOPHRENIA

Several studies have compared the responses of different types of schizophrenics. Some of these investigations have contrasted subjects grouped according to the diagnostic subclassifications of schizophrenia—e.g., acute versus chronic, or paranoid versus hebephrenic. Others have divided the subjects on the basis of a social-behavioral variable—such as good premorbid adjustment versus poor premorbid adjustment, or social interaction on the ward versus social isolation—or of a cognitive variable—such as impaired abstraction ability. For example, Sommer et al. (1960) compared the responses of acute and chronic schizophrenics to Kent-Rosanoff stimuli, and noted that while the two subject groups did not differ in terms of response commonality (as determined by associative-response frequency on the 1910 Kent-Rosanoff norms), the chronic subjects gave more idiosyncratic responses than did the acute schizophrenic group. Wynne (1964) compared acute and chronic schizophrenics with normal subjects for responses to 54 Kent-Rosanoff stimuli, selected for three levels of Primary response strength. He found what while data for normal subjects did not differ from normative data (Russell & Jenkins, 1954) in terms of the frequency of occurrence of Primary response, both schizophrenic groups gave fewer Primary responses than expected from the normative data and fewer than did the normal subjects, for all levels of Primary response strength. Furthermore, when the schizophrenic subjects were subdivided, acute schizophrenics were found to give more Primary responses than chronic schizophrenics. However, this rather neat rank order—of normal greater than acute greater than chronic—for number of Primary responses, is confounded by the fact that all the normal subjects were female, while all the chronic subjects were male, with the acute schizophrenics being equally divided for sex. Since females have been shown to give more Primary responses than males (see Chapter 7), it is difficult to determine to what extent pathology, and not sex, was the critical variable in this study.

This negative relationship between number of Primary responses and chronicity (versus acuteness) in schizophrenics also has been noted by Higgins, Mednick, and Philip (1965). In this study, the responses of 47 male schizophrenics varying in length of hospitalization from 8 to 21 years, were compared with the Palermo-Jenkins norms (1964). Length of hospitalization (the index of chronicity) was negatively correlated with number of Primary responses and with overall associative-response strength, and was positively related to number of idiosyncratic responses (all correlations significant at .01 level; with age held constant, the correlations were virtually unchanged). The authors concluded that these data indicate that there is greater associative disturbance in schizophrenia with increasing chronicity.

Although these results would appear to provide support for Wynne's findings, the Higgins *et al.* study unfortunately also confounds two variables (although the problem of sex differences is eliminated by the use of only male schizophrenics). In this study, chronicity is confounded with length of hospitalization, so that it is difficult to determine which of these two conditions is responsible for the increasing associative disturbance. Whether chronic schizophrenics who had not been isolated from the language culture of an ongoing society would show this same pattern of increasing associative disturbance has not been determined.

In a more carefully controlled study, Lester (1960) matched 15 male and 15 female patients diagnosed as paranoid, hebephrenic, or epileptic with 30 normal control subjects, for age, education, IQ, and length of hospitalization. The subjects were instructed to produce as many names of colors as possible for a 10-minute period. The continuous controlled association responses thus produced were contrasted with the same subjects' performance in *re*producing a 40-word list, consisting entirely of food words. Responses were scored with both a lenient criterion (any response given was scored) and a strict criterion (only those responses clearly meeting the criterion were scored). The study made use of Bousfield, Sedgewick, and Cohen's (1954) formula for describing the production of continuous, controlled associative responses. This formula was based on the assumption that the subject has a limited supply of available associates which belong to the response category established by the instructions, and that the *rate* at which the supply is depleted is proportional to the number of associates remaining in the pool. To this formulation, Lester added the assumption that the *rate* of depletion depends also on the subject's capacity for supraordination. Based on these assumptions, Lester formulated different predictions for different pathological groups. For example, paranoids show little disturbance in ability for supraordination and hence their rate of depletion should approximate that of normal subjects, although their total supply of associates would be expected to be less. On the other hand, both hebephrenics and epileptics would be expected to be weak in capacity for supraordination, in addition to having a reduced supply of associates; hence both of these groups should show a slower rate of depletion than either normal or paranoid subjects, and of the two, epileptics should be even slower than hebephrenics, since both functional and organic factors contribute to the epileptic's pathology.

The results were highly consistent with these hypotheses. In terms of total responses emitted (similar to *m*), the control subjects exceeded the paranoids, who gave more responses than the hebephrenics, who in turn gave more responses than the epileptic patients. This rank order (reversed) was again found for amount of "interference" manifest in producing the associative responses (holding constant the total number of items available). Furthermore, the difference among the subject groups increased directly as the task and/or the criterion became more restrictive. Thus on the color-production association task, using the lenient criterion, there was no difference among the subject groups; using the strict criterion, the epileptic subjects showed significantly more interference than either paranoid or control subjects. With the more restricted task of reproducing items from the food list, the number of significant differences among groups increased, and increased again with the application of the stricter scoring criteria.

The same rank order—of controls being followed by paranoids, hebephrenics, and then by epileptics—occurred for "efficiency" in responding; this measure was based on the relationship between the supply of items and the amount of interference manifest in their production (with sheer output of responses held constant). Here, however, there was no difference among groups in the associative production of "color" responses. Rather, the groups differed in ability to reproduce the words on the food list; the increased discrimination provided by applying the strict scoring criterion to the food responses suggested that irrelevant intrusions accounted for the reduction in efficiency of the paranoid and hebephrenic groups. The consistent rank order of normal, paranoid, hebephrenic, and epileptic subjects for total number of responses emitted, lack of interference, efficiency, and absence of irrelevant instructions is strikingly consistent with the initial hypotheses regarding the nature of the associative disorders connected with these pathological groups, as well as with Bousfield *et al.*'s formulation of the processes involved in continuous, controlled association.

Finally, Doust and Schneider (1955), in an extensive study, compared the stress reaction of constitutional and paranoid schizophrenics to emotional and neutral stimuli. Different from other diagnostic groups (see pp. 202 and 207) and from normals (see Chapter 1), these schizophrenics did not show any difference in stress reaction (as measured by percentage of blood oxygen saturation) to the two types of stimuli. However, further examination of responses to the *first half* of the WAT indicated that the paranoid subjects did show an initial differential reactivity, but that this difference disappeared during the second half of testing—a change which the authors interpret as an attempt at "coping" on the part of these subjects.

Two studies have used a social-behavioral criterion to divide schizophrenic patients into subtypes. Dokecki *et al.* (1965) compared the associative responses of male schizophrenics who had a history of good premorbid adjustment with those of male schizophrenics of poor premorbid adjustment; male TB patients were used as a control group. The Kent-Rosanoff stimuli were administered twice, with a 48-hour interval separating the two tests; subjects were scored for number of Primary responses given to Horton's 33-item commonality scale (Horton et al. 1963) and for stability of response (number of responses repeated on the second test). For both measures, the good premorbid schizophrenics did not differ from the control subjects, but the poor premorbid schizophrenic group gave significantly fewer Primaries and had less stable responses than either of the other two groups.

In the other study dividing schizophrenics on a social-behavioral criterion, M.J. Goldstein and Jones (1964) compared patients who were socially isolated on the ward with those who were socially engaged. Isolated female schizophrenics were found to give more autistic and clang associative responses than nonisolated females, and isolated males gave more distant associative responses and made more response reproduction errors than nonisolated males. Furthermore, these associative-response characteristics were better predictors of ward behavior than was any MMPI score.

Finally, in this discussion of the associative responses of different subtypes of schizophrenia. Meadow, Greenblatt, and Solomon (1953) had chronic schizophrenics give continuous, free associations for 30 minutes. The response protocols were then scored for "looseness of association," which was a defined as the number of "abnormal shifts" between "units of thought." This measure was found to be positively related to other measures of impairment in abstraction ability, leading the authors to conclude that these two cognitive abilities (or disabilities)—i.e., looseness of association and impairment in abstraction—are closely related aspects of the thought disorder characteristically found in chronic schizophrenics.

Schizophrenia versus Other Pathologies

Several studies of word association have compared psychotic patients (predominantly schizophrenics) with a number of other diagnostic groups, including neurotics, character disorders, epileptics, and brain-damaged patients. The latter two groups will be discussed in the following section, which deals with the effects of organic pathology on association. It should be pointed out that the variations among the studies both in terms of diagnostic groups tested and response measures used precludes any precise comparison or ranking of the several pathologies.

The strength of associative responses in schizophrenics, in depressives and alcoholics, and in normals, were studied by Sommer et al. (1960). Both for number of Primary responses (Primary determined for each group separately), and for response commonality (as determined by the 1910 Kent-Rosanoff normative response frequency), the three groups were significantly different; nonschizophrenic patients (depressives and alcoholics) showed the greatest response strength and schizophrenics showed the least, with the associative-response strength of normal subjects falling in between these two groups. The occurrence of idiosyncratic responses followed this same pattern, with schizophrenics giving more of these responses than normals, who in turn gave more than the depressive and alcoholic patients.

This study also attempted to determine the relative *awareness* of the different subject groups for the commonness or idiosyncrasy of their associative responses. Subjects were asked to rate their responses for commonness on a 4-point scale, and these ratings were compared with the actual frequency with which the response occurred on the 1910 Kent-Rosanoff norms. From this data, the authors reached the conclusion that schizophrenics do not differ from other individuals in terms of their insight into the uncommonness of their associative responses. The first support of this assertion is based on the correlation (ϕ coefficient) between the subjects' ratings of response commonness and the actual Kent-Rosanoff response frequency; the authors state that, although insignificant, schizophrenics showed greater concordance between their ratings and the actual empirical response frequency than did nonschizophrenic patients; however, both subject groups were less "aware" (accurate) than normals. Examination of the reported statistics, however, suggests to the present author that while normal subjects were the most accurate, the nonschizophrenic patients and the schizophrenic patients were approximately equal in their awareness of response commonness.

The second basis for the assertion of schizophrenic insight is based on the number of common responses (responses with a Kent-Rosanoff frequency of 20% or greater) which were rated by the subjects as being idiosyncratic. The results of this analysis indicated that nonschizophrenic patients rated 19% of their "common" responses as being idiosyncratic, while the occurrence of this rating was less for chronic schizophrenics (10%), acute schizophrenics (4%), and even less for normals (3%). From these findings the authors conclude that schizophrenics are aware their response are more uncommon than those of normals.* However, to the present author it seems that the authors have misinterpreted the meaning of their findings.†

---

*The authors do not discuss the fact that the nonschizophrenic (depressive and alcoholic) patients scored even higher (19%) on this measure.

†Apart from the question of the suitability of using 1910 norms.

The data tell us that schizophrenics think their *common* associations are uncommon, but they tell us nothing about whether schizophrenics think their *un*common associations are uncommon—, i.e., they tell us nothing about the schizophrenics' "insight." According to the present author's interpretation of the correlational data, this insight is shown to be poorer in schizophrenics than in normal subjects.

Commonality of associative responses in chronic schizophrenics and alcoholics also was investigated by Sommer *et al.* (1962); in addition, this study was concerned with the relative ability of the two groups ($N = 9$ and 5, respectively) to learn to give common responses. After an initial test to determine baseline response commonality (frequency of occurrence of the top three responses in the 1910 Kent-Rosanoff norms), subjects were subsequently tested on two alternating lists of 33 Kent-Rosanoff stimuli, and were reinforced for giving common (top three) responses. For the alcoholic subjects, this training was continued for 8 trials over a period of 2 weeks; the schizophrenic subjects were trained for 17 trials over 4 weeks. The results indicated that the response commonality of alcoholics was initially higher, and that it increased significantly over the training trials. Schizophrenics, on the other hand, showed only a slight (insignificant) increase in commonality from the beginning to the end of training. When these subjects were then tested with a new (third) list of stimuli, only the alcoholics showed an increase in response commonality. Subsequently, a new group of alcoholic patients ($N = 5$) were reinforced for giving *uncommon* responses (any response other than the top three on the 1910 norms); there was a significant increase in the number of uncommon responses given from the first to the seventh day (trial). Obviously, the design problems of this experiment—the small N's, the absence of nonreinforced control groups,* and the varying intervals between training and test—make the results difficult to interpret. The results only may be considered to *suggest* that it is more difficult to effect a lasting change in the associative habit hierarchy of schizophrenics than in that of alcoholics.

In addition to these studies of response strength, the types of responses made by various diagnostic groups also have been investigated. In the study reported earlier (see p. 153), Peters (1952) administered a controlled-association test with instructions to give supraordinate or subordinate responses. Consistent with the hypothesis† that giving supraordinate responses is related to maladjustment, psychotic subjects gave relatively

---

*This is a critical problem since Maltzman *et al.* (1958, 1962) have found that reinforcement was no more effective in producing unusual responses than was practice without reinforcement (see Chapter 4).

†From Korzybski's general semantic theory (1933).

more supraordinate responses than did neurotic subjects. (However, it should be recalled that when this test was presented as a multiple-choice procedure, the relationship between preference for supraordinate responses and maladjustment was equivocal; see p. 155).

Two other studies have used a multiple-choice WAT to determine the category of preferred responses. The first (Crown, 1952) used a WAT consisting of one "normal" and one "abnormal" response alternative, for an extensive study of several "normal" (total $N = 3345$) and "abnormal" (total $N = 505$) subject groups. The number of "abnormal" responses given by psychotic patients exceeded that of normal subjects; however, neurotic subjects were noted to give the greatest number of abnormal responses. In addition, the author cited some evidence which suggested that certain psychosomatic and psychopathic groups also give more "abnormal" responses than psychotic patients. In the second study, Gottesman (1964) constructed a 51-item multiple-choice WAT in which the three response alternatives consisted of the adult Primary (Russell & Jenkins, 1954), the child Primary (Woodrow & Lowell, 1916), and an irrelevant response. Sixteen schizophrenics were matched with sociopathic and normal subjects, and their relative preference for child responses (corrected for random marking by subtracting the number of irrelevant responses) was determined. The results indicated that the schizophrenic subjects gave the child response significantly more often than did the normal subjects ($p < .05$) and than did the sociopathic subjects ($p < .10$), while the latter two groups did not differ. (The irrelevant response was rarely chosen by any subject group.) However, the author makes the interesting observation that the preference of schizophrenics for child, as opposed to adult, responses, was largely due to the effect of the 25 opposite-evoking stimuli in the list. That is, the schizophrenics did not choose adult Primaries which were high strength *contrast* responses, although they did choose adult Primaries which were of equally high association strength when these were noncontrast responses.*

STUDIES OF LESS SEVERE FUNCTIONAL PATHOLOGY

Fewer studies of the effects of less severe functional pathology have been conducted. Those involving character disorder have been discussed above and will not be repeated here (cf. Crown, 1952; Sommer *et al.*, 1960, 1962). Instead, several investigations of the associative reactions of neurotic subjects will be presented. Clarke (1955) contrasted 43 neurotic soldiers, about to be discharged from the army for psychiatric disability, with 43

---

*Cf. the study by Kjeldergaard and Carroll (1963), cited in Chapter 8, for evidence of this same response style in normal subjects.

normal ones. The stimuli (predominantly emotional) were presented visually; the subject was to respond orally and at the same time to press a reaction time lever. On measures of response latency, motor disturbance, and failure to make a motor response, the neurotic subjects scored significantly higher than the normals; however, part of these findings were due to the fact that the neurotic subjects were less intelligent. When the effects of intelligence were partialed out, the relationship of the associative measures with neuroticism decreased. It was further demonstrated that the relative disturbance to various stimuli was the same for both subject groups, the difference being only in terms of degree, or magnitude.

At the end of testing, without warning, the subjects also were asked for a written recall of the stimuli. The tendency to be disturbed by the same words was also found in the stimulus recall results; a rank order correlation of .96 between the two subject groups for stimuli remembered and forgotten was obtained. Overall, the neurotic subjects recalled significantly fewer of the stimulus words than did the normals; however, when the effects of intelligence were partialed out, the recall difference was insignificant. For neither subject group was there a relationship between motor response disturbance to a stimulus word and the subsequent recall (or forgetting) of that word.

Kline and Schneck (1951) also found reaction time to be an effective discriminator between neurotic and normal subjects. In this study, the Menninger WAT was administered twice to 10 neurotic patients and to 10 normal students; during the second administration, half the subjects of each group were under hypnosis. As indicated, the neurotic subjects had longer reaction times on the first, prehypnosis test; with hypnosis, both subject groups showed a decreased response latency. When the responses to the emotional stimuli (only) of the second test were analyzed, the groups were significantly different. The greatest number of response disturbances occurred in the hypnotized-neurotic subject group (32%); the next greatest number occurred in the control-neurotic group (20%), followed by the hypnotized-normal subjects (18%), and the control-normal subjects (10%).

Bodin and Geer (1965) selected hospitalized psychiatric patients who scored high and low on the MMPI Depression scale, *D*; other aspects of pathology were randomly distributed. Half of each group was then administered a WAT with two standard response reproduction trials, and the other half a WAT with modified reproduction tests (the subject was to give a *different* response on trials 2 and 3). The results indicated that depression was negatively related to reproduction errors but positively related to errors on the modified test. Surprisingly, the authors found no relationship between trial 1 reaction time and depression. Equally unexpected was the finding that subjects with high *D* scores had *shorter* reaction times of trials 2 and 3. However, as all of the subjects in this study were hospitalized patients, the various other pathologies of the low *D* subjects may have caused an increase in their reaction times, thus producing an *apparent* decrease in the reaction time of the high *D* subjects.

Finally, two studies have used physiological measures to study the associative behavior of neurotic subjects. Herr and Kobler (1953), analyzing only the reactions to the emotional stimuli of a mixed-list WAT, found no difference in the mean GSR of neurotic and normal subjects, but did find that the GSR variance was greater for the neurotic group. Doust and Schneider (1955) used another physiological measure (percentage of blood oxygen saturation) to compare the stress reactions of a number of diagnostic groups to emotional stimuli (see Chapters 1 and 9 above). By using each subject as his own control (i.e., by subtracting the reaction to neutral stimuli from that to emotional stimuli), it was determined that neurotic subjects showed greater anoxemia than did normals.

Altered States of Consciousness

Another topic to be considered in this chapter is the effect of altered states of consciousness on the production of associative responses. Such changes in level of consciousness have been studied through the use of hypnosis and of drugs, and through the presentation of stimuli at subthreshold levels. The changes in thinking induced by such procedures are frequently assumed to approximate the type of thinking found in pathological conditions.

Hypnosis

Of three investigations made of the effects of hypnosis on associative responses, two were studies of individual patients. Dittborn (1954) presented to one hypnotized subject a list of stimuli, two of which were related to previous psychopathic behavior of the patient. In accord with the hypnotic suggestion, Dittborn found that the presentation of the "disagreeable" stimuli resulted in awakening from the hypnotic trance; no other differences between waking and hypnotic responses were noted for the one subject studied. Schneck and Kline (1952) studied the imagery responses of two patients to those Kent-Rosanoff stimuli which elicited either common or unusual responses from the subjects. The results were discussed in terms of the case analyses of the patients and it was noted that the visual images obtained to both control and critical stimuli corroborated the results of other psychological tests on these patients. In the third study (Kline &

Schneck, 1951, using 10 experimental and 10 control subjects), hypnosis was shown to decrease associative response latency and to increase both the number of response changes* and respose disturbances on a second (uninstructed) successive association trial.

Drugs

The effect of LSD on associative responses has been investigated in two studies by Weintraub *et al.* (1959, 1960). As compared to control subjects, LSD was found to increase both the number of association disturbances and response latency, for both neutral stimuli (significant) and emotional stimuli (insignificant). Furthermore, the number of "serious" deviant responses, "close" responses, and "serious" reproduction disturbances were all significantly increased by LSD, and to a lesser (insignificant) degree, there was an increase in the number of "minor" deviant responses, "distant" responses, and "minor" reproduction disturbances. Overall, LSD subjects showed an equal number of association disturbances for neutral and emotional stimuli, while for control subjects the occurrence of such disturbances to emotional stimuli exceeded that to neutral stimuli. In the second (1960) study, LSD and normal subjects were readministered the WAT after a 1-week interval. While normal subjects tended to eliminate unusual responses on the retest, this corrective tendency was not found in LSD subjects; rather, both unusual and common responses from the first test were maintained.

Although not strictly a word-association experiment, one other study relevant to the effect of drugs on associative processes will be mentioned here. Luria and Vinogradova (1959) have shown that the generalization of a vascular conditioned response to a verbal conditioned stimulus ordinarily, in normal subjects, proceeds along a "meaning," or semantic continuum (cf. Lacey & Smith, 1954, discussed in Chapter 4). However, if the subjects were given chloral hydrate (a cortical inhibitor), the system of associative links was changed, and generalization proceeded along a phonic continuum, such that words similar in sound to the conditioned stimulus elicited a conditioned response, but words similar in meaning did not.

Sub-Threshold Stimuli

The effects of altered states of consciousness on associative responses may also be studied by presenting stimuli at sub-threshold levels.† In a

---

*The direction of response change—toward popularity versus toward idiosyncrasy—was not specified.

†That is, the stimulus is presented at such a low level of intensity and/or so rapidly that the subject reports he is unable to perceive it.

pilot study reported by Dixon (1956, 1958), neutral and emotional stimuli were presented at sub-threshold levels to seven subjects, who were required to give either a discrete free-association response or to choose a response from 12 alternatives. The author reports that the emotional stimuli elicited a longer reaction time (insignificant) and a larger GSR (significant), as typically found with supraliminal emotional stimuli. Furthermore, the author cites some evidence from a stimulus-response matching test to support the hypothesis that the associative responses to the subliminal stimuli were not random, but were actually determined by the stimuli.

However, in a controlled, more extensive study, Fuhrer and Eriksen (1960) were unable to replicate Dixon's matching test results; instead, they found some evidence that partial stimulus cues (such as the greater length of emotional stimuli) may have accounted for the differential results.

Finally, Ricklin (1955) has presented an interesting clinical study in which WAT response disturbances are found to be related to both content and structure of the patient's dreams.

Organic Pathology

In addition to the studies of mental retardation discussed previously (see pp. 159–161), several investigations of the effects of organic pathology on associative processes have been carried out. These investigations have been concerned almost entirely with comparing the effects of organicity with those of other types of pathology. Of special interest have been those aspects of the response process which depend on memory and on the ability to change response sets.

It has been found, for example, that when intelligence is equated, brain-damaged patients do not differ from normal subjects in ability to repeat their initial association on a second, reproduction trial (Appelbaum, 1960b). However, when the subject is given a third association trial and asked to produce a *different* response, the two groups are differentiated; brain-damaged subjects more often repeat the first response, give multiword responses, give no response, or show evidence of blocking or other response disturbance. A second study by Appelbaum (1963) demonstrated that the ability to give a different response on the third association trial did not differentiate between normal subjects and nonpsychotic psychiatric patients, while again brain-damaged patients had significantly more difficulty than either of these groups. Furthermore, brain-damaged patients showed disturbances just as often to neutral as to emotional stimuli, while the other two subject groups had significantly more disturbances to emotional stimuli. In this latter study, however, brain-damaged patients also showed more response reproduction errors on trial 2 than did either the normal or psychiatric subjects (although trial-3 disturbances were still better diagnostic discriminators than trial-2 errors). The author suggests that this finding, discrepant with the first study, may be a function of the type of stimuli used. In the first investigation, Kent-Rosanoff stimuli with Primaries not exceeding a 25% response strength were used; in the second study, stimuli approximating those of the Menninger list, including emotional words, were used. It was suggested that the presence of these emotional stimuli disrupted the passive process which is usually involved in the reproduction of neutral responses, and made necessary the use of an *active* recall process, for which the brain-damaged patient was incapacitated.

Milgram (1960), comparing brain-damaged, schizophrenic (predominantly paranoid), and normal male subjects approximately matched for age, IQ, and education, also found that brain-damaged patients are significantly less able to give a different response on the third association trial than are schizophrenic or normal subjects, while these latter two groups do not differ from each other. On the other hand, when the subjects were given a stimulus word with seven response alternatives and were asked to pick the three responses which were related to the stimulus, brain-damaged subjects did as well as schizophrenic subjects, although normal ones were significantly better than both pathological groups.

Additional tests of the subjects' ability to shift response sets were carried out in this study. Using two forms of the Terman-Miles multiple-choice WAT (consisting of one masculine, one feminine, and two neutral response alternatives), the subjects were instructed to give the "masculine" response on one form and the "feminine" response on the other. Similarly, using two forms of an Abstract-Concrete multiple-choice WAT, subjects were instructed to choose the "adult" response on one form and the "child" response on the other. In all cases, the brain-damaged subjects appeared less able than normal subjects to adopt the appropriate response set, while schizophrenic subjects did as well as normals, with the exception of instructions to pick the "masculine" response. However, when the difference between brain-damaged and schizophrenic subjects for ability to give *any* different response* was accounted for, then brain-damaged subjects did better than schizophrenics in giving "masculine" responses and did as well in giving "feminine" and "child" responses. They still, however, were poorer in ability to pick "adult" (i.e., abstract, as opposed to concrete) responses.

In addition to these studies of associative memory and of maintenance

---

*As determined from performance on association trial 3, on which a "new" response was requested.

and ability to shift response set, an extensive study of the number of associative responses available, as well as the rate and efficiency of their emission in a continuous-association task, has been investigated by Lester (1960); the results of this study were reported in the section on functional pathology (see pp. 196–197). Beyond this study which used epileptic patients, the only other studies of the effect of organic pathology on associative responses have been those of Milgram (1961), comparing categories of response, and of Doust and Schneider (1955), using anoxemia as a measure of stress reaction to different types of stimulus words. In Milgram's study, which used Kent-Rosanoff stimuli, brain-damaged subjects were found to make more multiword and fewer "attribute" responses than normal subjects; compared to schizophrenics, brain-damaged subjects made more "meaningful-perseverative" and verb responses, and fewer "irrelevant-perseverative" responses. Furthermore, the correspondence of the frequency of certain categories of response was greater between the two pathological subject groups than it was between either group and the normal subjects. On the other hand, in Doust and Schneider's study, although organic (epileptic) patients showed relatively greater anoxemia to emotional stimuli (relative to their reaction to neutral stimuli) than did normal subjects, schizophrenic subjects (constitutional and paranoid) showed less reactivity to emotional stimuli (i.e., they showed equal anoxemia to neutral and to emotional stimuli).* For this type of stimulus, then, with this type of response measure, organic and schizophrenic patients react quite differently, while with neutral, Kent-Rosanoff stimuli, their qualitative style of response was quite similar.

Effect of Treatment

Two studies have investigated the effects of electroshock therapy (ECT) on the associative processes of schizophrenics. Moran, Mefferd, and Kimble (1960b) administered 30 different forms of a WAT to schizophrenic subjects for 240 consecutive days. During the first 100 days, the typical responses for each subject were established; during the next 20-days "control" period, it was noted that 38% of the responses were "new" (never given before). Following this, ECT was begun; during this treatment period, 84% of the responses were "new," and were more "normal," as determined both by normative frequency (Russell & Jenkins, 1954) and by judges' ratings. Two weeks after the cessation of ECT, 66% of the responses were still "new"; however, following this period, a gradual return of the old associations was noted, and this change paralleled a decline in the overall psychiatric condition of the patients.

*Between these two extremes were, in order of decreasing anoxemic reactivity, neurotics, normals, high-grade aments, senile dements, and depressives.

In the second study (Janis, 1950), the schizophrenic ECT patients were compared with a schizophrenic control group, who were matched for diagnosis, age, education, and length of hospitalization. The WAT consisted of 23 Kent-Rosanoff stimuli, 37 stimuli from the Menninger list, and 20 stimuli individually selected for emotional relevance to each subject; it was administered twice to each subject group. For the experimental group, ECT treatments intervened during the 12-week period between tests; for the control group, a period of 11 weeks elapsed between tests. The results of the second test indicated a decrease for both subject groups in the number of responses with delayed reaction times (reaction time $\geqslant$ 3 seconds). This decreased latency was slightly greater for the ECT subjects than for the controls, but the difference was not significant.

This finding of more rapid responding then made it possible to rule out blocking as the cause of the response disturbances which were subsequently noted for the ECT group. When the second-test responses of ECT subjects were compared with their first-test responses, on overall increase in response disturbance was noted; specifically, stimulus repetition and remote, idiosyncratic, and multiword responses increased, while other types of response disturbance remained at their pre-ECT level. On the other hand, the control schizophrenic subjects showed a decrease in number of response disturbances from test 1 to test 2. A comparison of the two subject groups, holding level of initial response disturbance constant, indicated significantly more response disturbances for the ECT group.

Similarly, response reproduction errors were greater for the ECT subjects than for the controls. This finding was interpreted not to be due to a disturbance of immediate memory, since other studies of ECT effects have shown that immediate memory is not affected. Rather, the author interpreted these results as indicating a failure of *set*; that is, he suggests that the subject has given a "spurious reaction," rather than a "genuine," well-established response on the association test proper, and that on the reproduction trail he either give a "genuine" response or another spurious response, either of which behaviors results in fluctuating, unstable responses. In general the author concludes that ECT association disturbance is not due to blocking, but rather to an inhibition or supplantation of the habitual associative response.

Summary and Discussion

The following is a summary of the findings relating pathology to various word-association response measures. These results have been grouped under several general headings: response strength, other aspects of the associative-response domain, response variability, response consistency over time, physiological measures of response, and the effect of the WAT format.

I. RESPONSE STRENGTH

(1) Primary response frequency
   (A) is greater for depressives and alcoholics than for normals, who in turn show a greater frequency than schizophrenics;
   (B) is greater in acute than in chronic schizophrenics, although in these studies there is a problem of confounding variables;
   (C) is the same for schizophrenics with a good premorbid history as for normals, and is greater for both of these groups than for poor premorbid schizophrenics.
(2) Response commonality
   (A) is greater for depressives and alcoholics than for normals, who in turn show a greater frequency than schizophrenics;
   (B) in schizophrenics has been found to increase during ECT treatment (but cf. II (3) (A) (a);
   (C) Errors in *rating* responses as idiosyncratic, when in fact they are common (frequency $\geqslant 20\%$) occur most often with depressives and alcoholics, followed by chronic schizophrenics, and then by acute schizophrenics, who make only a slightly greater number of such errors than do normals.
(3) Reaction time
   (A) is longer in schizophrenics than in normals, especially for multi-meaning stimuli;
   (B) is longer for neurotics than for normals;
   (C) is decreased by hypnosis;
   (D) is increased by LSD.

II. OTHER ASPECTS OF THE ASSOCIATIVE-RESPONSE DOMAIN

(1) Response availability, m, (on a controlled association test) is greater for normals than for paranoids, followed by hebephrenics, followed by epileptics.

(2) Idiosyncratic responses are more frequent with schizophrenics than with normals, and least frequent in depressives and alcoholics.

(3) Unusual responses and other types of response disturbance
   (A) are greater in schizophrenics than in normals—
      (a) they are also more common in socially isolated schizophrenics than in nonisolated schizophrenics, and
      (b) also, unusual responses have been found both to decrease

as a result of ECT (when schizophrenics were tested during treatment and immediately following) and to increase as a result of ECT (when schizophrenics were tested following treatment);
- (B) are greater in neurotics than in normals;
- (C) are greater in organics than in normals;
- (D) are greater under hypnosis and LSD, and are maintained on a second testing (vs. normal "corrective" tendency).

(4) There is some suggestion that certain semantic and/or response disturbance categories may discriminate among diagnostic groups.

III. Response Variability

(1) Response reproduction errors
- (A) are greater in schizophrenics than in normals, for both neutral and emotional stimuli—
    - (a) they are also greater in socially isolated male schizophrenics than in non-isolated male schizophrenics, and
    - (b) they are more common for schizophrenics who have had ECT than for those who have not;
- (B) are equal for organics and normals for neutral stimuli, but are greater for organics for emotional stimuli.

(2) Response changes on a second, uninstructed trial are greater under hypnosis.

(3) Stimulus reproduction errors have been found to be greater in neurotics than in normals, but this result was largely a function of IQ.

(4) Stimulus recognition errors are greater for schizophrenics than for normals, for both emotional and neutral stimuli.

IV. Response Consistency over Time

(1) Response commonality has been found to
- (A) remain the same in schizophrenics tested at 4-month intervals over a 16-month period, but increase in normals when retested after 2 weeks;
- (B) remain the same in normals but increase in certain schizophrenics,* over a period of 4 days.

(2) The type of response disturbance is more consistent over time for normals than for schizophrenics.

(3) The number of identical responses
- (A) is greater for normals than for schizophrenics, when retested after a week;

---

*Those with "object-referent" or "concept-referent" response sets.

(B) is equivalent for normals and schizophrenics with a good premorbid history, and less for poor premorbid schizophrenics, when retested after 48 hours.

V. PHYSIOLOGICAL MEASURES

(1) When the GSR to emotional stimuli is determined
   (A) neurotics and normals are equal in mean amplitude of response, but
   (B) neurotics show greater variability of response than do normals.

(2) Responses of anoxemia to emotional stimuli are greatest for epileptics, followed, in terms of decreasing responsivity, by neurotics, normals, high-grade retardates, senile dements, depressives, paranoids, and constitutional schizophrenics.

VI. TEST FORMAT

(1) When a multiple-choice test format is used
   (A) With response alternatives of "normal" versus "abnormal," the number of "abnormal" responses is greatest for neurotics, less for psychotics, and fewest for normals, and
   (B) with response alternatives of "adult," "child," and "irrelevant," the number of "child" responses is greatest for schizophrenics and less for sociopaths and normals, who are about equal.

(2) With a discrete WAT, when subjects are *instructed*
   (A) to give a different, second response
      (a) organics
         (i) have more difficulty than normals, and
         (ii) make an equal number of errors on emotional and neutral stimuli;
      (b) normals, nonpsychotic psychiatric patients, and schizophrenics
         (i) do not differ in overall number of errors, but
         (ii) normals and nonpsychotic patients make more errors on emotional than on neutral stimuli;
   (B) to give a particular *kind* of response, normals are more successful than schizophrenics.
   (C) to give either supra- or sub-ordinate responses, psychotics show a greater increase in supraordinate responses than do neurotics.

(3) There have been several studies of the effect of instructions to give a particular kind of response, using a multiple-choice test.
   (A) In general, organics make more errors than schizophrenics, who do not differ from normals.

(B) However, schizophrenics make as many errors as organics when instructed to choose a "masculine" response, or to choose the three responses (out of seven) which are most appropriate to the stimulus.

(C) Moreover, when ability to give *any* different response is partialed out (cf. VI. (2) (A) (a), schizophrenics make more errors than organics in choosing "masculine" responses, and an equal number of errors in choosing "feminine" and "child" responses.

This discussion of the effects of pathology on associative behavior is organized around one general question: what can be said about the associative-response domains of different pathological groups? The concept of associative-response domain will be discussed more fully in the final chapter of the book. As an approximate definition, it will suffice to indicate that by associative-response domain is meant the collection and organization of all those responses which make up the response hierarchy to a particular stimulus word.

With regard to organically based pathology, the most characteristic finding is of a severe restriction in the number of associative pathways which can be activated by a stimulus. Perhaps more accurately stated, organic pathology is characterized by a marked reduction in the number of responses available to any one stimulus. This is conceptualized as involving an extreme and involuntary restriction of the associative-response domain, perhaps as the result of the physical dissolution of associative pathways. It should be noted that this process does not involve an overall *weakening* of associative connections, but rather seems to reflect the *elimination* of pathways. This last assertion is inferred from the finding that the limited responses which are available are often of low normative frequency, whereas if the restriction phenomenon being described depended on an overall associative weakening, then the organic subject should be restricted to give only the most popular responses. Nor can it be assumed that the response restriction is only a behavioral epiphenomenon, reflecting extreme response inhibition due to heightened response competition. If it were true that the associative-response domains of organic patients consisted of many competing responses, then it should also be true that their associative responses would be highly variable from one testing to the next. In fact, the opposite results are found. Not only are individuals with organic pathology no more variable in associative responses than are normals, but in fact they are less able to change their associative responses *even when this is requested.* This latter response rigidity differentiates organics from schizophrenics, although in certain other ways their associative behavior is similar, as will be seen below.

The phenomenon of associative-response domain restriction is also characteristic of depressive and alcoholic pathologies. The processes involved in these two groups, however, appear to be rather different from those of the organic condition. As noted above, the restriction of associative pathways in the organic individual is independent of response commonality. For depressive and alcoholic individuals, the associative domain is restricted to the most common, or Popular, responses. In fact, the associative-response commonality of depressive and alcoholic patients has been found to exceed that of normals. This finding suggests to the present author that these individuals may be operating under a self-imposed response set to give the association which they think would be most likely to satisfy, or please, the examiner—that is, to give the most socially acceptable response.

This hypothesis is further supported by the finding that, despite their giving more common responses, depressive patients have longer reaction times,* whereas highly frequent responses are usually given more rapidly. It is suggested, then, that this increased reaction time reflects, in part, the individual searching for an appropriate response. Furthermore, it is hypothesized that the restriction of the associative response domain is a functional one which is partly under the voluntary control of the individual.†

There have been a few attempts to use hypnosis or drugs to induce altered states of consciousness, often with the belief that these correspond more closely to pathological cognitive states—such as, for example, found in schizophrenia. Rather little work has been done in this area, and even fewer carefully controlled experimental studies have been carried out. Tentatively, it appears that an alteration in the level of consciousness may affect the organization of associative domains. This is seen in the increase in the frequency of responses from outside the normal domain—i.e., of unusual responses—which suggests a breakdown in the domain boundary. It is also seen in the increase in response variability which, in addition to changing boundary conditions, suggests a breakdown of the associative hierarchy within the domain.

However, this disorganization of associative domains has different

---

*Reaction time data for alcoholics is not available in the literature. However, at least one investigator has noted that alcoholics appear to have longer reaction times than do normals (R. I. Story, personal communication, 1966). It is true, of course, that the reaction time of depressives to a number of tasks is generally slower. To note this fact, however, is not to explain it.

†as compared with the involuntary restriction based on physiological changes postulated for the organic.

effects when level of consciousness is modified by hypnosis as opposed to modification by LSD. Although both hypnosis and LSD result in an increased number of associative-response disturbances, reaction time is decreased with hypnosis but increased with LSD. Presumably, the hypnosis findings represent a weakening of ego-defenses and/or of the response-searching process. On the other hand, the LSD findings may represent some attempt at control of responses, or they may reflect an increase in response competition.

The kind of disorganization of associative domains found to result from altered states of consciousness is also found to be characteristic of schizophrenics. In contradistinction to organic, depressive, and alcoholic pathological conditions, one of the main difficulties which the schizophrenic manifests in his associative behavior is his *inability* to restrict the associative domain. The breakdown in the normal boundaries is seen in the finding that the associative domains of schizophrenics contain more different responses of an idiosyncratic nature, and that these responses are characterized as being "unusual" or "distant"—i.e., from outside of the usual domain. This breakdown in domain boundaries may also help explain why schizophrenics judge their common responses to be uncommon. That is, if the schizophrenic does not have some subjective sense of the average, or normal limits of an associative domain, it is very difficult for him to make a judgment as to whether his response falls inside or outside of that domain—i.e., whether it is a common or uncommon response.

As was true for LSD subjects, the associative domain disorganization found in schizophrenics is accompanied by an increase in associative reaction time. Again, different from depressives and alcoholics, this increased reaction time appears to be a function of the schizophrenic's inability to restrict his associative domain. That is, the greater number of response alternatives results in greater response competition, and it is this competition among potential responses which is responsible for the delay. Unlike the depressive or alcoholic, the schizophrenic's delayed reaction time does not result from searching for an acceptable response, but rather represents his inability to choose *a* response from among too many. This hypothesis is supported also by the finding that the reaction time of schizophrenics to multiple-, as opposed to single-, meaning stimuli is significantly longer, while for normal subjects the reverse is true. That is, schizophrenics have difficulty in restricting the activation of associative pathways, and this difficulty is increased when the stimulus itself is connected with several different associative domains.

Another way to describe this phenomenon of breakdown of boundaries of the associative domain is to say that schizophrenics have difficulty in applying and maintaining a response set in order to restrict associative responses. This is seen, for example, in the finding that schizophrenics have especial difficulty on *controlled*-association tests. When the test instructions require the subject to limit his responses, schizophrenics are less able to give a particular *kind* of response, and they have fewer responses available (as opposed to the free-association situation, in which they have too many responses available). The schizophrenic individual, then, is not able to limit his responses to those which fit the instructions by imposing an appropriate response set. However, if the experimental situation itself limits the responses possible—as in a multiple-choice test—then the schizophrenic is as successful, generally, as the normal individual in choosing the appropriate response.

Studies of schizophrenic associations also suggest that in addition to the breakdown of the domain boundary there is a breakdown of the associative hierarchy within the domain. This is seen, for example, in the fewer number of Primary responses and the lower response commonality of schizophrenic associations. Whether these findings are the result of a reduction in the associative strength of previously strong responses, or of an increase in the strength of weak responses due to heightened internal arousal* cannot be determined directly from the associative data. However, the increased number of responses which occur to a free-association test would suggest that the latter condition—increased strength of weaker responses—may better represent the situation. In either case, however, the decreased differences in relative associative response strength (i.e., the increased response competition postulated above), is seen in the increased response variability which characterizes the associative behavior of schizophrenics on response reproduction tests—a finding which distinguishes schizophrenic from neurotic individuals. The breakdown of the associative hierarchy within the domain is also seen in the schizophrenic's decreased ability to identify the most common responses which make up an associative domain—i.e., the three top responses in the associative hierarchy.

To summarize, then, studies of word association in different pathological groups indicate that they differ as to the kind of associative domains which occur in each pathology. Thus in organic patients, as well as in depressives and alcoholics, there is a restriction of the associative domain. However, in the former case this can be understood as an involuntary physical dissolution of associative connections, independent of the prior strength of those connections. One consequence of this is that the organic is unable to shift to a different response when requested. In the case of depressives and alcoholics, the domain is voluntarily restricted by eliminating weak responses and maintaining only the strongest (i.e., most popular) responses.

*As suggested, e.g., by Broen and Storms (1961).

The associative domains of schizophrenics, however, demonstrate the opposite state of affairs. The problem of the schizophrenic is that he is unable voluntarily to restrict his associations, and as a consequence is flooded with competing responses, many of which fall outside of the usual—i.e., normal—associative domain. The increased associative reaction time of the schizophrenic is understood as the result of this response competition, while the increased reaction time of the depressive and alcoholic—and, incidentally, of the normal individual with emotional stimuli—is understood as reflecting the time required to search for an acceptable response.

We would suggest that this (postulated) multiple causality of the same associative-response behavior has contributed to the difficulties investigators have encountered in trying to determine response measures which would discriminate among the various pathological conditions.

Chapter 9

CULTURAL DIFFERENCES

The effect of cultural differences on associative responses has been studied in two ways. First, the effect of changes across different chronological periods has been investigated. In these studies, the associative responses obtained in, for example, 1910, are compared with those obtained in the 1920's and the 1930's, on up until the current time.

In addition to these investigations of the changes in associative responses related to "changing times," there have also been studies contrasting the responses obtained from different cultural groups of subjects. These cross-cultural studies are presented later in this chapter.

Chronological Changes

Associative responses have been noted by several investigators to have changed with "changing times." Subsequent to Kent and Rosanoff's study in 1910, a number of other normative studies have been published through the years. These have been used for a series of investigations of cultural-chronological changes in the associations of adults and children.

ADULTS

The changes in adult responses over time was noted by Dörken (1956), who compared subjects tested in 1910 (Kent and Rosanoff, 1910), 1925 (O'Connor, 1928), 1953 (Tresselt and Leeds, 1953), and 1952 (Russell and Jenkins, 1954), for their responses to ten stimuli with strong Primaries. The results of this comparison indicated that the (percentage) frequency of Primary responses increased with each year sampled. In a more extensive study, J. J. Jenkins and Russell (1960) contrasted the 1910, 1925, 1927 (Schellenberg, 1930), 1933 (Keene, 1951), and 1952 normative data; they noted that the associative responses changed slowly but systematically over time, with the strongest responses being the most stable. They also found an increase in the frequency of the Primary response and a decrease in the number of supraordinate responses over time; method of testing* also appeared important, with individual-oral tests increasing Primary response frequency. A comparison of the 1927 and 1952 data, both based on University of Minnesota students, indicated a large increase in Primary response frequency, with 71% of the actual Primary responses being identical, and with the relative strengths among stimuli showing some consistency ($r = .70$). Measures of response commonality also reflected the general increase in response stereotype; in 1927, the first three associates to each stimulus accounted for 49% of the responses, while in 1954 this had increased to 59%.

A subsequent investigation by J. J. Jenkins and Palermo (1965) adds data from two additional sets of norms—1942 (Wilson, 1942) and 1960 (Palermo and Jenkins, 1964) to the previous comparison. The findings of this study supported the earlier results. In addition, the authors suggest that a plateau may have been reached with respect to both the increase in Primary responses and the decrease in supraordinate responses, noting that the 1942 data had the strongest mean Primary response strength (mean = 38.2%); it was also the strongest of all the individual-oral tests. However, a comparison of the 1942 mean Primary strength (38.2%) with the 1952 strength (37.5%) and the 1960 strength (34.8%) indicates that the frequency of Primary responses is still quite high in the latter groups, especially considering the fact that these responses were obtained under conditions of group-written testing, which has been shown to produce fewer Primary responses.

Finally, in this comparison of adult responses, Tressel and Leeds (1955) administered individual-oral tests to approximately 100 men and women from different regions and occupations and compared their responses with those of the 1927 group. They noted that 55 out of the 100 stimuli had a higher frequency of Primary response in 1955, and that, of these, 45% involved contrast responses.

CHILDREN

Several investigations have compared the changes in childrens' responses from those published by Woodrow and Lowell (1916)† to those obtained in more recent investigations. Entwisle et al., (1964) compared the oral responses of a current sample of 5-to-11-year-old children with the 1916 data. Although different stimuli were used in two studies, the authors arrived at the general conclusion that the current data indicated an acceleration by 4 to 5

---

*1910, 1925, 1933, and 1942 were individual-oral tests; for 1953, information about test format was not provided by the authors; presumably, it was individual-oral.

†Oral stimulus, written response.

years of the sequence of development of word-association behavior, with, for example, syntagmatic responses occurring earlier in children today. They concluded that the differences found between children and adults noted in the 1916 study are not found today between children who are just beginning school and those in the fifth grade. Increasing urbanization and availability of mass media for communication are suggested as explanatory factors.

Koff (1965) tested 8-to-12-year-old children on 51 stimuli selected from the 1916 list on the basis of two criteria: the stimulus had a different Primary response from children in 1916 than from adults in 1954, and the stimulus had a Primary response which was strong enough to account for a significant (.05 level) percentage of all responses given to that stimulus. The results indicated that only four of the 51 stimuli elicited identical Primary responses from the 1916 and 1963 groups; for these four, the 1916 response strength was (insignificantly) greater. For the 47 stimuli with changed Primaries, the 1963 data showed significantly stronger Primaries (mean 1916 = 22.5%, 1963 = 39.7%). This same (significant) difference was found for measures of response commonality, based on the frequency of the first three responses (mean 1916 = 42.5%, 1963 = 60.9%), and for number of opposite responses (mean 1916 = 3%, 1963 = 46%).

In this study, Koff used a written-stimulus, written-response procedure, while the 1916 data were based on an oral-stimulus, written-response procedure. The author suggests that the difference in procedure has little importance for the results. However, a study by Palermo and Jenkins (1965b) indicates this is not a valid conclusion. In this latter study, data reported by Palermo (1963) on fourth- and fifth-grade subjects who were tested in 1961 by a written-stimulus, written-response method were compared both with the oral-stimulus, written-response data of 1916 and with current (1963) data collected to replicate the 1916 method. The results of this comparison indicated that both the number of Primary responses and the number of contrast responses increased over time *and* increased with the use of oral stimuli; the rank order of the three subject groups for these two measures was 1963 stimulus-oral > 1961 stimulus-written > 1916 stimulus-oral. For number of heterogeneous, D, and idiosyncratic responses, there was an increase over time (1961 stimulus-written and 1963 stimulus-oral > 1916 stimulus-written). For supraordinate responses, 1961 stimulus-written exceeded 1916 stimulus-oral, which approximately equalled 1963 stimulus-oral; here, the apparent current increase of supraordinate responses in children which was noted in an earlier paper (Palermo & Jenkins, 1963) appeared to be a function of the different method of stimulus administration. Comparisons of the number of paradigmatic responses indicated that, for noun stimuli, 1963 stimulus-oral > 1961 stimulus-written > 1916 stimulus-oral; thus both method of administration and time were determining variables. However, for adjective stimuli, only time appeared to be a critical variable, for 1961 stimulus-written and 1963 stimulus-oral had approximately the same number of paradigmatic responses, while both exceeded 1916 stimulus-oral. Comparisons also were made for paradigmatic responses to transitive and intransitive verbs and to participles, but these were based on few stimuli, and each yielded a different rank order of subject groups.

Adult-Child

Several studies have contrasted the effects of changes due to time for adult and for child samples, in order to assess the relative effects of changes due to "changing times" and changes due to changing age, as well as the interaction of these two factors. Riegel (1965) compared the Primary responses to Kent-Rosanoff stimuli for normative data arranged on an age continuum (children, young adults, and adults) and a time continuum (1910, 1916, 1925, 1954, and 1958). The percentage of agreement among the groups so ordered was determined by constructing a simplex matrix of intercorrelations, first for age and then for time. When the data were ordered according to age, 15 interchanges were needed to meet the criteria for a simplex; when the data were ordered for time, 26 interchanges were needed, leading the author to conclude that age is a more important variable than chronological period of testing, in determining associative responses.*

Palermo and Jenkins (1963, 1965b) compared the number of supraordinate responses of adults and children tested earlier (1910, 1916) and later (1961, 1963), and determined that while in the earlier period adults gave more superordinate responses than children, the trend is now reversed. That is, while the frequency of superordinate responses has decreased for adults from 1910 to 1961, it has remained unchanged for children (Grades 4 and 5) from 1916 to 1963 (when method of testing is equated). The overall results of this change, however, is that children now give relatively more superordinate responses than do adults.

Koff (1965) has made a similar comparison for the occurrence of contrast responses. The largest number of these occurred for adults tested in 1954 (60%), followed by adults of 1933 (51%), children of 1963 (46%), adults of 1925 (44%), adults of 1910 (32%), and children of 1916 (3%).† The difference between 1963 children and the earliest child and adult groups was highly significant ($p < .001$).

*Note, however, the comment on this study in the discussion.
†See note, p. 218.

NORMAL-ABNORMAL

One final study of changes over time and with subject groups is that by Sommer *et al.* (1960). Kent-Rosanoff stimuli were administered to normal and schizophrenic subjects, and their responses were compared with those reported by Kent and Rosanoff in 1910 for normal and "insane" subjects. The number of idiosyncratic responses for normal subjects was greater in 1960 than in 1910 (mean = 10.9% versus 8.3%, respectively); however, for schizophrenics, the 1910 subjects exceeded the 1960 subjects (mean = 29.3% versus 18%, respectively).

Cross-Cultural Studies

In addition to the studies of changes in the associative responses of the culture over time, there have also been several investigations of the associative responses of *different* cultures. The most extensive of these cross-cultural studies was carried out by Miron and Wolfe (1964). A restricted WAT, calling for modifier responses (e.g., The_____ car; or the car is_____) was administered in written form to 100 male high-school subjects in each of 12 linguistic communities. The study was designed to determine the shape of the frequency distribution of such restricted associative responses. Other investigations of language—for example, studies of vocabulary and of aphasic speech—characteristically have found frequency distributions of lognormal form. The results of this association study indicated that the frequencies of such associative responses also conform to a theoretical distribution of lognormal form. Furthermore, associations in some languages were noted to show much greater response stereotypy than in others; that is, one or a few responses would predominate, and the probability of other responses was quite low. Specifically, Japanese was found to be the most stereotyped of the languages studied, and Afghan-Farsi the least stereotyped, with Kannada, Arabic, French, Flemish, Iranian-Farsi, Finnish, Swedish, Dutch, Cantonese, and English falling in between.

Ervin and Landar (1963) studied the responses of Navahos, using a technique in which subjects were to repeat the stimulus and then add another word to it. The Primary responses to 47 stimulus words which also appeared on the Kent-Rosanoff WAT were compared with the Russell-Jenkins normative data (1954) for those stimuli. Twenty-four of the Primaries were identical; the mean response strength based on the 47 words was 17% for the Navaho group, as compared to 45% for the Minnesota subjects. The Navaho responses tended to be paradigmatic contrasts, except when the variety of contexts in which the stimulus could be used was limited;

however, the proportion of paradigmatic responses in the Navaho group was as low as among non-Indian American primary-school children.

Rosenzweig (1959, 1961) compared the Primary responses of English, French, German, and Italian subjects to translated Kent-Rosanoff stimuli.* He noted a "strong tendency" for the Primary response to corresponding stimuli to be equivalent in meaning for the four language groups; this was more likely to be true if the Primary response were very strong, if the stimulus and response were adjectives, or if a contrast response was involved. These findings led to the conclusion that the more a particular response predominates in one sample, the more likely it is to appear as a Primary response in another sample.

In this regard, it is interesting to consider a study by Kolers (1963), in which bilingual subjects were given four forms of a WAT. These forms differed in terms of whether the stimuli were administered either in the subjects' native language or in English, and in whether responses were to be given in the native language or in English. The results indicated that only one-third of the responses in one language translated those in the other, and the proportion of similar-meaning responses did not differ very much regardless of whether the associations were intra- or inter-lingual. This finding led the author to conclude that verbal memories are not stored in some supralinguistic form, but are "tagged and stored separately in the language S used to define the experience to himself" (p. 300).

Finally, Rosenzweig (1964) compared the responses of both French college-aged workmen and students with those of both U.S. workmen (data from M. E. Tresselt, 1951–1952) and students. For number of identical Primary responses, U.S. workers and students were most similar (68 out of 100 responses); French students and U.S. students were next most similar (48/99); and French workers and French students least similar (39/98). Measures of response commonality, based on the frequency of the first three responses, found the greatest response similarity among U.S. students (59.1%); next most similar were U.S. workers (54.4%), and then French students (37.0%), and then French workers (33.3%). Supraordinate responses were more frequent among U.S. subjects than among the French, and were more frequent among workers than among students.

Measures of group associative overlap (mutual frequency measure applied to subjects; see Prologue, p. 35) based on *all* responses given to each stimulus indicated that U.S. workers and students were more similar than French workers and students, that U.S. workers and professional men were slightly more similar than U.S. workers and students, and that most similar

---

*It should be noted that these data were collected by different experimenters at different times.

were French men and French women students. To determine within-subject-group communality, Postman and Adams' measure (1960) was used (see Prologue, p. 35). Greatest within-group agreement was found for U.S. students, followed by U.S. workers, French students, and French workers. The author concluded from these findings that the language habits of adults differ according to social groupings within the community.

Summary and Discussion

The following is a summary of the findings regarding changes in associative responses, as these are related to cultural differences.

I. CHRONOLOGICAL CHANGES WITHIN ONE CULTURE

(1) For adults, studies of changes over time have indicated that
   (A) Primary responses
      (a) have increased in frequency,
      (b) were identical for 71% of the Kent-Rosanoff stimuli (1927 versus 1954), and
      (c) of greatest strength are most stable;
   (B) response commonality has increased; and
   (C) number of opposite responses has increased;
   (D) there is some evidence that the frequency of idiosyncratic responses has increased for normal subjects and decreased for psychiatric subjects.

(2) For children, studies of changes over time have indicated
   (A) Primary responses
      (a) have increased in frequency, and
      (b) were identical for only 7.8% of the Woodrow-Lowell stimuli (1916 versus 1963);
   (B) response commonality has increased;
   (C) response heterogeneity, D, and idiosyncrasy has increased;
   (D) number of opposite and paradigmatic responses has increased.

(3) When the relative importance of changes due to "changing times" versus changes due to different ages, is determined,
   (A) for the increase in Primary response frequency, age is the more important determiner;
   (B) for the increase in contrast responses, age is the more important determiner—however, 1963 children gave significantly more contrast responses than did 1910 adults;
   (C) For number of supraordinate responses, both age and time are important determinants—that is, number of supraordinate

responses has decreased over time for adults but remained un-unchanged for children.

II. CHANGES ACROSS CULTURES

(1) Primary responses
   (A) are more frequent among Americans than Frenchman;
   (B) are more frequent among non-Indian Americans than Navajos;
   (C) which are very strong in one language are more likely than are weak Primaries to be the Primaries in another language;
   (D) However, intra-subject comparison of bilingual subjects found only one-third of the responses given in one language to translate those in the other language.

(2) Response stereotypy varies across cultures, with Japanese being the most, and Afghan-Farsi the least, stereotyped (of the 12 language cultures studied).

(3) Paradigmatic responses are more frequent among non-Indian Americans than among Navajos.

(4) Supraordinate responses are more frequent among Americans than Frenchmen.

The cultural-chronological studies of word association indicate that the responses of both children and adults have become more stereotyped over the years. This increased response consistency is most marked in the associative behavior of children, who today by the fifth grade are as advanced, in comparison to first graders, as were adults in comparison to children some 50 years ago. However, while for adults this increasing stereotypy appears to reflect more people responding in the way that most people were already doing, for children there has been a striking qualitative change. It is not just that today's children are more consistent in the responses they give; they also give a different set of responses than did the children of earlier times.

In addition to this increased stereotypy, there is also evidence that there are more idiosyncratic responses among today's children (and possibly among adults, also). This finding suggests a polarization of individuals, in terms of associative behavior, such that the flexible middle of earlier times has been replaced by the extremes of response stereotypy (high-commonality subjects) and response idiosyncrasy (low-commonality subjects). Despite these striking changes with "changing times," it has been suggested (Riegel, 1965) that the age of the subject, rather than the chronological period of testing, is the more important determinant of associative responses. However, in the study on which this conclusion was based, the variable of age was confounded with that of method of testing, such that the older subjects gave oral responses, while the younger subjects gave written responses. Since giving oral responses is known to elicit more Primaries, it is possible that it was the response mode, rather than age, which was responsible for the greater response consistency among the older subjects of this study.

Cross-cultural studies indicate that different linguistic groups differ in the predictability of their associative behavior, with, for example, the responses of Americans being more stereotyped than those of Frenchmen. There is also some evidence that stimuli tend to elicit the same Primary responses across linguistic groups, especially when these are responses of high associative frequency. On the other hand, comparison of the responses of bilingual subjects to the same stimulus presented in two languages showed relatively little correspondence.

Chapter 10

CONCLUDING REMARKS

When considering these many studies, the author has found a particular conceptualization of associative organization to be helpful. This approach to word association conceives of associative hierarchies as a number of intersecting sets, and includes, in part, some ideas put forth elsewhere by Deese (e.g., 1962b, 1965) and by Noble (1952, 1953). The work of these authors and of other investigators in this area has influenced, in a variety of ways, the thinking reflected in the present formulation. However, both the general model and the manner in which a variety of studies are coordinated with it are the responsibility of the present author.

It is postulated, first of all, that there is some general, nonspecific repository of verbal memories, which includes all the verbal responses which are *potentially* available to the individual, irrespective of any particular stimulus. In other words, the general verbal universe is roughly equivalent to the vocabulary of the individual. The size of this universe—that is, the number of elements (words) in it—will vary both with age and from individual to individual.

Each of these elements is conceived of as having a nonspecific, general probability of occurrence—that is, of being emitted as an overt response—again, independent of any particular stimulus. This nonspecific response probability is most likely best estimated from some measure of the frequency with which that word appears in the language—such as the Thorndike-Lorge word count.

The general verbal universe just described is further conceptualized as consisting of a number of subsets, or associative domains. These domains are defined in terms of the existence of associative connections between several words and one particular stimulus. The same word may be repeatedly represented within one associative-response domain, depending on the strength of its associative connection with the stimulus. That is, a strong associative connection means multiple representation of that response in the domain. The concept of an associative-response domain, then, roughly corresponds to that of an associative response hierarchy.

In the simplest case, the associative response probability of a word from one domain is superimposed on the general response probability of that word in the verbal universe. Then, when a stimulus word is presented, all the elements in the associative domain are activated, but the final occurrence or nonoccurrence of a response is seen, in the simplest case, as the outcome of the interaction between these two factors of associative- and general-response probability.

In fact, this simple state of affairs rarely obtains. More often, additional factors interact with these two in determining overt response probability. Again, it has been helpful to use the associative domain concept to understand this interaction. If the general verbal universe consists of a fixed number of different words, then certain words must be represented in more than one associative domain. This means that the associative-response domains for certain stimuli must overlap, or intersect. If it happens that two stimuli with overlapping response domains are presented at the same time, then the area of overlap will be doubly activated, and hence the probability of a response from that area will be increased. At the same time, the relative probability of a response from outside the domain will be decreased, with a resulting restriction of the range of different responses which occur. On the other hand, if the associative-response domains of two stimuli presented in proximity are nonoverlapping, then the associative arousal of the two domains will result in the occurrence of a greater number of different responses than would be given to either single stimulus. As a corollary of this increased response heterogeneity, the relative probability of any single response will be decreased.

This theoretical conception accurately describes the empirical findings regarding the effect of changing the verbal context which surrounds the association test. When this context is chosen on the basis of knowledge that (at least) one associative response to the contextual stimuli overlaps with those responses given to the test stimulus—as, for example, in studies of mediated priming—the probability of that response is increased markedly. When the context is chosen without this consideration, the range, or heterogeneity, of responses is increased, and this is accompanied by a relative decrease in the probability of responses which frequently occur to either the context or test stimulus.

The conception of an increased probability of responses from the area of overlap between two associative domains is also helpful in explaining certain findings regarding associative reaction time. This explanation is based on the idea that the smaller the area from which the response may be chosen, the fewer the response alternatives, and hence the more rapidly the response can be made. Such an explanation is consistent with the finding that responses to controlled-association tests are given more quickly than to free-association tests. It is also consistent with the finding that subjects who operate within one response set have faster reaction times than those who change from one set to another. In both cases of decreased reaction time, the size of the domain which is available for selecting responses has been reduced.

This same approach is useful in understanding the associative response effects of the interaction between objective, external stimuli and subjective, internal—i.e., intra-subject—stimuli. Thus far, we have been considering associative domains organized on the basis of associative connections with stimuli—such as words—which are capable of objective representation. However, it is also possible for associative domains to be defined in terms of the associative connections of a set of words to certain subjective, intra-subject factors—such as emotional or motivational states, interests, or values. What is being suggested, then, is that there are different bases for the organization of the elements of thought. The distinctions being made here between an organization based on cognitive connections and an organization based on affective connections has been described in more detail by Bruner *et al.* (1962),* by Hilgard (1962), and by Rapaport (1951).†

Just as the presentation of a word may serve as an external stimulus to activate an associative domain, so may intra-subject factors activate associative domains. Then, to the extent that the associative-response domain of the external stimulus overlaps with that of the internal stimulus, we would expect to find the same kind of increased response probability in the area of associative overlap as occurs when two external stimuli with overlapping associative domains are presented.

The results of investigations of the effects of subjective values on associative responses are consistent with this point of view. First, support for the idea that subjective factors, as values, can serve as sources for organizing associative-response domains comes from the finding that responses representative of particular values are more likely to be given by subjects for whom those values are strong than by subjects for whom they are weak.‡ Secondly, the interaction between the associative domain based on external and on internal stimuli can be seen in those studies in which the stimulus

---

*In this book, Bruner distinguishes among three bases for grouping experience: affective, functional, and formal (p. 4).

†Cf. especially pp. 696-697.

‡Machover and Schwartz' study (1952) of the relationship between affective mood and associative response also supports this point of view. They found that, regardless of the affective quality of the stimulus, subjects gave responses from that affective associative domain which corresponded to their predominant mood.

words were preselected to represent different values. In these situations, subjects with strong values had both shorter reaction times and more responses available to those stimuli which represented their strongest values. This associative facilitation can be thought of as the result of the double activation of overlapping associative domains, once as a result of the external stimulus, and once as a result of the internal state of the subject. The multiple activation of the responses in the area of overlap results in a temporary increase both in the response potential of the Primary response (and hence a shorter reaction time), as well as in the number of other responses from that area which exceed threshold (and hence more responses, m, available).

In this discussion of associative domains, we have not yet considered the question of the size of the domain, apart from the suggestion that the size of the overall verbal universe roughly corresponds to the size of the individual's vocabulary. Nevertheless, it should be clear that the predictions made about the occurrence of responses from these domains will depend on the way in which the size of the domain is conceptualized. As noted in earlier chapters, estimates of domain size typically have been based on two different response measures. The importance of distinguishing between estimates of size based on the average number of responses made by a single individual, m, as opposed to estimates based on the number of different discrete responses made by different individuals, D, has been pointed out. It has been found, for example, that some experimental variables produce opposite effects on m and D. Thus, emotional stimuli elicit fewer continued responses, m, but more different discrete responses, D, than do neutral stimuli. A similar inverse relationship of decreasing m but increasing D has been found in studies of the associative behavior of males (versus females) and of older (versus college-aged) adults. An inverse relationship also has been found with the variable of stimulus familiarity, where the more familiar stimuli elicit more m responses but fewer D responses.

On the other hand, there are situations in which m and D both are related in the same manner to the same variables. Thus, like m, D has been found to increase with increasing subject anxiety, to increase from kindergarten to pre-adolescence, and to be less for adjectives and nouns than for other grammatical classes.

Measures such as m and D are clearly only approximations to the size of the "true" associative domain, and both are partly determined by the method used to obtain the associative data. That is, m will in part depend on the amount of time allowed the subject to continue giving associations, while D will in part depend on the number of subjects included in the total sample. Using a type-token ratio measure (number of different kinds of responses / total number of responses) does not fully solve this latter problem, since it is difficult to know how many subjects it is necessary to add to the sample before a new response would be expected to appear.*

However, there is a more serious consequence which derives from the method used to determine domain size. If domain size is estimated on the basis of the number of discrete responses given by a fixed number of subjects, then the domain size will not be determined only by the number of subjects in the sample. This technique also will result in a conception of associative domains in which the overall total associative strength of every domain is assumed to be equal. It has been suggested† that the use of this type of model has been responsible for the seemingly paradoxical situation that the strongest associative responses are also the most variable responses. That is, in this model, the strength of an associative response is based on the percentage of subjects within a sample who emit that discrete response. In this case, the estimate of strength of any one response is dependent on the estimate of strength of each other response. In other words, estimates of response strength based on the *percentage* of subjects giving that response result in a model in which the overall maximum response strength is fixed—i.e., the total associative strength, summed over all responses given to any one stimulus, must equal 100%.

It is questionable whether this fixed maximum strength model (FMS) is an adequate representation of the associative domain. As discussed earlier, it is likely that there are some domains in which there are several relatively strong responses, such that the sum of their individual associative strengths is greater than 100%. This could be determined by using a continued-association task to estimate associative response strength. For example, a continued-association task might reveal that 70% of the subjects gave the same first response, 70% gave the same second response, 70% gave the same third response, and so on. On the basis of these three responses alone, we would estimate that the total associative response strength of that domain exceeds 210%. This variable maximum strength model (VMS), then, can take into account the fact that some stimuli may have several equally strong associative responses which may, in turn, be responsible for the paradoxical response variability noted above.

In other words, it appears that the FMS model may markedly underestimate the associative strength of certain responses (as would be true for R_2 and R_3 in the example). An experiment by Wicklund, Palermo, and Jenkins (1964) provides supporting data for this point of view. In a paired-associate $(A-B)$ learning study, they found that responses, B, of equally low

---

*A modification of Horvath's application (1963) of the Yule Distribution to predict the expected associative hierarchy might be helpful with this problem.

†See Chapter 1.

normative strength (4%) were learned more easily if they came from a response hierarchy which had a strong Primary, as opposed to one having a weak Primary. They suggest that this is due to an underestimation of the A-B strength of the former type pairs, due to the "forced-frequency" approach which necessitates that lower-rank responses appear to be of weaker strength if the Primary response is very strong.

On the other hand, it has been pointed out (D. S. Palermo, personal communication, 1966) that the VMS model is open to the criticism that R_2-R_n are not being given to the stimulus alone, but to the stimulus plus all the preceding elicited responses. Empirical studies of the effects of prior verbal context would support this assumption. However, if we believe that the presentation of a stimulus activates the entire hierarchy of implicit associative responses, this criticism would not appear to be so serious. That is, if we believe that on a single presentation of the stimulus, R_2 is being activated at the same time as is R_1, and that R_1 and R_2 are activated at the same time as R_3, and so on, then the joint effects of the stimulus plus R_1 on R_2, and of the stimulus plus R_1 and R_2 on R_3 are already playing a part in determining the nature of the response hierarchy. If this is so, then making these implicit responses explicit (by giving repeated association trials) should not seriously distort the response hierarchy obtained.

The studies which *have* demonstrated changes in the response hierarchy as a result of verbal context have done so when the context words have been chosen specifically to increase the probability of a particular response or have been selected such that they activate a different associative domain. In the first case, the result has been to narrow the range of responses obtained (i.e., increase the probability of one response). In the second case, the number of different responses obtained has been increased.

However, in studies in which the context has been chosen from the *same* associative domain—e.g., a compound stimulus consisting of a stimulus and its R_1 (Grooms & Osipow, 1963), the responses obtained to the compound were very similar to those obtained to either stimulus presented independently. This would seem to suggest that overt presentation of responses within the same hierarchy does not necessarily change the hierarchy. Whether this would be true for all S-R_1 compounds, or whether it was a function of the particular compounds used in this study (see p. 88) remains to be determined.

Another criticism which might be raised regarding the VMS approach also is related to the use of repeated stimulus presentation. Since there is some evidence which suggests that this procedure may result in stimulus satiation, it might be argued that it would not be an appropriate method for establishing the true nature of the associative domain. It should be pointed out that both of these criticisms—the effects of preceding context and the possibility of stimulus satiation—have been discussed in connection with the interpretation of originality-training effects. In fact, the continued-association method being proposed to determine VMS is very similar to that used in originality training. Thus, to the extent that it can be argued that the results of originality training are due to increased contextual complexity and stimulus satiation, it may also be argued that these factors will modify the responses to the later VMS association trials.

While these factors cannot be ignored, their effect is probably less important for the determination of VMS than it is for the interpretation of originality training. This is because the VMS method makes use of all the responses given to the stimulus over successive trials, while the effects of originality training are determined only by the responses given to the final trial, on which the cumulative effects of context and satiation are maximal. It is suggested, then, that the VMS approach may be a better method for determining both the number and associative strength of responses which constitute an associative domain.

The problem of qualitatively characterizing the responses which make up an associative domain is somewhat more difficult. In terms of the developmental formation of associative domains, it appears fairly clear that the responses of young children are established on the basis of associative contiguity. Two events (e.g., objects, or elements of speech) which often occur contiguously come to be associated. Such syntagmatic associations are characteristic of the associations of young children. It has been suggested (Glucksberg & Cohen, 1965; McNeill, 1963) that the development of paradigmatic associations results from these words having occupied the same grammatical position in sentences.* In any case, the qualitative explanation of paradigmatic responses requires reference to some third concept. For example, responses are characterized as being synonyms, or antonyms, or members of a particular conceptual class.

This switch from syntagmatic to paradigmatic association may well be another aspect of the processes described by Kendler and Kendler (1962) to explain concept formation and problem solving in younger and older children. Younger children use an approach to problem solving which can be characterized as developing *S-R* associations, or automatic associative habits. The transfer of original learning (problem solution) to new situations then depends on the same laws of primary stimulus generalization as apply in studies of animal learning. However, this automatic approach eventually gives way to a "thinking" approach, where problem solving responses become conceptually mediated. It is suggested here that the shift from syntagmatic associations, based on the associationistic law of contiguity, to paradigmatic associations, based on conceptual relationships and

---

* But see footnote on p. 72 for the change in McNeill's viewpoint.

represented by the more structural association laws of similarity and contrast, may be another aspect of this process.

The increasing occurrence of conceptually mediated associations with increasing age in childhood is paralleled by an increase in these associations with increasing intellectual level. Both within groups of mental retardates and within groups of normal children, the brighter individuals give more responses based on conceptual links between the stimulus and response. At the same time, the brighter individuals of both groups show greater response commonality.

Subsequently, however, in normal adults it appears that the mediating link for a number of these conceptual associations is short-circuited, such that many of the responses can be characterized as depending on automatic, direct word-word associative habits. These are not, however, necessarily of the same type as the automatic, nonmediated responses of young children. In the case of adults, the former cognitive mediator can be reconstructed; in the case of children, the association is based on principles of spatial or temporal contiguity.

The development of these short-circuited responses complicates the relationship between intellectual level and response commonality in adults. That is, to the extent that adult Primary responses are conceptually mediated, and to the extent that conceptual mediation is positively related to intelligence, then the occurrence of Primary responses will be a positive function of intellectual level. However, empirical studies have not found response commonality in normal adults to be a function of intelligence. This result has suggested to the present author that the absence of a relationship between response commonality and intelligence in adulthood is due to the fact that a number of adult Primary responses are not conceptually mediated.

Apart from these and certain other developmental findings regarding qualitative changes in associative responses, other attempts to use categories or classifications as a response variable have not been very successful. Characteristically, a great deal of time and effort has been spent on classifying responses into a large number of response categories, only to find that not more than three or four of these bear any consistent relationship to the variables under study, or that a factor analysis of the results indicates that three or four general factors will account for the results based on the extensive category list. These discouraging results have not been due to the unreliability of the clasifications, since inter-rater reliability is generally quite high. Nor, on reflection, do they seem to be due to the wrong categories being used. Rather, it is suggested that these findings are closely related to the results of studies of response sets. If it is true that there are only three or four sets that a subject may adopt when taking a WAT, then it is not surprising that a factor analysis of some 60 response categories reduces to three or four factors. That is, it is suggested that each of these factors reflects a different response set. Nor is it difficult to understand, in this context, why only a few categories relate to the other variables of the study. It may be that each category represents a different response set, each of which, in turn, is related to the variables under study in some particular way. Alternatively, the several categories may represent one response set, which is the only one which is related to the other variables.

Although a variety of verbal labels has been used to describe the several response sets identified in different studies, it appears that these sets, or styles of response, can be grouped into two general categories. These larger categories have been identified by Nunnally as representing either a semantic relationship or an associative relationship between the stimulus and response. In turn, the semantic category is comprised either of a set to give functional responses or a set to give conceptual responses. The associative category, on the other hand, is based on a speed set—i.e., is based on a set to give responses as quickly as possible. In fact, the responses which occur under such a set are primarily contrast and contiguity associations.

These findings fit very well with the distinction made above between the mediated and the short-circuited (nonmediated) associative responses found in adults. As has been suggested in Chapter 8, functional and conceptual responses are examples of mediated associations, while speed responses—i.e., contrast and contiguity responses—are made possible by the elimination of the mediating link. It also has been suggested that this distinction is a useful way to conceptualize the difference in associative responses obtained from subjects who differ in predominating personality factors or values. Extraverted, impulsive, and socially oriented individuals typically show higher response commonality. It is postulated that this reflects a greater number of nonmediated responses in these individuals as a result of the greater amount of interaction which they have had with (verbal) society. On the other hand, the lower response commonality of introverted, inhibited, and introspective individuals is hypothesized to be due to their giving more conceptually mediated responses which, in part, reflects their lesser degree of social interaction.

In addition to the issues of the development of associative domains and the conditions which may cause a temporary rearrangement of the response hierarchy within the domain, the preceding chapters also have pointed to several factors which disrupt normal associative functioning. One such factor is the nature of the stimulus word itself. A second disruptive factor is that of stress—whether experimentally created or internally produced (subject anxiety). A third cause of disordered associative processes is subject pathology. The associative response effects of each of these variables may be thought of as the result of certain modifications which they produce in the associative-response domains of the individual.

In Chapter 1 it was suggested that emotional stimuli produce implicit avoidance responses which then generalize to other words of the same semantic category—i.e., to other conceptually related responses in that associative domain. It was postulated that the empirical finding of decreased response availability, m, to emotional stimuli was one consequence of this generalization of avoidance responses. Support for the hypothesis that this decrease reflects an underlying process of generalization of avoidance responses comes from studies of the effects of negative reinforcement on word association (as reported in Chapter 4). These studies have demonstrated that what might be termed autonomic avoidance responses—e.g., increased heart rate following shock—can be conditioned to neutral stimuli when these are paired with negative reinforcement. More crucial to the present argument is the further finding that these autonomic avoidance responses generalize to other words of the same semantic category.* That is, meaningfully related words now produce the same avoidance responses as did the original conditioned stimulus, or, to restate this finding in terms of the above hypothesis, implicit avoidance responses generalize to other conceptually related elements of the associative domain.

A second consequence of the generalization of implicit avoidance responses to other conceptually related responses in the associative domain is the disruption of a characteristic response set—i.e., the disruption of the functional-conceptual response set. This disruption may make little difference if the response set to give contrast responses (i.e., the speed set) can be easily adopted. However, not all stimuli have a contrast response available, and not all subjects may be able to adopt this set.† Furthermore, this response set is less (or not at all) effective when the task calls for more than one response to the same stimulus, since most words have but one antonym. In any case, if it is not feasible to adopt a contrast response set and if the conceptual response set is rendered inoperative due to generalized implicit avoidance responses, the subject must then use a new response strategy in order to find an associative response. In turn, this may require the subject to go outside the usual associative domain. The effects of this

---

*Semantic generalization as a basis for explaining autonomic responses has been discussed by Luria and Vinogradova (1959) and by Razran (1961).

†It is interesting to note, as an aside, that although it has been suggested that nonmediated automatic responses occur as the result of a defensive maneuver of the normal individual (e.g., Siipola et al., 1955), it has been the author's experience that among schizophrenics there are some who scrupulously avoid making these responses. This observation is empirically supported by Gottesman's study (1964), in which schizophrenics avoided choosing high-strength Primary contrast responses, while they did choose noncontrast Primary responses of equally high associative strength.

"searching" process are seen in the increased reaction time, the increased number of idiosyncratic responses, and, perhaps, the increased number of response reproduction errors which occur with these stimuli.*

In the discussion above, it is hypothesized that due to the nature of the stimuli, implicit avoidance responses generalize to certain other elements in the associative response domain. However, it also has been found that the particular responses which are avoided are due to an interaction between stimulus and subject variables. This idea is of course implicit in Geer and Mollenauer's hypothesis (1964) that increased reaction time to emotional stimuli is due to the subject searching for a socially acceptable response. Here, the criterion of what constitutes an acceptable response is based on subjective factors within the individual. However, more subtle interactions between subject variables and avoided responses have been demonstrated. For example, Machover and Schwartz (1952) found that positively or negatively toned emotional stimuli will be responded to with a semantically congruent response if the stimulus is consonant with the subject's emotional state. However, these responses will be avoided, and a contrast response given instead, if the emotional tone of the stimulus is opposite to that of the subjective feeling-state of the subject.

An interaction between experimental variables and subject variables in producing a disruption of associative processes also has been characteristic in studies of the effects of stress on associative behavior. Thus, several attempts to relate anxiety to measures of response heterogeneity, response availability, or reaction time were unsuccessful, when these measures were based on the associative responses to an undifferentiated collection of stimuli. However, when the stimuli were divided according to the pre-experimental size of their associative-response domains (high D versus low D), or to their affective values (emotional versus neutral), then significant interactions between subject anxiety and associative responses were found. Stimuli with large response domains elicited more heterogeneous responses, with longer reaction times, from anxious subjects, but anxiety was unrelated to reaction time, and it decreased response heterogeneity to stimuli with small response domains. Similarly, emotional stimuli resulted in decreased response availability and longer reaction times for anxious subjects, but these relationships were not found with neutral stimuli.

We would interpret these findings as indicating that the disorganization of associative domains which results from internal sources of stress (subject anxiety) may not be sufficient to produce reliable changes in response

---

*These findings parallel the results of other studies (independent of the question of stimulus emotionality) of the effects of subjects adopting a nonpreferred response set.

measures. However, presenting stimuli which are themselves sources of associative domain disorganization may increase the disorganization to a sufficient degree that its effects become manifest on the response measures.

It has been suggested earlier (see Chapter 5) that anxious individuals will have developed a variety of methods to avoid the arousal of anxiety-producing ideas. On the one hand, the associative domain may be sharply constricted, such that connections to disturbing associative responses are functionally eliminated. On the other hand, the individual may avoid the anxiety-producing ideas by developing associations to a series of substitute, conflict-free ideas. The impoverished associative domains which result from the repression and/or denial in the former type of individual will result in different associative behavior than will be found associated with the latter method of coping by rationalization and/or intellectualization.

Thus, determining the nature of the associative disruption as a result of the interaction of stimulus and subject variables is more complicated than simply summing the effect of each separate variable. While it is true that certain stressful stimuli or task conditions have consistent effects on the disorganization of associative domains, when dealing with the effects of subject anxiety it is, in addition, necessary to take into account the different methods of coping with that anxiety which the individual has developed over the years. As has been pointed out, this coping may involve a marked constriction of the associative-response domain. On the other hand, it may result in an expansion (by substitution) of the associative domain. These two methods clearly will produce different effects on response measures.

Thus far we have discussed external factors—such as the nature of the stimulus word—which disrupt associative processes, and we have considered what happens when these factors interact with the characteristic mechanisms the individual has developed to cope with anxiety-arousing situations. There are, in addition, sources of associative disruption which are nearly exclusively determined by internal, intra-subject factors. These causes of associative disorganization fall under the general heading of pathology, and include—among others—conditions of mental retardation, of brain damage, and of schizophrenia.

It has been hypothesized earlier that the associative responses of the retarded individual are qualitatively different from those of persons of normal intelligence. Among higher-level retardates, it was suggested that this difference is seen in the absence of short-circuited, nonmediated responses* from their associative domains. Among lower-level retardates, it appears that many associative domains are not organized on the basis

---

*Which are derived originally from conceptually mediated responses.

of conceptual links. Rather, they often are formed on the basis of phonic similarity between the stimulus and the elements which make up the domain—as seen, for example, in the number of clang responses which these individuals give.

In this sense, then, retardation is connected with the disruption of normal associative response domains. It is interesting to note that administering chloral hydrate (a cortical inhibitor) to normal subjects can produce this same kind of disorganization. That is, while under normal conditions the generalization of a conditioned vascular response occurs along associative pathways which are semantically determined, following chloral hydrate the conditioned response no longer is elicited by semantically related words but rather occurs to words which are similar in sound (Luria & Vinogradova, 1959).

The effects of brain damage also have been discussed in terms of modifications of the associative-response domain. Although it is likely that damage to different areas of the brain will have specific effects on associative processes, there does seem to be a more general organic syndrome with regard to associative behavior. We have characterized this as a marked restriction of the associative domain, most likely due to a physical dissolution of associative pathways. The consequences of this restriction are seen especially in the reduction of response availability and in a rigidity of response, both of which are characteristic of this group.

Unlike the restriction of the associative-response domain which is postulated for the organic individual, it appears that the disorganization which characterizes the associative behavior of the schizophrenic is due to his *inability* to restrict the associative domain. The breakdown in the boundaries of the domain—alternatively described as the inability to apply and maintain a response set—is, then, one source of associative disorganization in this pathological group.* A second source of this disorganization is postulated to reflect a breakdown of the associative hierarchy within the response domain. The observed response effects of these (postulated) changes in the associative domains of the schizophrenic have been presented in an earlier chapter. In the following discussion, an attempt is made to relate these ideas to certain forms of thinking which have been described as characteristic of schizophrenics.

It has been noted that schizophrenic thinking is often overinclusive. Too many ideas are grouped under the same rubric.† In considering this problem, we again have made use of the concept of the associative domain. To begin with, we have noted that stimuli characteristically differ in the number

---

*As has been pointed out in Chapter 8, if the design of the experiment provides an experimental restriction of the subject to a limited number of responses, the associative behavior of schizophrenics and normals does not differ.

†E.g., cf. Cameron, in Kasanin (1964).

of different *types* of responses, D, in the domain. Under normal circumstances, the most frequently occurring type in the domain will "represent" that domain—i.e., will be the response which is elicited by the stimulus on which that domain is based. However, under special conditions (e.g., with drugs, hypnosis, or pathology), it appears that other responses which occur less frequently in the domain may be elicited by the stimulus. These responses may then come to represent the domain and/or each other.

Following this line of reasoning, it can be seen that the greater the number of response types in the domain, the greater the number of ideas which may be used to represent that stimulus. Since it has been shown that stimuli from some areas of psychological functioning (e.g., emotional stimuli) have significantly larger associative domains (larger here refers to more different types of responses), this means that the number of symbolic equivalents available to represent some psychological areas exceeds those available in other areas.

The author has noted, from an unpublished study, some further differentiations which may be made among emotional stimuli with regard to associative domain size. A comparison of the number of responses elicited by Rapaport's emotional and neutral words (Rapaport *et al.*, 1946) indicated that emotional stimuli elicited more different responses, D, for both normal and schizophrenic subjects (Cramer, 1965b). However, when the 60 stimuli were rank-ordered for size of associative domain, it was found, for both subject groups, that stimuli classified as representing sexual, anal, and aggressive emotional areas* were responsible for producing large associative domains, while not one of the nine "oral" stimuli fell within the top 20% of the rank order. On the other hand, among the words which elicited the fewest different responses (bottom 20%), there were three emotional stimuli, all of which belonged to the oral category. According to the present argument, this finding implies that the psychological areas of sexuality, anality, and aggressivity may be represented by a relatively large number of symbolic equivalents, while orality has relatively fewer substitutes. This hypothesis is also supported by the reaction time findings of Smock and Thompson (1954), in which a comparable rank order of stimuli was obtained. That is, stimuli which are suggested above as having the larger number of symbolic equivalents available to choose from, were found by Smock and Thompson to have longer reaction times, while oral stimuli had the shortest reaction time. Since reaction time and associative domain size, D, are positively related (M. J. Goldstein, 1961; Wiggens, 1957), these data offer some independent support for the reliability of the domain size findings.

Using this conception of stimuli as differing in the number of symbolic

---

*In descending rank order.

substitutes available, let us now return to the question of overinclusive thinking. We would suggest that stimuli, or concepts, with many available symbolic equivalents are more likely to be subject to overinclusive thinking. That is, the nature of the associative domain of certain concepts, when these constitute the content of cognitive tasks, may make it more likely that overinclusive thinking will occur in the individual's attempt to solve the task.

On the other hand, overinclusive thinking may also reflect the case in which the boundary of the associative domain breaks down, and elements which are ordinarily outside of the domain are now included in it. As discussed earlier, this is conceived of as characterizing the state of affairs in the schizophrenic.*

It will be noted that this change in domain boundary also has been suggested as a mechanism which some (nonpsychotic) individuals develop to cope with anxiety. To this extent, individuals who rely on intellectualization and rationalization may be expected to be prone to overinclusive thinking, under conditons of stress. However, according to the theoretical conception being put forth here, the associative domains of these individuals can be differentiated from those of schizophrenics. The nonpsychotic intellectualizer, it will be recalled, is postulated to have *substituted* elements outside of the associative domain in order to avoid anxiety-arousing elements within the domain. This means that the overall *size* of the associative domain is not enlarged, and that certain affectively toned responses are avoided. With the schizophrenic, on the other hand, these responses are not avoided, and hence the overall domain size is enlarged.†

Apart from the differences in the *content* of the associative domains of nonpsychotic and of schizophrenic individuals, there are also differences in the formal aspects of their thinking. It has been pointed out by several investigators‡ that schizophrenics, when faced with a problem in syllogistic reasoning, often do not adhere to classical logic. Rather than following the "All men are mortal; Socrates is a man; Therefore Socrates is mortal" paradigm, in which identity is accepted only on the basis of identical subjects, the schizophrenic may use a paralogic. In this form of reasoning, identity is accepted on the basis of identical predicates. Von Domarus offers as an example of this form of thinking the following: "Certain Indians are swift; . . . Stags are swift; . . . [Therefore] Certain Indians are stags" (p. 110).

---

*This conception roughly corresponds to that of the decreased response ceiling, postulated by Broen and Storms (1966).

†It also has been pointed out (footnote, p. 235) that certain schizophrenics avoid giving contrast responses, which would not be expected of the nonpsychotic intellectualizer.

‡E.g., cf. von Domarus, in Kasanin (1964).

The identical predicate *swift* is sufficient for the paralogician to assume an identity of subjects.

To the extent that this form of logic is used, knowledge of the different predicates attached to various stimuli should facilitate an understanding of certain otherwise incomprehensible groupings of ideas—i.e., should help explain unusual symbolic equivalences. Thus, if we try to understand the bizarre statement "Certain Indians are stags" as a single communication, we will have a good deal more difficulty than if we know the common predicate—"swift"—which connects the two ideas. What is being suggested is that it is possible to consider the associative domain of any stimulus word as constituting an atlas of the predicates attached to that word. Knowledge of associative-response overlap between two stimuli would give us some idea, then, of the basis on which two conceptually different ideas might be treated as equivalents by the paralogician.

EPILOGUE

The author has attempted to review a series of studies on word association which appeared in the literature during a period of rapid growth of interest in verbal behavior. The WAT is perhaps the simplest of tasks meant to represent cognitive processes, in the sense that we are looking at a single link in the complex chain of ideas we refer to as thinking. Nevertheless, we have seen that the factors which determine the single-word response are many, and that the effects of their interaction are not always predictable as a simple summation of separate effects.

A number of recent studies in the areas of verbal learning, concept formation, recall, and recognition have made use of associative connections among words as a basis for selection of stimulus materials. It is hoped that this review will be of benefit to future investigations of this type, in pointing out variables which may be expected to modify associative strengths and connections. It also is hoped that some of the interpretative comments and attempts at explanation made by the author may help draw together under a more general framework a wide range of empirical findings regarding word association. If the conception of the associative domain, as developed in this book, is a meaningful one for describing word association— as the author believes it to be—it should help in formulating future research in this area. Where there are discrepant findings, it should suggest explanations which can then be tested. Where there are consistent findings assumed to be explained by this model, it should suggest variables which would modify those results. The author has attempted in a few places, to apply the model in this way. Further development along this pathway remains for a future time and will depend on the overlapping efforts of a number of investigators—just as the material for this book has depended on the past studies of so many different individuals. It is hoped that collecting them together has, through organization, enriched this domain of investigation.

BIBLIOGRAPHY

WORD ASSOCIATION: 1950–1965

Albright, R. W., & Albright, J. B. Chain associations of pre-school children to picture stimuli. *Journal of Genetic Psychology,* 1951, **79,** 77–93.

Amster, H., & Battig, W. F. Effect of contextual meaningfulness on rated association values (m'), number of associations (m), and free recall. *Psychonomic Science,* 1965, **3,** 569–570.

Anderson, N. S. Word associations to individual letters. *Journal of Verbal Learning and Verbal Behavior,* 1965, **4,** 541–545.

Appelbaum, S. A. The word association test expanded. *Bulletin of the Menninger Clinic,* 1960, **24,** 258–264. (a)

Appelbaum, S. A. Automatic and selective processes in the word associations of brain-damaged and normal subjects. *Journal of Personality,* 1960, **28,** 64–72. (b)

Appelbaum, S. A. The end of the test as a determinant of responses. *Bulletin of the Menninger Clinic,* 1961, **25,** 120–128.

Appelbaum, S. A. The expanded word association test as a measure of psychological deficit associated with brain-damage. *Journal of Clinical Psychology,* 1963, **19,** 78–84.

Archer, E. J. Re-evaluation of the meaningfulness of all possible CVC trigrams. *Psychological Monographs,* 1960, **74** (10, Whole No. 497).

Baker, S. J. Autonomic resistances in word association tests. *Psychoanalytic Quarterly,* 1951, **20,** 275–283.

Becher, B. A. A cross-sectional and longitudinal study of the effect of education on free association responses. *Journal of Genetic Psychology,* 1960, **97,** 23–28.

Beck, H. S. The relationship of colors to various concepts. *Journal of Educational Research,* 1960, **53,** 194–196.

Bersh, P. J., Notterman, J. M., & Schoenfeld, W. N. The effect of experimental anxiety upon verbal behavior. *U.S. Air Force School of Aviation Medicine Report,* 1957, No. 57–26.

Birren, J. E., Riegel, K. F., & Robbin, J. S. Age differences in continuous word associations measured by speech recordings. *Journal of Gerontology,* 1961, **17,** 95–96.

Block, J. Commonality in word association and personality. *Psychological Reports,* 1960, **7,** 332.

Bodin, A. M., & Geer, J. H. Association responses of depressed and non-depressed patients to words of three hostility levels. *Journal of Personality,* 1965, **33,** 392–408.

Bousfield, W. A., & Barclay, W. D. The relationship between order and frequency of occurrence of restricted associative responses. *Journal of Experimental Psychology,* 1950, **40,** 643–647.

Bousfield, W. A., & Barclay, W. D. The application of Zipf's analysis of language to sequences of restricted associative responses. *Journal of General Psychology,* 1951, **44,** 253–260.

Bousfield, W. A., & Samborski, G. The relationship between strength of values and the meaningfulness of value words. *Journal of Personality,* 1955, **23,** 375–380.

Bousfield, W. A., Sedgewick, C. H. W., & Cohen, B. H. Certain temporal characteristics of the recall of verbal associates. *American Journal of Psychology,* 1954, **67,** 111–118.

Bousfield, W. A., Steward, J. R., & Cowan, T. M. The use of free associational norms for the prediction of clustering. Technical Report No. 36, 1961, Contract Nonr-631(00), Office of Naval Research and University of Connecticut.

Deterline, W. A. Verbal responses and concept formation. *Psychological Reports*, 1957, **3**, 372.
Dittborn, J. Dehypnotization and associated words. *Journal of Clinical and Experimental Hypnosis*, 1954, **2**, 136–138.
DiVesta, F. J. The distribution of modifiers used by children in a word-association task. *Journal of Verbal Learning and Verbal Behavior*, 1964, **3**, 421–427. (a)
DiVesta, F. J. A simplex analysis of changes with age in responses to a restricted word-association task. *Journal of Verbal Learning and Verbal Behavior*, 1964, **3**, 505–510. (b)
Dixon, N. F. Symbolic associations following subliminal stimulation. *International Journal of Psychonalysis*, 1956 , **37**, 159–170.
Dixon, N. F. The effect of subliminal stimulation upon autonomic and verbal behavior. *Journal of Abnormal and Social Psychology*, 1958, **57**, 29–36.
Dokecki, P. R., Polidoro, L. G., & Cromwell, R. L., Commonality and stability of word association responses in good and poor premorbid schizophrenics. *Journal of Abnormal Psychology*, 1965, **70**, 312.
Dörken, H. Frequency of common associations. *Psychological Reports*, 1956, **2**, 407–408.
Doris, J., Sarason, S., & Berkowitz, L. Test anxiety and performance on projective tests. *Child Development*, 1963, **34**, 751–766.
Doust, J. W., & Schneider, R. A. Studies on the physiology of awareness: An oximetrically monitored controlled stress test. *Canadian Journal of Psychology*, 1955, **9**, 67–78.
Dunn, S., Bliss, J., & Siipola, E. Effects of impulsivity, introversion and individual values upon associations under free conditions. *Journal of Personality*, 1958, **26**, 61–76.
Entwisle, D. R., & Forsyth, D. F. Word associations of children: Effect of method of administration. *Psychological Reports*, 1963, **13**, 291–299.
Entwisle, D. R., Forsyth, D. F., & Muuss, R. The syntactic-paradigmatic shift in children's word associations. *Journal of Verbal Learning and Verbal Behavior*, 1964, **3**, 19–29.
Epstein, S., & Fenz, W. D. Theory and experiment on the measurement of approach-avoidance conflict. *Journal of Abnormal and Social Psychology*, 1962, **64**, 97–112.
Eriksen, C. W. Defense against ego-threat in memory and perception. *Journal of Abnormal and Social Psychology*, 1952, **47**, 230–235.
Eriksen, C. W., & Kuethe, J. L. Avoidance conditioning of verbal behavior without awareness: A paradigm of repression. *Journal of Abnormal and Social Psychology*, 1956, **53**, 203–209.
Eriksen, C. W., & Lazarus, R. S. Perceptual defense and projective tests. *Journal of Abnormal and Social Psychology*, 1952, **47**, 302–308
Ervin, S. M. Changes with age in verbal determinants of word association. *American Journal of Psychology*, 1961, **74**, 361–372.
Ervin, S. M. Correlates of associative frequency. *Journal of Verbal Learning and Verbal Behavior*, 1963, **1**, 422–431.
Ervin, S. M., & Landar, H. Navaho word-associations. *American Journal of Psychology*, 1963, **76**, 49–57.
Faibish, G. M. Schizophrenic response to words of multiple meaning. *Journal of Personality*, 1961, **29**, 414–427.
Fillenbaum, S. Verbal satiation and changes in meaning of related items. *Journal of Verbal Learning and Verbal Behavior*, 1963, **2**, 263–271.
Fillenbaum, S., & Jones, L. V. Grammatical contingencies in word association. *Journal of Verbal Learning and Verbal Behavior*, 1965, **4**, 248–255.
Flaugher, R. L. Detection value: A measure of verbal relatedness applied to free association. *Journal of Verbal Learning and Verbal Behavior*, 1965, **4**, 309–314.
Flavell, J. H., Draguns, J., Feinberg, L. D., & Budin, W. A microgenetic approach to word association. *Journal of Abnormal and Social Psychology*, 1958, **57**, 1–7.

Fosmire, F. R. Clustering as a function of associative commonality. *American Journal of Psychology*, 1965, **78**, 39–47.
Fosmire, F. R., & Tryk, H. E. Word association: Common and original response. *Science*, 1963, **139**, 415–416.
Freedman, J. L. Increasing creativity by free-association training. *Journal of Experimental Psychology*, 1965, **69**, 89–91.
Fuhrer, M. J., & Eriksen, C. W. The unconscious perception of the meaning of verbal stimuli. *Journal of Abnormal and Social Psychology*, 1960, **61**, 432–439.
Gallup, H. F. Originality in free and controlled association responses. *Psychological Reports*, 1963, **13**, 923–929.
Garskof, B. E. Relation between single word association and continued association response hierarchies. *Psychological Reports*, 1965, **16**, 307–309.
Garskof, B. E., & Houston, J. P. Measurement of verbal relatedness: An idiographic approach. *Psychological Review*, 1963, **70**, 277–288.
Garskof, B. E., & Marshall, G. R. Relationship between two measures of verbal relatedness: Preliminary report. *Psychological Reports*, 1965, **16**, 17–18.
Geer, J. H., & Mollenauer, S. O. Meaning class and affective content in word association. *Psychological Reports*, 1964, **15**, 900.
Gillhooly, W. B. The effect of familiarization on associative latency. *Psychonomic Science*, 1965, **3**, 235–236.
Glanzer, M. Grammatical category: A rote learning and word association analysis. *Journal of Verbal Learning and Verbal Behavior*, 1962, **1**, 31–41.
Glucksberg, S., & Cohen, J. A. Acquisition of form-class membership by syntactic position. *Psychonomic Science*, 1965, **2**, 313–314.
Goldstein, A. G. Spatial orientation as a factor in eliciting associative responses to random shapes. *Perceptual and Motor Skills*, 1961, **12**, 15–25.
Goldstein, M. J. The relationship between anxiety and oral word association performance. *Journal of Abnormal and Social Psychology*, 1961, **62**, 468–471.
Goldstein, M. J., & Jones, R. B. The relationship among word association test, objective personality test scores and ratings of clinical behavior in psychiatric patients. *Journal of Projective Techniques*, 1964, **28**, 271–279.
Gottesman, L. E. Forced-choice word associations in schizophrenia. *Journal of Abnormal and Social Psychology*, 1964, **69**, 673–675.
Greenbaum, R. S. A note on the use of the word association test as an aid to interpreting the Bender Gestalt. *Journal of Projective Techniques*, 1955, **19**, 27–29.
Grooms, R. R., & Osipow, S. H. The effect of experimentally controlled verbal chains on word association. Paper presented at Eastern Psychological Association, New York City, 1963.
Gumenik, W. E., & Spencer, T. Verbal repetition and changes in meaning of synonyms: Satiation or set? *Journal of Verbal Learning and Verbal Behavior*, 1965, **4**, 286–290.
Hall, J. F., & Ugelow, A. Free association time as a function of word frequency. *Canadian Journal of Psychology*, 1957, **11**, 29–32.
Hare, R. D. Suppression of verbal behavior as a function of delay and schedule of severe punishment. *Journal of Verbal Learning and Verbal Behavior*, 1965, **4**, 216–221.
Harrison, K. Preliminary report on a multiple choice word-picture association test. *Diseases of the Nervous System*, 1960, **21**, 147–148.
Havron, M. D., Nordlie, P. G., & Cofer, C. N. Measurement of attitudes by a simple word association technique. *Journal of Social Psychology*, 1957, **46**, 81–89.
Herr, V. V., The Loyola language study. *Journal of Clinical Psychology*, 1957, **13**, 258–262.
Herr, V. V., & Kobler, F. J. A psychogalvanometric test for neuroticism. *Journal of Abnormal and Social Psychology*, 1953, **48**, 410–416.

Higgins, J., Mednick, S. A., & Philip, F. J. Associative disturbance as a function of chronicity in schizophrenia. *Journal of Abnormal Psychology*, 1965, **70**, 451–452.

Hills, J. R. Controlled association scores and engineering success. *Journal of Applied Psychology*, 1958, **42**, 10–13.

Hinze, H. A. K. The individual's word associations and his interpretation of prose paragraphs. *Journal of General Psychology*, 1961, **64**, 193–203.

Holtzman, W. H., Gorham, D., & Moran, L. J. A factor-analytic study of schizophrenic thought processes. *Journal of Abnormal and Social Psychology*, 1964, **69**, 355–364.

Horan, E. M. Word association frequency tables of mentally retarded children. *Journal of Consulting Psychology*, 1956, **20**, 22.

Horowitz, L. M., Brown, Z. M., & Weissbluth, S. Availability and the direction of associations. *Journal of Experimental Psychology*, 1964, **68**, 541–549.

Horton, D. L., Marlowe, D., & Crowne, D. P. The effects of instructional set and need for social approval on commonality of word association responses. *Journal of Abnormal and Social Psychology*, 1963, **66**, 67–72.

Horvath W. J., A stochastic model for word association tests. *Psychological, Review.*, 1963, **70**, 361–364.

Houston, J. P., & Garskof, B. E. Correlation between word association strength and associative overlap. *Psychological Reports*, 1963, **13**, 866.

Howard, K. I., & Fiske, D. W. Changes in relative strength of naturally acquired responses as a function of intervening experience. *Journal of Personality* 1961, **29**, 73–80.

Howe, E. S. Uncertainty and other associative correlates of Osgood's D_4. *Journal of Verbal Learning and Verbal Behavior*, 1965, **4**, 498–509.

Howes, D. On the relation between the probability of a word as an association and in general linguistic usage. *Journal of Abnormal and Social Psychology*, 1957, **54**, 75–85.

Howes, D., & Osgood, C. E. On the combination of associative probabilities in linguistic contexts. *American Journal of Psychology*, 1954, **67**, 241–258.

Howes, D. H., & Solomon, R. L. Visual duration threshold as a function of word-probability. *Journal of Experimental Psychology*, 1951, **41**, 401–410.

Hsü, E. H. A method for isolating presumptive personality profiles from changes in skin conductivity during word association tests. *Psychosomatic Medicine*, 1951, **13**, 260–261.

Jacobs, A. Formation of new associations to words selected on the basis of reaction-time-GSR combinations. *Journal of Abnormal and Social Psycholoy*, 1955, **51**, 371–377.

Jacobs, A. The recurrence of multiple verbal associations. *Psychology Newsletter, N.Y.U.*, 1959, **10**, 237–239.

Janis, I. L. Psychologic effects of electric convulsive treatments. (II. Changes in word association reactions.) *Journal of Nervous and Mental Disease*, 1950, **111**, 383–397.

Jenkins, J. J. Effects of word-association on the set to give popular responses. *Psychological Reports*, 1959, **5**, 94.

Jenkins, J. J. Commonality of association as an indicator of more general patterns of verbal behavior. In T. A. Sebeok (Ed.), *Style in language*. New York: Wiley, 1960. Pp. 307–329.

Jenkins, J. J., & Palermo, D. S. A note on scoring word association tests. *Journal of Verbal Learning and Verbal Behavior*, 1964, **3**, 158–160.

Jenkins, J. J., & Palermo, D. S. Further data on changes in word-association norms. *Journal of Personality and Social Psychology*, 1965, **1**, 303–309.

Jenkins, J. J., & Russell, W. A. Basic studies on individual and group behavior. Annual technical Report; 1956, Contract No. N8-onr -66216 between the Office of Naval Research and the University of Minnesota.

Jenkins, J. J., & Russell, W. A. Systematic changes in word association norms: 1910–1952. *Journal of Abnormal and Social Psychology*, 1960, **60**, 293–304.

Jenkins, J. J., Russell, W. A., & Suci, G. J. An atlas of semantic profiles for 360 words. *American Journal of Psychology*, 1958, **71**, 688–699.

Jenkins, P., & Cofer, C. N. An exploratory study of discrete free association to compound verbal stimuli. *Psychological Reports*, 1957, **3**, 599–602.

Johnson, D. M. Word-association and word frequency. *American Journal of Psychology*, 1956, **69**, 125–127.

Johnson, P. E. Associative meaning of concepts in physics. *Journal of Educational Psychology*, 1964, **55**, 84–88.

Johnson, R. C. Latency and association value as predictors of rate of verbal learning. *Journal of Verbal Learning and Verbal Behavior*, 1964, **3**, 77–78. (a)

Johnson, R. C. Mean associative latencies of 200 CVC trigrams. *Journal of Psychology*, 1964, **58**, 301–305. (b)

Johnson, R. C., & Lim, D. Personality variables in associative production. *Journal of General Psychology*, 1964, **71**, 349–350.

Johnson, R. C., Weiss, R. L., & Zelhart, P. F. Similarities and differences between normal and psychotic subjects in responses to verbal stimuli. *Journal of Abnormal and Social Psychology*, 1964, **68**, 221–226.

Johnson, T. J., Meinke, D. L., Van Mondfrans, A. P., & Finn, J. Word frequency of synonym responses as a function of word frequency of the stimulus and list position of the response. *Psychonomic Science*, 1965, **2**, 235–236.

Johnson, W. R. Psychogalvanic and word association studies of athletes. *Research Quarterly of the American Association for Health Physical Education*, 1951, **22**, 427–433.

Jones, R. M. The differential effects of negated word associations on ability to recall "traumatic" and "non-traumatic" stimulus words. *Journal of Projective Techniques*, 1958, **22**, 55–63.

Kagan, J., Rosman, B. L., Day, D., Albert, J., & Phillips, W. Information processing in the child: significance of analytic and reflective attitudes. *Psychological Monographs*, 1964, **78** (1, Whole No. 578).

Kanfer, F. H. Word-association and the drive hypothesis of anxiety. *Journal of Clinical Psychology*, 1960, **16**, 200–204.

Kanungo, R., & Lambert, W. E. Semantic satiation and meaningfulness. *American Journal of Psychology*, 1963, **76**, 421–428.

Kimbrough, W. W., & Cofer, C. N. A method for evaluating discrete, continuous associations. *Journal of Psychology*, 1957, **44**, 295–298.

Kimbrough, W. W., & Cofer, C. N. Attitudes and stimuli as determiners of responses. *Psychological Reports*, 1958, **4**, 61.

Kintz, B. L. Rated association values of pronounced items. *Perceptual and Motor Skills*, 1964, **19**, 452–454.

Kjeldergaard, P. M. Commonality scores under instructions to give opposites. *Psychological Reports*, 1962, **11**, 219–220.

Kjeldergaard, P. M. & Carroll, J. B. Two measures of free association response and their relations to scores on selected personality and verbal ability tests. *Psychological Reports*, 1963, **12**, 667–670.

Kline, M. V., & Schneck, J. M. Hypnosis in relation to the word association test. *Journal of General Psychology*, 1951, **44**, 129–137.

Koen, F. Polarization, *m* and emotionality in words. *Journal of Verbal Learning and Verbal Behavior*, 1962, **1**, 183–187.

Koff, R. H. Systematic changes in children's word association norms, 1916–1963. *Child Development*, 1965, **36**, 299–305.

Kolers, P. A. Interlingual word associations. *Journal of Verbal Learning and Verbal Behavior*, 1963, **2**, 291–300.

Kollar, E. J., Slater, G. R., Palmer, J. O., Docter, R. F., & Mandell, A. J. Measurement of stress in fasting man. *Archives of General Psychiatry*, 1964, **11**, 113–125.

Kuethe, J. L. The interaction of personality and muscle tension in producing agreement on commonality of verbal associations. *Journal of Abnormal and Social Psychology*, 1961, **62**, 696–697.

Kundu, R. A study of accident susceptibility by word association test. *Indian Journal of Psychology*, 1958, **33**, 249–257.

Lacey, J. I., & Smith, R. L. Conditioning and generalization of unconscious anxiety. *Science*, 1954, **120**, 1045–1052.

Laffal, J. The learning and retention of words with association disturbances. *Journal of Abnormal and Social Psychology*, 1952, **47**, 454–462.

Laffal, J. Response faults in word association as a function of response entropy. *Journal of Abnormal and Social Psychology*, 1955, **50**, 265–270.

Laffal, J. The use of contextual associates in the analysis of free speech. *Journal of General Psychology*, 1963, **69**, 51–64.

Laffal, J. Linguistic field theory and studies of word association. *Journal of General Psychology*, 1964, **71**, 145–155.

Laffal, J., & Feldman, S. The structure of single word and continuous word association. *Journal of Verbal Learning and Verbal Behavior*, 1962, **1**, 54–61.

Lambert, W. E. Associational fluency as a function of stimulus abstractness. *Canadian Journal of Psychology*, 1955, **9**, 103–106.

Lehmann, H., & Dörken, H. The clinical application of the Verdun Projective Battery *Canadian Journal of Psychology*, 1953, **7**, 69–80.

Lester, J. R. Production of associative sequences in schizophrenic and chronic brain syndrome. *Journal of Abnormal and Social Psychology*, 1960, **60**, 225–233.

Levinger, G., & Clark, J. Emotional factors in the forgetting of word associations. *Journal of Abnormal and Social Psychology*, 1961, **62**, 99–105.

Levy, S. Sentence completion and word association tests. In D. Brower & L. E. Abt (Eds.), *Progress in clinical psychology*. Vol. 2. New York: Grune & Stratton, 1956.

Luria, A. R., & Vinogradova, O. S. An objective investigation of the dynamics of semantic systems. *British Journal of Psychology*, 1959, **50**, 89–105.

Machover, S., & Schwartz, A. A homeostatic effect of mood on associative abstractness and reaction time. *Journal of Personality*, 1952, **21**, 59–67.

Maltzman, I., Belloni, M., & Fishbein, M. Experimental studies of associative variables in originality. *Psychological Monographs*, 1964, **78**, (3, Whole No. 580).

Maltzman, I., Bogartz, W., & Berger, L. A procedure for increasing word association originality and its transfer effects. *Journal of Experimental Psychology*, 1958, **56**, 392–398.

Maltzman, I., Cohen, S., & Belloni, M. Associative behavior in normal and schizophrenic children. Technical Report No. 11, July, 1963.

Maltzman, I., & Gallup, H. F. Comments on "originality" in free and controlled association responses. *Psychological Reports*, 1964, **14**, 573–574.

Maltzman, I., Seymore, S., & Licht, L. Verbal conditioning of common and uncommon word associations. *Psychological Reports*, 1962, **10**, 363–369.

Maltzman, I., & Simon, S. A recency effect between word association lists. *Psychological Reports*, 1959, **5**, 632.

Maltzman, I., Simon, S., Raskin, D., & Licht, L. Experimental studies in the training of originality. *Psychological Monographs*, 1960, **74** (6, Whole No. 493).

Mandler, G., & Mandler, J. M. Associative behaviour and somatic response. *Canadian Journal of Psychology*, 1962, **16**, 331–343.

Mandler, G., & Parnes, E. W. Frequency and idiosyncrasy of associative responses. *Journal of Abnormal and Social Psychology*, 1957, **55**, 58–65.

Marshall, G. R., & Cofer, C. N. Associative indices as measures of word relatedness: A summary and comparison of ten methods. *Journal of Verbal Learning and Verbal Behavior*, 1963, **1**, 408–421.

Martin, J. G. Word-association frequency and the proximity effect. *Journal of Verbal Learning and Verbal Behavior*, 1964, **3**, 344–345.

Martin, R. B., & Dean, S. J. Word familiarity and avoidance conditioning of verbal behavior. *Journal of Personality*, 1965, **1**, 496–499.

Matthews, W. A. The relation between association norms and word frequency. *British Journal of Psychology*, 1965, **56**, 391–399.

McGinnies, E. Personal values as determinants of word association. *Journal of Abnormal and Social Psychology*, 1950, **45**, 28–36.

McNeill, D. The origin of associations within the same grammatical class. *Journal of Verbal Learning and Verbal Behavior*, 1963, **2**, 250–262.

Meadow, A., Greenblatt, M., & Solomon, H. C. "Looseness of association" and impairment in abstraction in schizophrenia. *Journal of Nervous and Mental Disease*, 1953, **118**, 27–35.

Mednick, M. T., Mednick, S. A., & Jung, C. C. Continual association as a function of level of creativity and type of verbal stimulus. *Journal of Abnormal and Social Psychology*, 1964, **69**, 511–515.(a)

Mednick, M. T., Mednick, S. A., & Mednick, E. V. Incubation of creative performance and specific associative priming. *Journal of Abnormal and Social Psychology*, 1964, **69**, 84–88. (b)

Mednick, S. A. The associative basis of the creative process. *Psychological Review*, 1962, **69**, 220–232.

Messick, S., & Solley, C. M. Word association and semantic differentiation. *American Journal of Psychology*, 1957, **70**, 586–593.

Milgram, N. A. Cognitive and empathic factors in role-taking by schizophrenic and brain-damaged patients. *Journal of Abnormal and Social Psychology*, 1960, **60**, 219–224.

Milgram, N. A. Microgenetic analysis of word associations in schizophrenic and brain-damaged patients. *Journal of Abnormal and Social Psychology*, 1961, **62**, 364–366.

Milgram, N. A. & Goodglass, H. Role style versus cognitive maturation in word associations of adults and children. *Journal of Personality*, 1961, **29**, 81–93.

Miron, M. S., & Wolfe, S. A cross-linguistic analysis of the response distributions of restricted word associations. *Journal of Verbal Learning and Verbal Behavior*, 1964, **3**, 376–384.

Mooherjee, K. Studies in word-association test. *Indian Journal of Psychology*, 1950, **25**, 49–57.

Moran, L. J., Mefferd, R. B., & Kimble, J. P. The objective measurement of psychopathology in longitudinal studies. *Transactions of the Fifth Research Conference on Cooperative Chemotherapy Studies in Psychiatry and Research Approaches to Mental Illness*, 1960, **5**, 106–111. (a)

Moran, L. J., Mefferd, R. B., & Kimble, J. P. Standardization of psychometric and psycho-diagnostic tests for daily measurements in psychopharmacological research. *Transactions of the Fourth Research Conference on Chemotherapy in Psychiatry*, 1960, **4**, 135–318. (b)

Moran, L. J., Mefferd, R. B., & Kimble, J. P. Idiodynamic sets in word association. *Psychological Monographs*, 1964, **78** (2, Whole No. 579).

Musgrave, B. Context effects on word associations using one-word, two-word and three-word stimuli. Paper presented at the meetings of the Eastern Psychological Association, 1958.

Nakamura, C. Y., & Wright, H. D. Effects of experimentally induced low drive, response mode, and social cues on word association and response speed. *Journal of Experimental Research in Personality*, 1965, **1**, 122–131.

Noble, C. E. An analysis of meaning. *Psychological Review*, 1952, **59**, 421–430.

Noble, C. E. The meaning-familiarity relationship. *Psychological Review*, 1953, **60**, 89–98.

Noble, C. E. Measurements of association value (*a*), rated associations (*a'*), and scaled meaningfulness (*m'*) for the 2100 CVC combinations of the English alphabet. *Psychological Reports*, 1961, **8**, 487–521.

Noble, C. E. Meaningfulness and familiarity. In C. N. Cofer & B. S. Musgrave (Eds.), *Verbal behavior and learning*. New York: McGraw-Hill, 1963. Pp. 76–119.

Noble, C. E., & Parker, G. V. C. The Montana scale of meaningfulness (*m*). *Psychological Reports*, 1960, **7**, 325–331.

Nunnally, J. C., Flaugher, R. L., & Hodges, W. E. Measurement of semantic habits. *Educational and Psychological Measurement*, 1963, **23**, 419–434.

Nunnally, J. C., & Hodges, W. E. Some dimensions of individual differences in word association. *Journal of Verbal Learning and Verbal Behavior*, 1965, **4**, 82–88.

Osgood, C. E., & Anderson, L. Certain relations among experienced contingencies, associative structure, and contingencies in encoded messages. *American Journal of Psychology*, 1957, **70**, 411–420.

Osgood, C. E., & Sebeok, T. A. Psycholinguistics. *Journal of Abnormal and Social Psychology* 1954, **49**, No. 4, Supplement, 1–203.

Osgood, C. E., Suci, G. J., & Tannenbaum, P. H. *The measurement of meaning*. Urbana, Ill.: University of Illinois Press, 1957.

Osipow, S. H., & Grooms, R. R. Reciprocal association to the Kent-Rosanoff primary associations. *Psychological Reports*, 1964, **14**, 106.

Osipow, S. H., & Grooms, R. R. Comparisons between cultural and individual response hierarchies. *Journal of Verbal Learning and Verbal Behavior*, 1965, **4**, 94–97. (a)

Osipow, S. H., & Grooms, R. R. Norms for chains of word associations. *Psychological Reports*, 1965, **16**, 796. (b)

Palermo, D. S. Word associations and children's verbal behavior. In L. P. Lipsett & C. C. Spiker (Eds.), *Advances in child development and behavior*. Vol. 1. New York: Academic Press, 1963. Pp. 31–68.

Palermo, D. S. Word associations and their influence upon the verbal behavior of children. Paper presented at the meeting of the American Psychological Association, Los Angeles, 1964.

Palermo, D. S. Characteristics of word association responses obtained from children in grades one through four. Paper presented at the Social Research of Child Development Conference, Minneapolis, 1965.

Palermo, D. S., & Jenkins, J. J. Superordinates, "maturity" and logical analyses of language. *Psychological Reports*, 1962, **10**, 437–438.

Palermo, D. S., & Jenkins, J. J. Frequency of superordinate responses to a word association test as a function of age. *Journal of Verbal Learning and Verbal Behavior*, 1963, **1**, 378–383.

Palermo, D. S., & Jenkins, J. J. Sex differences in word associations. *Journal of General Psychology*, 1965, **72**, 77–84. (a)

Palermo, D. S., & Jenkins, J. J. Changes in the word associations of fourth- and fifth-grade children from 1916 to 1961. *Journal of Verbal Learning and Verbal Behavior*, 1965, **4**, 180–187. (b)

Paul, C. Generalized inhibition of verbal associations. *Journal of Verbal Learning and Verbal Behavior*, 1962, **1**, 162–167.

Peak, H. Psychological structure and psychological activity. *Psychological Review*, 1958, **65**, 325–347.

Peters, H. N. Supraordinality of associations and maladjustment. *Journal of Psychology*, 1952, **33**, 217–225.

Peters, H. N. A multiple choice supraordinality test. *Journal of Clinical Psychology*, 1958, **14**, 416–418.

Peterson, M. S., & Jenkins, J. J. Word association phenomena at the individual level: A pair of case studies. Technical Report No. 16, 1957, under Contract N8-onr-66216, between the Office of Naval Research and the University of Minnesota.

Podell, H. A. A quantitative study of convergent association. *Journal of Verbal Learning and Verbal Behavior*, 1963, **2**, 234–241.

Pollio, H. R. Word association as a function of conditioned meaning. *Journal of Experimental Psychology*, 1963, **66**, 454–460. (a)

Pollio, H. R. A simple matrix analysis of associative structure. *Journal of Verbal Learning and Verbal Behavior*, 1963, **2**, 166–169. (b)

Pollio, H. R. Some semantic relations among word-associates. *American Journal of Psychology*, 1964, **77**, 249–256. (a)

Pollio, H. R. Composition of associative clusters. *Journal of Experimental Psychology*, 1964, **67**, 199–208. (b)

Pollio, H. R., & Lore, R. K. The effect of a semantically congruent context on word-association behavior. *Journal of Psychology*, 1965, **61**, 17–26.

Postman, L. The acquisition and retention of consistent associative responses. *Journal of Experimental Psychology*, 1964, **67**, 183–190.

Postman, L., & Adams, P. A. Studies in incidental learning. VII. The effects of contextual determination. *Journal of Experimental Psychology*, 1960, **59**, 153–164.

Powell, M. Age and sex differences in degree of conflict within certain areas of psychological adjustment. *Psychological Monographs*, 1955, **69** (2, Whole No. 387).

Rabin, A. I., & Haworth, M. R. (Eds.) *Projective techniques with children*. New York: Grune & Stratton, 1960.

Rankin, R. E., & Campbell, D. T. Galvanic skin response to Negro and White experimenters. *Journal of Abnormal and Social Psychology*, 1955, **51**, 30–33.

Rapaport, D. (Ed.) The *organization and pathology of thought*. New York: Columbia University Press, 1951.

Rau, L. C. Variability in response to words: An investigation of stimulus-ambiguity. *American Journal of Psychology*, 1958, **71**, 338–349.

Ricklin, F. Jung's association test and dream interpretation. *Journal of Projective Techniques*, 1955, **19**, 226–235.

Riegel, K. F. Age and cultural differences as determinants of word associations: Suggestions for their analysis. *Psychological Reports*, 1965, **16**, 75–78.

Riegel, K. F., & Birren, J. E. Age differences in associative behavior. *Journal of Gerontology*, 1965, **20**, 125–130.

Riegel, K. F., & Riegel, R. M. Changes in associative behavior during later years of life: A cross-sectional analysis. *Vita Humana*, 1964, **7**, 1–32.

Riley, D. A., & Phillips, L. W. The effects of syllable familiarization on rote learning, association value, and reminiscence. *Journal of Experimental Psychology*, 1959, **57**, 372–379.

Robertson, J. P. S. The time-limit version of the word association test. *Journal of Clinical Psychology*, 1952, **8**, 405–408.

Rocklyn, E. H., Hessert, R. B., & Braun, H. W. Calibrated materials for verbal learning with middle- and old-aged subjects. *American Journal of Psychology*, 1957, **70**, 628–630.

Rosen, E., & Russell, W. A. Frequency characteristics of successive word-association. *American Journal of Psychology*, 1957, **70**, 120–122.

Rosenbaum, M. E., Arenson, S. J., & Panman, R. A. Training and instructions in the facilitation of originality. *Journal of Verbal Learning and Verbal Behavior*, 1964, **3**, 50–56.

Rosenzweig, M. R. Comparisons between French and English word association norms. *American Psychologist*, 1959, **14**, 363.

Rosenzweig, M. R. Comparisons among word association responses in English, French, German, and Italian. *American Journal of Psychology*, 1961, **74**, 347–360.

Rosenzweig, M. R. Word associations of French workmen: Comparisons with associations of French students and American workmen and students, *Journal of Verbal Learning and Verbal Behavior*, 1964, **3**, 57–69.

Rotberg, I. C. Effect of schedule and severity of punishment on verbal behavior. *Journal of Experimental Psychology*, 1959, **57**, 193–200.

Rothkopf, E. Z. Two predictors of stimulus equivalence in paired associate learning. *Psychological Reports*, 1960, **7**, 241–250.

Rothkopf, E. Z., & Coke, E. U. Intralist association data for 99 words of the Kent-Rosanoff word list. *Psychological Reports*, 1961, **8**, 463–474.

Rouse, R. O., & Verinis, J. S. Compound verbal stimuli and word association. *Psychological Reports*, 1965, **17**, 403–406.

Saltz, E. The effect of induced stress on free associations. *Journal of Abnormal and Social Psychology*, 1961, **62**, 161–164.

Sarason, I. G. Relationships of measures of anxiety and experimental instructions to word association test performance. *Journal of Abnormal and Social Psychology*, 1959, **59**, 37–42.

Sarason, I. G. A note on anxiety, instructions, and word association performance. *Journal of Abnormal and Social Psychology*, 1961, **62**, 153–154.

Schafer, R. Tests of personality: Word association test. In A. Weider (Ed.), *Contributions toward medical psychology*. Vol. 2. New York: Ronald Press, 1953. Pp. 577–589.

Schlosberg, H., & Heineman, C. The relationship between two measures of response strength. *Journal of Experimental Psychology*, 1950, **40**, 235–247.

Schneck, J. M., & Kline, M. V. Hypnotic scene visualization and the word association test. *Journal of Genetic Psychology*, 1952, **46**, 29–42.

Schulz, R. W., & Thysell, R. The effects of familiarization on meaningfulness. *Journal of Verbal Learning and Verbal Behavior*, 1965, **4**, 409–413.

Secord, P. F. Objectification of word association procedure by the use of homonyms: A measure of body cathexis. *Journal of Personality*, 1953, **21**, 479–495.

Secord, P. F., & Jourard, S. M. The appraisal of body-cathexis: Body cathexis and the self. *Journal of Consulting Psychology*, 1953, **17**, 343–347.

Segal, S. J., & Cofer, C. N. The effect of recency and recall on word association. *American Psychologist*, 1960, **15**, 451. (Abstract)

Shakow, D. Segmental set. A theory of the formal psychological deficit in schizophrenia. *Archives of General Psychiatry*, 1962, **6**, 1–17.

Shakow, D. Psychological deficit in schizophrenia. *Behavioral Science*, 1963, **8**, 275–305.

Shakow, D., & Jellinek, E. M. Composite index of the Kent-Rosanoff free association test. *Journal of Abnormal Psychology*, 1965, **70**, 403–404.

Shapiro, S. S. Word associations to CVCs by grade-school-aged children. M.S. thesis, Department of Psychology, University of Massachusetts, 1963.

Shapiro, S. S. Meaningfulness values for 52 CVCs for grade-school-aged children. *Psychonomic Science*, 1964, **1**, 127–128. (a)

Shapiro, S. S. Word associations and meaningfulness values for grade-school-aged children. *Psychological Reports*, 1964, **15**, 447–455. (b)

Shapiro, S. S. Changes in commonality scores as a function of task and time: Implications for PA learning. *Psychonomic Science*, 1965, **2**, 367–368.

Siipola, E., Walker, W. N., & Kolb, D. Task attitudes in word association, projective and nonprojective. *Journal of Personality*, 1955, **23**, 441–459.

Silverstein, A. B., & McLain, R. E. Associative processes of the mentally retarded. I. An exploratory study. *American Journal of Mental Deficiency*, 1961, **65**, 761–765.

Silverstein, A. B., & McLain, R. E. Associative processes of the mentally retarded. II. Effects of selected background variables. *American Journal of Mental Deficiency*, 1964, **69**, 440–445.

Smith, D. E. P., & Raygor, A. L. Verbal satiation and personality. *Journal of Abnormal and Social Psychology*, 1956, **52**, 323–325.

Smock, C. D., & Thompson, G. G. An inferred relationship between early childhood conflicts and anxiety responses in later life. *Journal of Personality*, 1954, **23**, 88–98.

Sommer, R., Dewar, R., & Osmond, H. Is there a schizophrenic language? *Archives of General Psychiatry*, 1960, **3**, 665–673.

Sommer, R., Witney, G. & Osmond, H. Teaching common associations to schizophrenics. *Journal of Abnormal and Social Psychology*, 1962, **65**, 58–61.

Staats, A. W., & Staats, C. K. Meaning and *m*: Correlated but separate. *Psychological Review*, 1959, **66**, 136–144.

Storms, L. H. Backward association: A situational effect. *Journal of Experimental Psychology*, 1958, **55**, 390–395.

Storms, L. H., & Broen, W. E., Jr. Verbal associative stability and appropriateness in schizophrenics, neurotics, and normals as a function of time pressure. *American Psychologist*, 1964, **19**, 460. (Abstract)

Tecce, J. J., & Glassco, J. A. Word association time as a function of anxiety (drive) and response competition. *Psychological Reports*, 1965, **16**, 40.

Terwilliger, R. F. Free association patterns and familiarity as predictors of affect. *Journal of General Psychology*, 1964, **70**, 3–12.

Tobiessen, J. E. A developmental study of the relationship between children's word associations and verbal achievement. Unpublished Doctorate of Education dissertation, The Pennsylvania State University, 1964.

Trapp, E. P., & Kausler, D. H. Association tendencies of groups differentiated on the Taylor. Manifest Anxiety Scale. *Journal of Consulting Psychology,* 1959, **23**, 387–389.

Trapp, E. P., & Kausler, D. H. Relationship between MAS scores and association values of nonsense syllables. *Journal of Experimental Psychology*, 1960, **59**, 233–238.

Tresselt, M. E., & Leeds, D. S. The Kent-Rosanoff word association. I. New frequencies for ages 18–21 and a comparison with Kent-Rosanoff frequencies. *Journal of Genetic Psychology*, 1955, **87**, 145–148.

Tresselt, M. E., Leeds, D. S., & Mayzner, M. S. The Kent-Rosanoff word association. II. A comparison of sex differences in response frequencies. *Journal of Genetic Psychology*, 1955, **87**, 149–153.

Tresselt, M. E., & Mayzner, M. S. The Kent-Rosanoff word association: Word association norms as a function of age. *Psychonomic Science*, 1964, **1**, 65–66. (a)

Tresselt, M. E., & Mayzner, M. S. Value and meaning beyond the first word associations. *Psychonomic Science*, 1964, **1**, 203–204. (b)

Underwood, B. J. Verbal learning in the educative process. *Harvard Educational Review*, 1959, **29**, 107–117.

Underwood, B. J., & Schulz, R. W. *Meaningfulness and verbal learning*. Philadelphia: Lippincott, 1960.

Vanderplas, J. M., & Garvin, E. A. The association value of random shapes. *Journal of Experimental Psychology*, 1959, **57**, 147–154.

Van Krevelen, A. Relationships between number of verbal associations to value words and subjective ratings of value. *Proceedings of the Iowa Academy of Science*, 1956, **63**, 576–580.

Veness, T. An experiment on slips of the tongue and word association faults. *Language and Speech*, 1962, **5**, 128–137.

Wallenhorst, R. Some relations between reaction time and choice of response in word association. *Psychological Reports*, 1965, **17**, 619–626.

Weinberg, J. R. A further investigation of body-cathexis and the self. *Journal of Consulting Psychology*, 1960, **24**, 277.

Weintraub, W., Silverstein, A. B., & Klee, G. D. The effect of LSD on the associative processes. *Journal of Nervous and Mental Disease*, 1959, **128**, 409–413.

Weintraub, W., Silverstein, A., & Klee, G. D. The "correction" of deviant responses on a word association test. *Archives of General Psychiatry*, 1960, **3**, 17–20.

Weiss, J. H., Goldfried, M. R., & Bayoff, I. The levels hypothesis and the study of stimulus value of projective test items. *Journal of Projective Techniques and Personality Assessment*, 1965, **29**, 445–453.

Wiggins, J. S. Two determinants of associative reaction time. *Journal of Experimental Psychology*, 1957, **54**, 144–147.

Wild, C. Creativity and adaptive regression. *Journal of Personality and Social Psychology*, 1965, **2**, 161–169.

Wilson, R. C., Guilford, J. P., & Christensen, P. R. The measurement of individual differences in originality. *Psychological Bulletin*, 1953, **50**, 362–370.

Winnick, W. A., & Ellner, M. "Meaningfulness" in tachistoscopic thresholds, serial learning, and association measurement. *Psychonomic Science*, 1965, **2**, 233–234.

Winnick, W. A., & Kressel, K. Tachistoscopic recognition thresholds, paired-associate learning, and free recall as a function of abstractness-concreteness and word frequency. *Journal of Experimental Psychology*, 1965, **70**, 163–168.

Wispé, L. G. Physiological need, verbal frequency, and word association. *Journal of Abnormal and Social Psychology*, 1954, **49**, 229–234.

Wolfensberger, W. Conceptual satiation: An attempt to verify a construct. *American Journal of Mental Deficiency*, 1963, **68**, 73–79.

Wolff, C. Manifest anxiety, reaction potential ceiling, and word association. *Journal of Personality and Social Psychology*, 1965, **2**, 570–573.

Worell, J., & Worell, L. Personality conflict, originality of response, and recall. *Journal of Consulting Psychology*, 1965, **29**, 55–62.

Worell, L. The ring of punishment: A theoretical and experimental analogue of repression-suppression. *Journal of Abnormal Psychology*, 1965, **70**, 201–209.

Wynne, R. D. Are normal word association norms suitable for schizophrenics? *Psychological Reports*, 1964, **14**, 121–122.

Wynne, R. D., Gerjuoy, H., & Schiffman, H. Association test antonym-response set. *Journal of Verbal Learning and Verbal Behavior*, 1965, **4**, 354–359.

Yamamoto, J., & Seeman, W. A psychological study of castrated males. In Explorations in the physiology of emotions. *Psychiatric Research Reports*, 1960, No. 12, 97–103.

Additional References

Amster, H. Semantic satiation and generation: Learning? Adaptation? *Psychological Bulletin*, 1964, **62**, 273–286.

Bleuler, E. *Textbook of psychiatry*. (Transl. A. A. Brill). New York: Macmillan, 1924.

Boring, E. G. *A history of experimental psychology*. (2nd ed.) New York: Appleton, 1950.

Broen, W. E., & Storms, L. H. Lawful disorganization: The process underlying a schizophrenic syndrome. *Psychological Review*, 1966, **73**, 265–279.

Bruner, J. E., Goodnow, J. J., & Austin, G. A. *A study of thinking*. New York: Science Editions, 1962.

Cofer, C. N. On some factors in the organizational characteristics of free recall. *American Psychologist*, 1965, **20**, 261–272.

Cofer, C. N., & Foley, J. P., Jr. Mediated generalization and the interpretation of verbal behavior. I. Prolegomena. *Psychological Review*, 1942, **49**, 513–540.

Ekstrand, B. R. Backward associations. *Psychological Bulletin*, 1966, **65**, 50–64.

Erikson, E. H. *Childhood and society*. New York: Norton, 1950.

Goodenough, F. L. The use of free association in the objective study of personality. In Q. McNemar & M. A. Merrill (Eds.), *Studies in personality*. New York: McGraw-Hill, 1942. Pp. 87–103.

Galton, F. Psychometric experiments. *Brain*, 1879–1880, **2**, 149–162.

Hilgard. E. R. Impulsive versus realistic thinking. *Psychological Bulletin*, 1962, **59**, 477–488.

Hull, C. L. Knowledge and purpose as habit mechanisms. *Psychological Review*, 1930, **37**, 511–525.

Hull, C. L. *A behavior system*. New Haven: Yale University Press, 1952.

Jenkins, J. J. Mediated associations: Paradigms and situations. In C. N. Cofer & B. S. Musgrave (Eds.), *Verbal behavior and learning*. New York: McGraw-Hill, 1963. Pp. 210–245.

Jenkins, J. J., & Russell, W. A. Associative clustering during recall. *Journal of Abnormal and Social Psychology*, 1952, **47**, 818–821.

Jung, C. G. *Studies in word-association*. London: Heineman, 1918.

Jung, J. Experimental studies of factors affecting word associations. *Psychological Bulletin*, 1966, **66**, 125–133.

Kasanin, J. S. (Ed.) *Language and thought in schizophrenia*. New York: Norton, 1964.

Kendler, H. H., & Kendler, T. S. Vertical and horizontal processes in problem solving. *Psychological Review*, 1962, **69**, 1–16.

Korzybski, A. *Science and sanity*. New York: Science Press, 1933.

Maslow, A. H. The dynamics of psychological Security-Insecurity. *Character and Personality*, 1942, **10**, 331–344.

McNeill, D. A study of word association. *Journal of Verbal Learning and Verbal Behavior*, 1966, **5**, 548–557.

Osgood. C. E. *Method and theory in experimental psychology*. London and New York: Oxford University Press, 1953.

Rapaport, D. (Ed.) *The organization and pathology of thought*. New York: Columbia University Press, 1951.

Rapaport, D., Gill, M., & Schafer, R. *Diagnostic psychological testing*. Vol. II. Chicago: Year Book Publ., 1946.

Razran, G. The observable unconscious and the inferable conscious in current Soviet psychophysiology, *Psychological Review*, 1961, **68** 99–109.

Robinson, E. S. *Association theory today*. New York: Century, 1932.

Russell, W. A. Assessment versus experimental acquisition of verbal habits. In C. N. Cofer & B. S. Musgrave (Eds.), *Verbal learning and verbal behavior*. New York: McGraw-Hill, 1961. Pp. 110–123.

Thorndike, E. L., & Lorge, I. *The teacher's word book of 30,000 words*. New York: Teacher's College, 1944.

Watson, J. B. Psychology as the behaviorist views it. *Psychological Review*, 1913, **20**, 158–177.

Wicklund. D. A., Palermo. D. S., & Jenkins, J. J. The effects of associative strength and response hierarchy on paired-associate learning. *Journal of Verbal Learning and Verbal Behavior*, 1964, **3**, 413–420.

Woodworth, R. S., & Schlosberg, H. *Experimental psychology*. New York: Holt, 1954.

Normative Data

The following is a listing of word association norms available for a variety of stimulus words and subject groups.

Amster, H. Convergent association norms for ten-year old children and college age adults. *Psychonomic Monograph*, 1967, **2**, Supplement, 1–32.

Amster, H. & Keppel, G. Letter association norms. *Psychonomic Monograph*, 1966, **1**, Supplement, 211–238.

Battig, W. F. Single-response free word-associations for 300 most frequent four-letter English words. Under Grant M-5769, between the National Institute of Mental Health and the University of Maryland, 1959.

Bilodeau, E. A., & Howell, D. C. Free association norms by discrete and continued methods. Technical Report No. 1, 1965, for Contract Nonr-475 (10), between Tulane University and the Office of Naval Research.

Bousfield, W. A., Cohen, B. H., Whitmarsh, G. A., & Kincaid, W. D. The Connecticut free associational norms. Technical Report No. 35, 1961, under Contract Nonr-631 (00) between the Office of Naval Research and the University of Connecticut.

Castaneda, A., Fahel, L. S., Lunneborg, P. W., & Koppe, R. J. Association norms for 239 adjectives for fourth, fifth, and sixth grade children. University of Texas.

Castaneda, A., Fahel, L. S., & Odom, R. Associative characteristics of sixty-three adjectives and their relation to verbal paired-associate learning in children. *Child Development*, 1961, **32**, 297–304.

Cieutat, V. J. Association indices for 446 randomly selected English monosyllables, bisyllables and trisyllables. *Journal of Verbal Learning and Verbal Behavior*, 1963, **2**, 176–185.

Cohen, B. H., Bousfield, W. A., & Whitmarsh, G. A. Cultural norms for verbal items in 43 categories. Technical Report No. 22, 1957, Contract Nonr 631(00), between the Office of Naval Research and the University of Connecticut.

Cramer, P. The Austen Riggs Center norms for responses to the revised Menninger word association test. Mimeo, 1964. (a)

Cramer, P. The New York norms for responses to the revised Menninger word association test. Mimeo, 1964. (b)

Cramer, P. Word association norms for 100 homographs. Institute of Human Learning, Berkeley, California, 1967.

Deese, J. Johns Hopkins norms to 444 stimulus words. Mimeo, 1960.

DiVesta, F. J. Norms for modifiers used by children in a restricted word-association task. Studies in Verbal Processes, Report No. 9, 1964, National Institute of Child Health & Human Development, U.S.P.H.S. Research Grant No. 00872, Syracuse University.

Duncan, C. P., & Wood, G. Norms for successive word associations. *Psychonomic Monograph*, 1966, **1**, Supplement, 203–206.

Galbraith, G. Unpublished free association norms for 50 words; 30 with both neutral and sexual connotations, and 20 with only neutral connotations.

Gerjuoy, I. R., & Gerjuoy, H. Preliminary word-association norms for institutionalized adolescent retardates. *Psychonomic Science*, 1965, **2**, 91–92.

Gerow, J. R., & Pollio, H. R. Word association, frequency of occurrence, and semantic differential norms for 360 stimulus words. Technical Report No. 1, 1965, Research Grant MH-08903 to the University of Tennessee.

Hall, J. F. Unpublished free association norms for 54 adjectives. Department of Psychology, Pennsylvania State University.

Horton, D. L. The Kentucky norms for responses to 100 words from the Kent-Rosanoff word association test. University of Kentucky, 1963.

Jenkins, J. J. Contrast responses to the stimulus words of the Palermo-Jenkins word association list. Research Bulletin No. 43, June 1964, Research Grant HD-00961 to Pennsylvania State University.

Jenkins, J. J., & Palermo, D. S. Superordinate responses to the stimulus words of the Palermo-Jenkins word association lists. Research Bulletin No. 53, 1965, Research Grant HD-00961 to the Pennsylvania State University. (a)

Jenkins, J. J., & Palermo, D. S. Coordinate response to the stimulus words of the Palermo-Jenkins word association list. Research Bulletin No. 54, 1965, Research Grant HD-00961 to the Pennsylvania State University. (b)

Jenkins, J. J., & Palermo, D. S. Synonym responses to the stimulus words of the Palermo-Jenkins word association lists. Research Bulletin No. 55, 1965, Research Grant HD-0091 to the Pennsylvania State University. (c)

Jenkins, J. J., & Palermo, D. S. Attribute responses to the stimulus words of the Palermo-Jenkins word association list. Research Bulletin No. 56, 1965, Research Grant HD-0091 to the Pennsylvania State University. (d)

Jones, L. V., & Fillenbaum, S. Grammatically classified word-associations. Research Memo No. 15, 1964. Psychometric Laboratory, Chapel Hill, North Carolina.

Jones, L. V., & Wepman, J. M. A spoken word count. Language Research Assoc., Chicago, Illinois, 1966.

Keene, C. M. Commonality of response on a word-association test: A study of standardization procedures and an attempt to forecast moderate emotional maladjustment. Unpublished doctoral dissertation, Stanford University, 1951.

Kent, G. H., & Rosanoff, A. J. A study of association in insanity. *American Journal of Insanity*, 1910, **67**, 37–96, 317–390.

Lachman, R., & Laughery, K. R. Letter association and sequence norms. *Psychonomic Science*, 1965, **2**, 103–104.

Lachman, R., & Laughery, K. R. Letter-word association: Lexical responses to alphabetic stimuli of 1180 college students. Technical Report No. 1, 1966, State University of New York, Buffalo.

Marshall, G. R. Word association norms. Mimeo. Brooklyn College, 1961.

Martin, D. R., & Clifton, C., Jr. A normative collection of opposite responses. Report No. 14, 1964, under Grant G-18690 between the National Science Foundation and the University of Minnesota.

Noble, C. E. Tables of the e and m scales. *Psychological reports*, 1958, **4**, 590.

Noble, C. E., & Parker, G. V. C. The Montana scale of meaningfulness (m). *Psychological Reports*, 1960, **7**, 325–331.

O'Connor, J. *Born that way*. Baltimore: Williams & Wilkins, 1928.

Palermo, D. S., & Jenkins, J. J. *Word association norms*. Minneapolis: University of Minnesota Press, 1964.

Palermo, D. S., & Jenkins, J. J. Oral word association norms for children in grades one through four. Research Bulletin No. 60, 1966, Pennsylvania State University.

Rapaport, D., Gill, M., & Schafer, R. *Diagnostic psychological testing*. Vol. 2. Chicago: Year Book Publ. 1946.

Riegel, K. F. The Michigan restricted association norms. Report No. 3, 1965, under Grant No. MH 07619 between the National Institutes of Mental Health and the University of Michigan. (a)

Riegel, K. F. Free associative responses to the 200 stimuli of the Michigan restricted association norms. Report No. 8, 1965, under Grant No. MH 07619 between the National Institutes of Mental Health and the University of Michigan. (b)

Rosenberg, S. Associative sentence norms. Report No. 3, 1965, Research Grant MH-08904-02. (a)

Rosenberg, S. Free association norms for the forty nouns used in the associative sentence norms. Report No. 4, 1965, Research Grant MH 08904-02. (b)

Rosenberg, S. Noun responses to adjectives from the Rosenberg-Carter norms under conditions of controlled association. Report No. 5, 1965, Grant MH 08904-02. (c).

Rosenberg, S. Associative sentence norms. II. Simple declarative sentences. Report No. 6, 1966, Research Grant MH 08904-02.

Rosenberg, S., & Carter, J. Controlled adjective responses to 53 nouns from the Kent-Rosanoff association test. Mimeographed paper, George Peabody College for Teachers, September, 1965.

Rothkopf, E. Z., & Coke, E. U. Intralist association data for 99 words of the Kent-Rosanoff word list. *Psychological Reports*, 1961, **8**, 463-474.

Russell, W. A., & Jenkins, J. J. The complete Minnesota norms for responses to 100 words from the Kent-Rosanoff word association test. Technical Report No. 11, 1954, Contract N8-onr-66216, the Office of Naval Research and the University of Minnesota.

Schellenberg, P. E. A group free-association test for college students. Unpublished doctoral dissertation, University of Minnesota, 1930.

Segal, S. J. The Brooklyn College norms for responses to 100 words from the Kent-Rosanoff word association test. Mimeo, 1960.

Shapiro, S. I., & Palermo, D. S. An atlas of normative free association data. Research Grant GB-2568 to the Pennsylvania State University.

Shapiro, S. S. Word associations to CVCs by grade-school-aged children. M. S. thesis, Department of Psychology, University of Massachusetts, 1963.

Shapiro, S. S. Word association norms: Stability of response chains of association. Technical Report No. 3, 1964-1965, Austen Riggs Center, Stockbridge, Massachusetts.

Tresselt, M. E. The Kent-Rosanoff word association test and the geographical location. *Psychology Newsletter NYU.*, 1958, **10**, 22-26.

Tresselt, M. E. The responses and frequencies of responses for 108 subjects (ages 34-41) to the Kent-Rosanoff word list. *Psychology Newsletter*, 1959, **10**, 176-212.

Tresselt, M. E. The responses and frequencies of responses for 122 subjects (ages 42-54) to the Kent-Rosanoff word list. *Journal of Psychological Studies*, 1960, **11**, 118-146.

Tresselt, M. E., & Leeds, D. S. The responses and frequencies of responses for 124 males and females (aged 18-21) to the Kent-Rosanoff stimulus words. *Psychology Newsletter*, 1953, **5**, 1-36. (a)

Tresselt, M. E., & Leeds, D. S. The responses and frequencies of 124 males and females (age 22-25) to the Kent-Rosanoff stimulus words. *Psychology Newsletter*, 1953, **5**, 39-74. (b)

Tresselt, M. E., & Leeds, D. S. The responses and frequencies of responses for males and females (ages 26-29) to the Kent-Rosanoff word list. *Psychology Newsletter*, 1954, **5**, 144-177.

Tresselt, M. E., & Leeds, D. S. The responses and frequencies of responses for males and females (ages 30-33) to the Kent-Rosanoff word list. *Psychology Newsletter*, 1955, **6**, 95-127.

Underwood, B. J., & Richardson, J. Some verbal materials for the study of concept formation. *Psychological Bulletin*, 1956, **53**, 84-95.

Underwood, B. J., & Schulz, R. W. *Meaningfulness and verbal learning*. Philadelphia: Lippincott, 1960.

Verinis, J. S., Tuttle, T. R., & Rouse, R. O. Williams College discrete association norms, 1963.

Wilson, D. P. An extension and evaluation of association word lists. Unpublished doctoral dissertation, University of Southern California, 1942.

Woodrow, H., & Lowell, F. Children's association frequency tables. *Psychological Monographs*, 1916, **22** (5, Whole No. 97).

Author Index

Numbers in italics refer to the pages on which the complete references are listed.

A

Adams, P. A., 35, 37, 223, *253*
Albert, J., 68, 147, 148, *249*
Albright, J. B., 143, 146, 148, *243*
Albright, R. W., 143, 146, 148, *243*
Amster, H., 2, 91, 97, *243, 256, 258*
Anderson, L., 19, 79, *252*
Anderson, N. S., 21, 56, 165, *243*
Appelbaum, S. A., 12, 13, 14, 30, 43, 44, 205, *243*
Archer, E. J., 12, 28, 152, *243*
Arenson, S. J., 100, 101, *253*
Austin, G. A., 228, *256*

B

Baker, S. J., 177, *243*
Barclay, W. D., 15, 73, *243*
Barnhart, C. I., 29
Battig, W. F., 91, 97, *243, 258*
Bayoff, I., 51, 55, *256*
Becher, B. A., 143, 154, *243*
Beck, H. S., 15, *243*
Belloni, M., 86, 103, 179, *250*
Berger, L., 92, 99, 100, 115, 200, *250*
Berko, J., 68, 69, 146, *244*
Berkowitz, H., 30, 36, *244*
Berkowitz, L., 45, 49, 126, 152, *246*
Bersh, P. J., 116, *243*
Bilodeau, E. A., *258*
Birren, J. E., 142, 143, 144, 145, *243, 253*
Bleuler, E., 4, *256*
Bliss, J., 165, 170, 172, *246*
Block, J., 169, 174, *243*
Bodin, A. M., 13, 42, 43, 45, 48, 51, 55, 170, 202, *243*

Bogartz, W., 92, 99, 100, 115, 200, *250*
Boldwin, M. V., 47, 127, *244*
Boring, E. G., 2, 4, *256*
Bousfield, W. A., 10, 15, 30, 32, 34, 36, 37, 73, 164, 196, *243, 244, 258*
Boyd, P. S., 30, 45, 46, 180, *244*
Boyer, R. A., 91, *244*
Braun, H. W., 144, *253*
Brody, N., 16, 17, 125, *244*
Broen, W. E., 215, 240, *244, 256*
Broen, W. E., Jr., 192, *255*
Brook, D. F., 167, *244*
Brown, R. W., 68, 69, 146, *244*
Brown, W. P., 43, 45, *244*
Brown, Z. M., 83, *248*
Brozek, J., 47, 127, *244*
Bruner, J. E., 228, *256*
Buchwald, A. M., 16, 20, 124, 125, 131, *244*
Budin, W., 30, 129, 148, 153, 155, 160, 193, *246*

C

Campbell, D. T., 22, *253*
Carlson, V. R., 60, 171, *244*
Caron, A. J., 103, *244*
Carroll, J. B., 78, 162, 169, 174, 201, *244, 249*
Carter, J., *260*
Carton, A. S., 78, 174, *244*
Castaneda, A., *258*
Cieutat, V. J., 12, *244, 258*
Chatterjee, B. B., 118, *244*
Christensen, P. R., 15, *256*
Clark, J., 43, 78, *250*
Clarke, A. D. B., 162, 201, *244*
Clifton, C., Jr., *259*

AUTHOR INDEX

Cobb, K., 169, 171, *244*
Cofer, C. N., 2, 5, 14, 16, 30, 33, 36, 37, 56, 67, 73, 74, 82, 87, 166, *244*, *247*, *249*, *251*, *254*, *257*
Cohen, B. H., 10, 196, *243*, *258*
Cohen, J. A., 70, 232, *247*
Cohen, S., *250*
Coke, E. U., 30, *254*, *260*
Colby, K. M., 22, *245*
Coleman, E. B., 85, *245*
Cook, T. H., 75, 91, 177, *245*
Cowan, T. M., 34, 37, *243*
Cramer, P., 42, 57, 59, 84, 85, 192, 239, *245*, *258*
Cromwell, R. L., 174, 197, *246*
Crown, S., 165, 201, *245*
Crowne, D. P., 26, 92, 168, 198, *248*

D

D'Alessio, G. R., 119, *245*
Danick, J. J., 32, 36, *244*
Davids, A., 56, 58, 60, 125, 126, 170, *245*
Davidson, R. S., 75, 143, *245*
Day, D., 68, 147, 148, *249*
Dean, S. J., 117, *251*
De, Bimaleswar, *245*
De Burger, R. A., 19, *245*
Deering, G., 41, 43, 44, 154, 192, *245*
Deese, J., 2, 31, 32, 33, 34, 37, 63, 68, 69, 147, 166, 226, *245*, *258*
DeLucia, J. J. 62, *245*
Deterline, W. A., 11, 76, *246*
Dewar, R., 191, 192, 195, 198, 201, 221, *255*
Dittborn, J., 203, *246*
DiVesta, F. J., 142, 143, 145, 148, 156, *246*, *258*
Dixon, N. F., 30, 46, 205, *246*
Docter, R. F., 47, 127, *250*
Dörken, H., 141, 191, 192, 217, *246*, *250*
Dokecki, P. R., 174, 197, *246*
Donahoe, J. W., 19, *245*
Doris, J., 45, 49, 126, 152, *246*
Doust, J. W., 30, 46, 161, 197, 203, 207, *246*
Draguns, J., 30, 129, 148, 153, 155, 160, 193, *246*
Duncan, C. P., *258*
Dunn, S., 165, 170, 172, *246*

E

Ekstrand, B. R., 44, *257*
Ellner, M., 57, *256*
Elton, C. F., 91, *244*
Entwisle, D. R., 21, 61, 67, 146, 147, 162, 218, *246*
Epstein, S., 30, 45, 46, 74, 127, *246*
Eriksen, C. W., 49, 62, 116, 117, 118, 125, 126, 171, 205, *244*, *245*, *246*, *247*, *257*
Ervin, S. M., 6, 69, 70, 146, 147, 221, *246*

F

Fahel, L. S., *258*
Faibish, G. M., 192, 193, *246*
Feinberg, L. D., 30, 129, 148, 153, 155, 160, 193, *246*
Feldman, S., 18, 34, *250*
Fenz, W. D., 30, 45, 46, 74, 127, *246*
Fillenbaum, S., 67, 69, 105, 108, 109, *246*, *259*
Finn, J., 63, *249*
Fishbein, M., 86, 103, 179, *250*
Fiske, D. W., 102, *248*
Flaugher, R. L., 15, 29, 34, 85, 175, 188, *246*, *252*
Flavell, J. H., 30, 129, 148, 153, 155, 160, 193, *246*
Foley, J. P., Jr., 5, *257*
Ford, T. J., 87, *244*
Forsyth, D. F., 21, 61, 67, 146, 147, 162, 218, *246*
Fosmire, F. R., 14, 28, *247*
Freedman, J. L., 83, 103, 153, *247*
Fuhrer, M. J., 205, *247*

G

Galbraith, G., *258*
Gallup, H. F., 100, 102, *247*, *250*
Galton, F., 4, *257*
Garskof, B. E., 16, 17, 32, 33, 36, 66, *247*, *248*
Garvin, E. A., 11, 76, *255*
Geer, J. H., 13, 42, 43, 45, 46, 47, 48, 51, 55, 170, 202, 236, *243*, *247*
Gerjuoy, H., 91, 92, *256*, *258*
Gerjuoy, I. R., *258*

AUTHOR INDEX

Gerow, J. R., *258*
Gill, M., 1, 10, 13, 93, 160, 239, *257, 259*
Gillhooly, W. B., 62, *247*
Glanzer, M., 67, 68, *247*
Glassco, J. A., 79, 126, 130, *255*
Glucksberg, S., 70, 232, *247*
Goldfried, M. R., 51, 55, *256*
Goldstein, A. G., 11, 76, 126, *247*
Goldstein, M. J., 43, 45, 78, 126, 132, 135, 175, 198, *247*
Goodenough, F. L., 169, *257*
Goodglass, H., 93, 149, *251*
Goodnow, J. J., 228, *256*
Gorham, D., *248*
Gottesman, L. E., 201, 235, *247*
Greenbaum, R. S., 11, *247*
Greenblatt, M., 198, *251*
Grooms, R. R., 14, 19, 87, 88, 152, 231, *247, 252*
Guetzkow, H., 47, 127, *244*
Guilford, J. P., 15, *256*
Gumenik, W. E., 106, 108, 109, 111, *247*

H

Hall, J. F., 57, 59, 61, 62, *247, 258*
Hare, R. D., 116, 122, *247*
Harrison, K., *247*
Havron, M. D., 166, *247*
Haworth, M. R., 1, *253*
Heim, A. M., 167, *244*
Heineman, C., 80, *254*
Herr, V. V., 149, 154, 162, 193, 194, 203, *247*
Hessert, R. B., 144, *253*
Higgins, J., 195, *248*
Hilgard, E. R., 228, *257*
Hills, J. R., 15, 179, *248*
Hinze, H. A. K., 48, *248*
Hodges, W. E., 34, 175, 176, 188, *252*
Holtzman, W. H., *248*
Horan, E. M., 159, *248*
Horowitz, L. M., 83, *248*
Horton, D. L., 26, 92, 168, 198, *248, 258*
Horvath, W. J., 230, *248*
Houston, J. P., 32, 36, *247, 248*
Howard, K. I., 102, *248*
Howe, E. S., 17, 50, 51, 52, 78, *248*
Howell, D. C., *258*
Howes, D., 16, 84, 97, *248*

Howes, D. H., 62, *248*
Hull, C. L., 4, *257*
Hsü, E. H., 177, *248*

J

Jacobs, A., 13, 30, 43, 45, 46, 60, 62, *248*
Janis, I. L., 208, *248*
Jellinek, E. M., 191, *254*
Jenkins, J. J., 2, 5, 10, 11, 12, 18, 19, 20, 21, 26, 27, 28, 29, 30, 47, 50, 78, 92, 104, 148, 149, 151, 152, 153, 164, 168, 169, 174, 195, 201, 207, 217, 218, 219, 221, 230, *248, 249, 252, 253, 257, 259, 260*
Jenkins, P. M., 30, 87, *249*
Johnson, D. M., *249*
Johnson, P. E., 179, *249*
Johnson, R. C., 42, 50, 55, 76, 124, 125, 138, 170, 191, 192, *249*
Johnson, T. J., 63, *249*
Johnson, W. R., 128, *249*
Jones, L. V., 67, 69, *246, 259*
Jones, R. B., 43, 45, 175, 198, *247*
Jones, R. M., 43, 61, 92, *249*
Jourard, S. M., 126, 172, *254*
Jung, C. C., 56, 67, 75, 79, 178, *251*
Jung, C. G., 1, *257*
Jung, J., 1, *257*

K

Kagan, J., 68, 147, 148, *249*
Kanfer, F. H., 125, 131, 133, *249*
Kanungo, R., 13, 101, 104, 108, 109, 110, 111, 112, 113, *249*
Kausler, D. H., 125, 126, *255*
Kasanin, J. S., 238, 240, *257*
Keene, C. M., 217, *259*
Kendler, H. H., 232, *257*
Kendler, T. S., 232, *257*
Kent, G. H., 93, 159, 193, 217, 221, *259*
Keppel, G., *258*
Kimble, J. P., 34, 45, 54, 101, 176, 188, 191, 192, 193, 207, *251*
Kimbrough, W. W., 74, 166, *249*
Kincaid, W. D., 10, *258*
Kintz, B. L., 20, *249*
Kjeldergaard, P. M., 78, 92, 162, 169, 174, 201, *244, 249*

Klee, G. D., 13, 45, 204, *256*
Kline, M. V., 202, 203, *249*, *254*
Kobler, F. J., 203, *247*
Koen, F., 14, 42, 50, 56, 58, 60, *249*
Koff, R. H., 219, 220, *249*
Kolb, D., 68, 129, 235, *254*
Kolers, P. A., 43, 75, 222, *250*
Kollar, E. J., 47, 127, *250*
Koppe, R. J., *258*
Korzybski, A., 200, *257*
Kressel, K., 60, 75, *256*
Kuethe, J. L., 116, 117, 124, 125, 129, 131, *246*, *250*
Kundu, R., 180, *250*

L

Lacey, J. I., 118, 204, *250*
Lachman, R., *259*
Laffal, J., 18, 28, 34, 41, 78, *250*
Lambert, W. E., 13, 67, 75, 101, 104, 108, 109, 110, 111, 112, 113, *249*, *250*
Landar, H., 221, *246*
Laughery, K. R., *259*
Lazarus, R. S., 49, *246*
Leeds, D. S., 217, 218, *255*, *260*
Lehmann, H., 191, 192, *250*
Lester, J. R., 15, 196, 207, *250*
Levinger, G., 43, 78, *250*
Levy, S., 1, *250*
Licht, L., 100, 101, 102, 103, 115, 116, 122, 200, *250*
Lim, D., 42, 55, 124, 125, 138, 170, *249*
Longo, N., 75, 143, *245*
Lore, R. K., 48, 51, 52, 54, 55, 90, *253*
Lorge, I., 29, *257*
Lowell, F., 149, 159, 201, 218, *260*
Lunneborg, P. W., *258*
Luria, A. R., 161, 204, 235, 238, *250*

M

McGinnies, E., 165, 166, *251*
Machover, S., 170, 172, 228, 236, *250*
McLain, R. E., 160, *254*
McNeill, D., 6, 72, 232, *251*, *257*
Maltzman, I., 86, 92, 99, 100, 101, 102, 103, 115, 116, 122, 179, 200, *250*
Mandler, G., 34, 76, 78, 125, 126, 128, 174, *250*, *251*
Mandler, J. M., 78, 125, 126, *250*

Mandell, A. J., 47, 127, *250*
Marlowe, D., 26, 92, 168, 198, *248*
Marshall, G. R., 30, 33, 37, *247*, *251*, *259*
Martin, D. R., *259*
Martin, J. G., 83, 90, *251*
Martin, R. B., 117, *251*
Maslow, A. H., 172, *257*
Matthews, W. A., 56, 58, 68, 75, 152, *251*
Mayzner, M. S., 73, 142, 143, 144, *255*
Meadow, A., 198, *251*
Mednick, E. V., 83, *251*
Mednick, M. T., 56, 67, 75, 79, 83, 93, 178, *251*
Mednick, S. A., 2, 15, 56, 67, 75, 79, 83, 85, 89, 93, 178, 188, *248*, *251*
Mefferd, R. B., 34, 45, 54, 75, 91, 101, 176, 177, 188, 191, 192, 193, 207, *245*, *251*
Meinke, D. L., 63, *249*
Messick, S., 74, *251*
Milgram, N. A., 12, 93, 149, 193, 194, 206, 207, *251*
Miron, M. S., 221, *251*
Mollenauer, S. O., 46, 47, 55, 236, *247*
Mooherjee, K., *251*
Moran, L. J., 34, 45, 54, 101, 176, 188, 191, 192, 193, 207, *248*, *251*
Musgrave, B., 85, 88, 89, *251*
Muuss, R., 146, 147, 218, *246*

N

Nakamura, C. Y., 22, 125, 126, 131, 133, 137, 169, 171, *251*
Noble, C. E., 2, 12, 17, 27, 56, 76, 144, 155, 226, *251*, *252*, *259*
Nordlie, P. G., 166, *247*
Notterman, J. M., 116, *243*
Nunnally, J. C., 34, 175, 176, 188, *252*

O

O'Connor, J., 217, *259*
Odom, R., *258*
Osgood, C. E., 5, 16, 19, 50, 69, 79, 84, 98, *248*, *252*, *257*
Osipow, S. H., 14, 19, 87, 88, 152, 231, *247*, *252*
Osmond, H., 115, 122, 191, 192, 195, 198, 200, 201, 221, *255*

AUTHOR INDEX

P

Palermo, D. S., 10, 12, 20, 21, 22, 26, 27, 28, 67, 68, 70, 141, 142, 143, 144, 147, 148, 151, 152, 153, 195, 218, 219, 220, 230, *248*, *252*, *257*, *259*, *260*
Palmer, J. O., 47, 127, *250*
Panman, R. A., 100, 101, *253*
Parker, G. V. C., 155, *252*, *259*
Parloff, M. B., 103, *244*
Parnes, E. W., 34, 76, 128, 174, *251*
Paul, C., 104, 108, 109, 110, 111, *252*
Peak, H., *252*
Peters, H. N., 15, 22, 30, 148, 153, 155, 162, 200, *252*
Peterson, M. S., 174, *252*, *253*
Philip, F. J., 195, *248*
Phillips, L. W., 57, 62, *253*
Phillips, W., 68, 147, 148, *249*
Podell, H. A. A., 89, *253*
Polidoro, L. G., 174, 197, *246*
Pollio, H. R., 34, 37, 47, 48, 50, 51, 52, 54, 55, 75, 90, 148, 157, *253*, *258*
Postman, L., 21, 35, 37, 57, 59, 60, 61, 64, 223, *253*
Powell, M., 45, 49, 146, 152, *253*

R

Rabin, A. I., 1, *253*
Rankin, R. E., 22, *253*
Rapaport, D., 1, 10, 13, 93, 160, 228, 239, *253*, *257*, *259*
Raskin, D., 100, 101, 102, 103, *250*
Rau, L. C., 78, *253*
Raygor, A. L., 104, 108, 109, 170, *255*
Razran, G., 235, *257*
Riegel, K. F., 142, 143, 144, 145, 220, 224, *243*, *253*, *259*
Riegel, R. M., *253*
Richardson, J., 15, 85, *260*
Ricklin, F., 205, *253*
Riley, D. A., 57, 62, *253*
Robbin, J. S., 143, *243*
Robertson, J. P. S., 14, *253*
Robinson, E. S., 2, *257*
Rocklyn, E. H., 144, *253*
Rosanoff, A. J., 93, 159, 193, 217, 221, *259*
Rosen, E., 16, 18, *253*
Rosenbaum, M. E., 100, 101, *253*

Rosenberg, S., *259*, *260*
Rosenzweig, M. R., 35, 37, 222, *253*, *254*
Rosman, B. L., 68, 147, 148, *249*
Rotberg, I. C., 116, 122, *254*
Rothkopf, E. Z., 30, 36, *254*, *260*
Rouse, R. O., 90, 94, 97, *254*, *260*
Russell, W. A., 5, 6, 10, 11, 16, 18, 19, 21, 29, 30, 47, 50, 78, 104, 152, 195, 201, 207, 217, 221, *248*, *249*, *253*, *257*, *260*

S

Saltz, E., 128, *254*
Samborski, G., 164, *243*
Sarason, I. G., 125, 126, 130, 131, 132, 133, 134, *254*
Sarason, S., 45, 49, 126, 152, *246*
Schafer, R., 1, 10, 13, 93, 160, 239, *254*, *257*, *259*
Schellenberg, P. E., 217, *260*
Schiffman, H., 91, 92, *256*
Schlosberg, H., 1, 2, 3, 4, 54, 80, *254*, *257*
Schneck, J. M., 202, 203, 204, *249*, *254*
Schneider, R. A., 30, 46, 161, 197, 203, 207, *246*
Schoenfeld, W. N., 116, *243*
Schulz, R. W., 27, 56, 57, 63, 64, 76, 78, *254*, *255*, *260*
Schwartz, A., 170, 172, 228, 236, *250*
Sebeok, T. A., 69, 98, *252*
Secord, P. F., 75, 126, 172, *254*
Sedgewick, C. H. W., 196, *243*
Seeman, W., 180, *256*
Segal, S. J., 82, *254*, *260*
Seymore, S., 115, 116, 122, 200, *250*
Shakow, D., 13, 191, 192, *254*
Shapiro, S. I., *260*
Shapiro, S. S., 12, 13, 102, 143, 144, 151, *254*, *260*
Shevitz, R., 14, 56, 67, *244*
Siipola, E., 68, 129, 165, 170, 172, 235, *246*, *254*
Silverstein, A. B., 13, 45, 160, 204, *254*, *256*
Simon, S., 100, 101, 102, 103, *250*
Slater, G. R., 47, 127, *250*
Smith, D. E. P., 104, 108, 109, 170, *255*
Smith, R. L., 118, 204, *250*
Smock, C. D., 45, 49, 124, 126, 239, *255*
Solley, C. M., 74, *251*

Solomon, H. C., 198, *251*
Solomon, R. L., 62, *248*
Sommer, R., 115, 122, 191, 192, 195, 198, 200, 201, 221, *255*
Spencer, T., 106, 108, 109, 111, *247*
Staats, A. W., 52, *255*
Staats, C. K., 52, *255*
Stagner, R., 62, *245*
Steward, J. R., 34, 37, *243*
Storms, L. H., 16, 82, 192, 215, 240, *244*, *255*, *256*
Suci, G. J., 29, 47, 50, *249*, *252*

T

Tannenbaum, P. H., 50, *252*
Tecce, J. J., 79, 126, 130, *255*
Terwilliger, R. F., 42, 56, 59, 61, *255*
Thompson, G. G., 45, 49, 124, 126, 239, *255*
Thorndike, E. L., 29, *257*
Thysell, R., 56, 57, 63, 76, 78, *254*
Tobiessen, J. E., 162, *255*
Tuttle, T. R., *260*
Trapp, E. P., 124, 126, *255*
Tresselt, M. E., 73, 109, 142, 143, 144, 217, 218, *255*, *260*
Tryk, H. E., 28, *247*

U

Ugelow, A., 57, 59, 61, 62, *247*
Underwood, B. J., 15, 27, 56, 64, 85, *255*, *260*
Unger, S. M., 103, *244*

V

Valentine, M., 30, 45, 46, 180, *244*
Vanderplas, J. M., 11, 76, *255*
Van Krevelen, A., 164, *255*
Van Mondfrans, A. P., 63, *249*
Veness, T., 42, 45, 57, 59, 62, 78, 177, *255*

Verinis, J. S., 90, 94, 97, *254*, *260*
Vinogradova, O. S., 161, 204, 235, 238, *250*

W

Walker, W. N., 68, 129, 235, *254*
Wallenhorst, R., 62, 79, 152, 175, 188, *255*
Watson, J. B., 4, *257*
Weinberg, J. R., 172, *255*
Weintraub, W., 13, 45, 204, *256*
Weiss, J. H., 51, 55, *256*
Weiss, R. L., 50, 191, 192, *249*
Weissbluth, S., 83, *248*
Wepman, J. M., *259*
Whitmarsh, G. A., 10, 30, 32, 36, *244*, *258*
Wicklund, D. A., 230, *257*
Wieland, B. A., 75, 91, 177, *245*
Wiggins, J. S., 78, 79, 239, *256*
Wild, C., 93, 179, 193, 194, *256*
Wilson, D. P., 218, *260*
Wilson, R. C., 15, *256*
Winnick, W. A., 57, 60, 75, *256*
Wispé, L. G., 47, 56, 58, 60, 127, *256*
Witney, G., 115, 122, 200, 201, *255*
Wolfe, S., 221, *251*
Wolfensberger, W., 104, 108, 109, 110, 111, 159, *256*
Wolff, C., 130, 131, 132, 133, 137, *256*
Wood, G., *258*
Woodrow, H., 149, 159, 201, 218, *260*
Woodworth, R. S., 1, 2, 3, 4, 54, *257*
Worell, J., 124, 126, 130, 131, 132, 137, *256*
Worell, L., 119, 124, 126, 130, 131, 132, 133, 134, 137, *256*
Wynne, R. D., 91, 92, 191, 193, 195, *256*
Wright, H. D., 22, 125, 126, 131, 137, 169, 171, *251*

YZ

Yamamoto, J., 180, *256*
Zelhart, P. F., 50, 191, 192, *249*

Subject Index

A

A-B associative frequency, 84, 88
A-B-C associative chain, 85, 88
Abstract-concrete stimuli, 50 n., 75
Adjective,
  categorized, 87
  negatively toned, 172
  Primary response strength, 68
  paradigmatic response to, 146–147
Adjective-noun compound stimulus, 87
Adverbs, Primary response strength of, 67
Affect arousal, 52 n.
Affective stimuli,
  versus neutral, 41–47
  types of, 47–50
Age,
  effects of, 141–151
  Primary response and, 141–142
  response heterogeneity and, 143
Aggressive stimuli, 49
Alcoholics,
  associative response commonality in, 200, 213
  reaction time in, 213 n.
Allport-Vernon Study of Values, 164, 181
Anoxemia, 207
Antonym Primary responses, 91–92, 98, 182
Anxiety,
  associative disruption and, 237
  control of, 139
  measures of, 124
  subject, 131, 137
Anxiety level, preexperimental, 8
Anxiety-producing ideas, 139
Anxiety stimuli, 127–128
Association,
  comparison of methods in, 16–20, 24–25
  continued in successive trials, 13
  continued versus continuous, 19–20
  continuous, 11–12, 14, 19–20
  controlled, 14–16, 19, 24
  discrete, 23
  discrete serial, 23
  free, *see* Free association
  hierarchies in, 18, 215
  laws of, 3
  number of, 20
  preexisting, 4
  preexperimental, 6
  primary laws of, 5
  successive, 12
  temporal sequence of, 5
  types of, 11–16
Association test,
  format of, 11–16
  multiple-choice, 11–16, 20, 22, 93
Associative chain, 88
Associative clusters, 19
Associative cohesiveness, 19
Associative domain, 229
Associative domain disorganization, 214
Associative environment, manipulation of, 82–86
Associative hierarchy, 18
  breakdown of, 215
Associative overlap, 30–35, 73, 227
Associative pathways,
  pathology of, 212
  short-circuiting of, 182, 189, 233–234
Associative response,
  age and, 156–158
  in brain-damaged patients, 205–206
  changes over time in, 217–220
  creativity and, 178–179
  cross-cultural studies in, 221–223

cultural differences and, 217–224
educational level and, 154–156
frequency of overlap in, 33–35
gradient in, 79
intelligence and, 159–164
in LSD users, 204, 214
organismic variables in, 159–190
originality of, 99–103
overlap in, 30–35, 73, 227
pathological conditions and, 191–216
personality and, 168–173
physiological measures of, 30
in schizophrenia, 193–195, 198–199, 203–204, 207–208
semantic level and, 73, 76–77
sex and, 151–154
short-circuiting of, 182, 189, 233–234
socioeconomic status and, 154–156
stimulus familiarity and, 56, 64
strength of, 26–27, 64–65
values and interests as factors in, 164–168
variability of, 28–29
see also Response; Stimulus; Stimulus-response
Associative-satiation hypothesis, 104, 110
Autistic responses, 45, 198
Availability, defined, 83, 96
Avoidance response, 52, 54
Awareness,
in reinforcement, 123
in schizophrenics, 199

B

"Bad" and "good" words, 50, 136, 138
Behavioristic psychology, 4
Belongingness, concept of, 74
Bipolar attributes, 74
Blocking, 45
Body-meaning, effect of, 75
Body-responses, personality and, 172
Brain-damaged patients, responses in, 205–206, 238
British empiricists, 3–4

C

Castrates, associative responses of, 180
Characteristic response set, 235
see also Response sets

Children,
associative continuity and, 232
changes in response over time, 218–220
syntagmatic response in, 146–148
see also Kindergarten subjects; Nursery-school subjects
Chronological changes, effect of, 217–221
Cognitive styles, 174–178
College students, responses of, 155
"Common" and "uncommon" response, 91, 95, 102, 109
Compound stimuli, 86–90, 94
Conceptual mediation, 183
Conceptual referent set, 188
Concrete response, preference for, 76
Conflict, stress and, 130–131
Conflict word, 49
Conjunctions, paradigmatic responses of, 73
Connotations, affective, 48
Consciousness, altered states of, 203–205
Continued association, 42
versus discrete, 16–18
Continuous association, 12–14, 23
versus continued, 19–20
stimulus familiarity and, 57
Contrast-coordinate, 176
Contrast response,
age and, 150, 163, 223
anxiety and, 132
changes over time and, 223
opposite-evoking stimuli and, 95
personality and, 173
reinforcement and, 120
sex and, 154, 163
values and, 168
verbal ability and, 163
Controlled association, 14, 19, 24
Coping mechanisms, 140
Creative individuals, responses of, 103, 178
Creativity,
associative basis of, 188
RAT, *see* Remote Associates Test
Cross-cultural studies, 221–223
Cultural differences, effect of, 217–225
CVC trigrams, 12, 47–48, 57 n., 62, 69–72
Cyclothymia, 171

D

Defense mechanisms, 140
Delay, in reinforcement, 118–120

Demographic variables, 8, 141–158
Different stimuli and responses, training in, 100–101
Discrete association, 11–12, 23
    versus continued, 16–18
    stimulus familiarity and, 57
Discrete serial association, 23
Distant responses, 45
Domain disorganization, 214
Drugs, associative response and, 204, 213–214
Dysmenorrheac patients, responses in, 46, 180

E

Educational level, effect of, 154–156
Ego-control, 169
Electroshock therapy, response following, 207–208
Emotional development, reaction time and, 49
Emotionality, stimulus familiarity and, 59
Emotional state, change in, 102
Emotional stimuli, 12
    avoidance response and, 54
    reaction time and, 236
    recalling of, 61
    respiration and, 46–47
    response method and, 41–44
Engineers, associative response in, 179–181
Environment,
    manipulation of, 82–86
    stress from, 127
    variables in, 41–81
Examples, use of, 91, 95, 101–102, 109
Extra-lingual responses, 177
Extraverted type, responses in, 186

F

Failure-stress situation, 128
Familiarity, stimulus, *see* Stimulus familiarity
Fixed maximum strength model (FMS), 230
Food deprivation, 47, 127, 134
"Food" words, 15
Foreign-language groups, responses in, 75, 221–222
Format, of association tests, 11–16, 211

Free-association test, 11–14, 23
    continued in successive trials, 13–14
    continuous, 11–12
    controlled, 92
    discrete, 11
    successive, 12
    time-limit version, 14
Functional disorders, 8, 191–205

G

Generalization, Index of, 32
"Good" and "bad" words, 50, 136, 138
Grammatical form, as stimulus characteristic, 67–73
Grammatical position, response and, 69–70, 232

H

Hebephrenics, response in, 195, 209
Hierarchies, associative, 18, 215
High-anxious subject, 124
High-conflict subject, 137
High-frequency stimuli, 57–59
Homonyms, 75, 97, 168
Hypnosis, associative response in, 203–204, 213
Hysteria, 171

I

Ideas, sequence of, 3
Idiosyncratic responses, 43, 55, 76, 78, 112 n., 113
    age and, 143
Impulsive type, 186
Index of Generalization, 32
Inhibited type, 186
Instruction, use of in tests, 91–92, 95, 151, 155, 172, 211
Intelligence, response and, 159–164
Intelligence quotient, *see* IQ
Interests, values and, 164–168
Intersection coefficient, 31 n., 34
Intra-subject stimuli, 228, 237
Introverted type, response in, 186
IQ, response and, 160, 180, 184

K

Kent-Rosanoff stimuli or word list, 17, 30 n., 67, 87, 90, 124–125, 128, 131, 142, 159, 169, 174, 195, 198–199, 207, 221–222
Kindergarten subjects, responses in, 143, 148

L

Language, response and, 75, 221
Law, concept of, 74
Law-relevant responses, 74
Leaders, response patterns in, 171–172
Lexical stimuli, 75
Low-anxious subject, 124
Low-conflict subject, 137
Low-frequency stimulus, 56–57
LSD,
    associative response and, 204
    domain disorganization and, 214

M

Meaning, loss of, 7
Meaningfulness factor, 12, 91
Mediated priming, 94
Mental defective, defined, 182
Mental retardate, see Retardate
m factor,
    age and, 144
    and associative domain, 229
    in continued association, 17
    in reinforcement, 123
    response sets and, 175
    satiation studies and, 104
    sex and, 153
    stimulus familiarity and, 58–60, 78, 80–81, 97
    stress and, 128–129
    values and interests in, 164
    see also Response availability
m' factor, 91
Multi-meaning stimuli, 75
Multiple-choice test or format, 11–16, 20, 22, 93, 211
    age and, 149
    for schizophrenics, 193

N

Negative reinforcement, 116–119
Negative words or stimuli, 55
Neurotic subjects, response in, 202
Neutral stimuli, 41–47
Nonoverlapping responses, 89
Noun stimuli, 62, 70
    in children, 157
    Primary response and, 68
Numeral homonyms, 75, 97
Nursery-school subjects, response in, 143, 146, 148

O

Object-referent set, in schizophrenics, 192
Opposite-Evoking Stimuli (OES), 54, 78, 174
    effect on antonym responses, 98
    Primary responses and, 78, 91
Opposite responses, see Contrast responses
Oral-individual testing, 21
Oral stimuli,
    changes in over time, 219
    emotionality and, 239
    sexual associations and, 47, 180
Organic pathology, 205–208
Organismic variables, 159–190
Originality training, 99–103, 106–107, 111–114
Overinclusive thinking, 238, 240
Overlapping responses, 30–35, 73, 227

P

Paired-associate paradigm, 3, 47–48, 83–84
Parachutists, responses in, 45, 74, 127
Paradigmatic-syntagmatic responses, 68–69, 71–72
    age and, 150, 223
    changes over time, 223
    commonality of subject and, 177, 178
    cultural differences and, 224
    familiarity of stimulus and, 63
    grammatical class of stimulus and, 71
    sex and, 154, 163
    values and, 168
    verbal ability and, 163
Pathological conditions, 191–216
    functional, 191–216
    organic, 205–208

SUBJECT INDEX

Personality,
    effects of, 168–173, 185–186
    primary response and, 168–173
Personality profile change, 169
Personality type, 185–186
Physics students, responses of, 179–180
Physiological measures of response, 30
    affectivity of stimulus and, 53, 134, 211
    anxiety and, 134
    high D stimuli and, 80
    psychopathology and, 211
    reinforcement and, 121
Pictorial stimuli,
    abstract-concrete dimension and, 75
    children's response to, 146
"Pleasant" and "unpleasant" words, 51
Polarization, on Semantic Differential, 50–55
Popular response, 14, 26,
    stress and, 129
    see also Response commonality
Predictability, of response, 96–97
Prepositions, and Primary response strengths, 67
Primary response,
    age and, 149, 150, 223
    anxiety and, 131, 132, 133
    bilingualism and, 224
    changes over time and, 223
    compound stimuli and, 94
    cultural differences and, 224
    familiarity of stimulus and, 63
    grammatical class of stimulus and, 71
    high D stimuli and, 80
    instructions and, 95, 172
    interests and, 167
    opposite-evoking stimuli and, 80, 95
    personality and, 172, 173
    psychopathology and, 209
    reinforcement and, 120
    sex and, 153, 154, 163
    values and, 167
    verbal ability and, 163
Priming,
    direct and indirect, 82–86
    mediated, 94
Pronouns, and Primary response strength, 67

R

RAT, *see* Remote Associates Test

Reaction time,
    affectivity of stimulus and, 53, 95, 133, 134, 154
    age and, 150
    anxiety and, 132, 133, 134
    clarity of stimulus and, 77
    compound stimuli and, 94, 95
    concrete verbal stimuli and, 77
    familiarity of stimulus and, 63
    flat response gradient of stimulus and, 80
    grammatical class of stimulus and, 71
    high D stimuli and, 80, 133
    hypnosis and, 209
    intelligence and, 163
    LSD and, 209
    multi-meaning stimuli and, 77
    personality and, 173
    psychopathology and, 209
    reinforcement and, 120, 121
    response set and, 178
    sex and, 154, 173
    strong response stimuli and, 80
    values and, 167
"Regulated" responses, 93
Reinforcement, 115–123
    awareness in, 123
    delay of, 118–120
    negative, 116–120
    positive, 115–116, 119–120
Relative Cohesiveness, measure of, 35
Remote Associates Test (RAT), 15, 24, 85–86, 107, 154
    creativity and, 178
    direct priming and, 83
    originality and, 113
Repeated stimulus presentation, 99–114
Reproduction errors, in emotional stimuli, 44
Reproduction response, 12–13
Response,
    associative, *see* Associative response
    availability of, *see* Response availability
    elicitation of, 21–22
    intersect of, 98
    mode of, 25
    nonmediated, 186–187
    order and frequency of, 15
    Popular, 14
    Primary, 14, 17–18
    relevant and irrelevant, 101
    shock accompanying, 115–117

supra- or sub-ordinate, 15, 22, 148, 153, 196
types of, 13–14
uncommon, 91, 95, 101–102, 109
see also Associative response
Response alternatives, 14
Response availability (m),
  affectivity of stimulus and, 53, 133, 173
  age and, 150, 154
  anxiety and, 132, 133
  clarity of stimulus and, 77
  concrete verbal stimuli and, 77
  creativity and, 180
  familiarity of stimulus and, 63
  flat response gradient of stimulus and, 80
  grammatical class of stimulus and, 71
  multi-meaning stimuli and, 77
  other stimuli on WAT and m', 95
  personality and, 173
  psychopathology and, 209
  reinforcement and, 121
  sex and, 154, 173
  values and, 167
Response category, 15
Response change, 102, 217–221
Response commonality,
  age and, 155, 163, 223
  anxiety and, 131, 133
  changes over time, 210, 223
  ECT and, 209
  education and, 155
  familiarity of stimulus and, 63
  grammatical class of stimulus and, 71
  instructions and, 95, 155
  intelligence and, 163
  mental retardation and, 163
  personality and, 173
  psychopathology and, 209, 210
  reinforcement and, 120
  response set and, 178
  sex and, 153, 154, 173
  socio-economic status and, 155
Response disturbances,
  affectivity of stimulus and, 53
  age and, 155, 163
  anxiety and, 132
  ECT and, 209, 210
  education and, 155
  high D stimuli and, 80
  hypnosis and, 210

LSD and, 210
mental retardation and, 163
psychopathology and, 209, 210
response set and, 178
Response familiarity,
  familiarity of stimulus and, 63
  high m stimuli and, 80
Response heterogeneity (D),
  affectivity of stimulus and, 53
  age and, 150, 223
  anxiety and, 132, 133
  changes over time, 223
  compound stimuli and, 94
  grammatical class of stimulus and, 71
  high D stimuli and, 133
  pictorial stimuli and, 77
  sex and, 154
Response idiosyncrasy,
  anxiety and, 134
  changes over time and, 223
  clarity of stimulus and, 77
  creativity and, 180
  education and, 155
  "food" stimuli and, 134
  high D stimuli and, 80
  high m stimuli and, 80
  instructions and, 107
  interpolated material and, 107
  mental retardation and, 163
  psychopathology and, 209, 223
  reinforcement and, 120
  repeated testing and, 107
Response latency, 80,
  see also Reaction time
Response measures, 25–30
Response predictability, 96–97
Response reproduction errors,
  affectivity of stimulus and, 53, 210
  anxiety and, 132, 134
  ECT and, 210
  familiarity of stimulus and, 63
  high D stimuli and, 80
  hypnosis and, 210
  psychopathology and, 210
  reinforcement and, 121
Response set, 98, 174–178, 188–189, 235
Response stereotype, age and, 156
Response strength, measure of, 27
Response variability,
  emotional stimuli and, 45

SUBJECT INDEX

number of responses and, 42
Response words, content and, 165
Retardate,
  nonmediated response and, 190
  reaction time in, 181
  response types in, 159–161

S

Satiation, verbal, 7, 103–106, 108–110, 173, 231
Schizophrenia, pathology of, 191–195, 198–201
Schizophrenics,
  association loosening in, 4
  domain disorganization in, 214
  electroshock therapy for, 207–208
  emotional stimuli in, 45
  overinclusive thinking in, 238–240
  Primary response in, 195–196
  responses in, 42, 57, 175–176, 191–194, 209–212
  subtypes of, 195–198
  syllogistic reasoning in, 240–241
Schizophrenic thinking, 238–241
S.D., see Semantic Differential
Secondary response,
  age and, 144
  conceptually mediated, 183
  reinforcement in, 115
Semantic Differential ratings or scale, 20, 29, 50–56
Semantic meaning, 176
Sentence frames, 69
Sex, response and, 151–154
Shock, stimulus with, 115–118
Short-circuited response, 182, 189, 233–234
Single-meaning stimuli, 75
Single-word stimuli, 94
Socioeconomic status, effect of, 21–22, 154–156
Sound similarities, 182
S-R see Stimulus-response
Stereotyped response, 12
Stimulus (-uli),
  affective versus neutral, 41–47, 138
  choice of, 10–11
  compound, 86–90, 94
  defined in terms of evoked response, 77–81
  food, 127, 134
  form and class of, 68
  "good" and "bad," 50, 136, 138
  grammatical form of, 67–73
  high-frequency, 57–59
  homosexual, 49
  hostile, 46, 48
  intra-subject, 228
  lexical, 75
  low-frequency, 56–57
  mode of presentation, 25
  multi-meaning, 75
  m value for, 78
  negative, 55
  neutral, 41–47
  nonbody-meaning, 75
  noun, 62, 68, 70, 146, 157, 172
  noun, 62, 68, 70, 146, 157, 172
  as part of speech, 67–73
  pictorial and lexical, 75, 146
  political economic, 166, 184
  positive, 55
  psychosexual, 128
  recognition of, 62–63
  religious, 166, 185
  remembered and forgotten, 171
  repeated presentation of, 99–114
  semantic level of, 73–77
  shock accompanying, 115–117
  single- versus multiple-meaning, 75
  single-word, 94
  subthreshold, 204–205
  value system and, 184–185
Stimulus affectivity, 41–56
Stimulus dual class membership, 98
Stimulus emotionality, 42
  see also Emotionality
Stimulus Equivalence, 34
Stimulus familiarity, 56–67, 163
Stimulus presentation, mode of, 20
Stimulus word, 7, 41–81
  associative responses to, 28
  lists of, 10, 111–112
Stress, 124–140
  experimentally induced, 127–131
  external, 132
  "good" and "bad" stimuli in, 137–138
  instructional, 129–131
  internal, 130–131
  as subject variable, 124
Subjective values, response and, 164–166

Successive association, 12, 23
Supraordinate responses,
  age and, 150, 151, 155, 223
  changes over time, 223
  cultural differences and, 224
  education and, 155
  sex and, 154
Supraordination, in schizophrenics, 196
Syllogistic reasoning, in schizophrenics, 240–241
Synonym-superordinate, 176
Syntagmatic responses, 63, 69
  age and, 146
  response sets and, 174
  switch to paradigmatic, 232
  values and interests in, 165

T

Task variables, 41–81
Tertiary response,
  age and, 144
  reinforcement and, 115
Thorndike-Lorge frequency, 17 n., 21, 29, 42, 50–51, 56–57, 60, 75, 84, 86, 97, 102, 107, 117, 120, 148, 159, 178
Thought processes, nature of, 2
Time-limit test, 14
T-L frequency, *see* Thorndike-Lorge frequency

U

Unusual or uncommon response, 91, 95, 101–102, 109

V

Values and interests, effect of, 164–168, 184–185
Variable maximum strength (VMS) model, 66, 230
Verbal ability, response and, 4, 159–164
Verbal context, 82–98
Verbal environment, manipulation of, 86–91
Verbal satiation, 7, 103–106, 108–110
Verbal universe, conceptualizing of, 226
Verbs, Primary response strength of, 67
Visual stimuli, presentation of, 20–21, 75, 146
VMS model, 66, 230

W

Word,
  "bad" and "good," 50, 136, 138
  grammatical position of, 68–70
  see also Stimulus; Stimulus word
WAT, *see* Word-association test
Word association,
  interest in, 1–2
  methods and techniques in, 10–22
Word-association test, 6
  format of, 11–16, 20, 22, 93
  instructions in, 91–96
  originality training in, 99–103
  reinforcement in, 115–123
  see also Associative response; Stimulus
Word lists, 10, 111–112